## More Praise for *Behind the Façade*

"According to the U.S. Small Business Administration, 70% of small businesses fail by year 10, and at any given time just 20% of small businesses have paid employees. While the challenges of scaling and sustaining a small business are numerous, many just don't know what it takes to wire a business for growth.

In *Behind the Façade*, Alicia Butler Pierre demystifies the process of building a solid business infrastructure using narrative and storytelling to demonstrate how her proven method has enabled her clients to achieve measurable success. It's a must read for anyone who is looking to take their business to the next level and build a company that is resilient, high-performing and sustainable."

— Kelly Burton, Ph.D., Huffington Post Contributor; CEO
of Nexus Research Group & Founders of Color

"A refreshing and enlightening reality check for any sized business. *Behind the Façade* opens us up to the reality and challenges every business leader has, but doesn't want revealed for fear of being considered weak. This is a book of strength through humility. It even inspired me to re-structure certain parts of my business. Great motivational read and breath of fresh air!"

— John M. Kamp, PMP, LSSBB, Founder and
CEO, The Business Kamp

# BEHIND THE

# FAÇADE

## How to Structure Company Operations for Sustainable Success

*To: Susan*
*So glad our paths have crossed! Thank you for being a guest on my podcast. Excited about the opportunity for us to collaborate in the near future.*
*Alicia Butler Pierre*
*09-17-20*

## ALICIA BUTLER PIERRE

**EAGLE EYE**
PUBLISHING

ATLANTA

Butler Pierre, Alicia C., 1976-
   Behind the Façade : how to structure company operations for sustainable success / Alicia Butler Pierre — 1st ed.
   Includes bibliographical references and index.
   ISBN: 978-1-7327392-0-8 (hardcover)
   ISBN: 978-1-7327392-1-5 (paperback)
   ISBN: 978-1-7327392-2-2 (ePub)
   ISBN: 978-1-7327392-3-9 (audio)
   SAN: 991-0794
   Library of Congress Control Number: 2018957802
   1. Business Infrastructure. 2. Small Business. 3. Operations Management. 4. Entrepreneurship.

Cover design by Milena Vitorovic
Original illustrations by Milena Vitorovic
Kasennu™ logo design by Vernell Mosley
Original charts, diagrams and tables by Alicia Butler Pierre

BehindTheFacadeBook.com

Printed in the United States of America

This book is dedicated to:

Olevia Durousseau, my beloved grandmother, who first described to me
what an entrepreneur is,

and

Sidney Butler, my father, for being a shining example of
what entrepreneurship is,

and

L. Carmele DeBaptiste, for demonstrating to me
what it means to truly be fearless,

and last,

The people who, despite the naysayers, criticisms and high
failure rates, dare to build businesses around their skills,
talents and abilities to share with the world.

# Contents

## PART ONE: INTRODUCING THE METHODOLOGY

An analogy to a fabled city foretells that all that glitters isn't gold as discovered when peeking behind the curtain of a fast-growing small business. A case is made for using the Kasennu methodology for business infrastructure as a way to match the tactical, operational back office to the strategic, marketing front office (façade).

## PART TWO: APPLYING THE METHODOLOGY

An appearance on a daytime talk show puts a non-profit on the map, but also exposes the founder's weakness. What is interpreted as an impending coup d'etat threatens to undermine what she's built. Implementing the Business Parts Analysis helps secure her future and reputation.

A software company's popularity is beginning to expand beyond its local market. You would never know the brains behind the operation is a teenager, that is, until he speaks publicly at a conference. The Business Design Blueprint is used to prove scalability to investors as well as his desire to show that this is more than a hobby.

Feuding siblings, equally smart and ambitious, are blind-sided when a malicious virus attacks their furniture store's network. Desperate to save face, they leverage an Electronic Records Management system as a preemptive strike against future disasters and as a tool to see who is really fit to succeed their father as CEO.

Twin sisters receive unexpected but welcomed attention to their mental rehabilitation facility following a cataclysmic natural disaster. Patients aren't the only individuals drawn to them; regulators are too. Taxes resulting from a failed audit forces them to develop a Paper Records Management system to avoid a shutdown.

Demand for a mortgage company's promise of fast loan processing is skyrocketing thanks to their recurring role on a new reality TV show. Unfortunately, customers are suffering because of the trio of business partners' conflicting objectives. Their Service Delivery Blueprint allows them to keep their promises and set priorities.

## 7 Veni, Vidi, Vici

Diversifying the client portfolio has proven to be a wise, and lucrative, move for an optimistic CEO. His company projects a "well-oiled machine" image and the contracts are pouring in. He wants to up the ante by taking his food distribution company public, but first he must battle some personal demons. The Work Space Logistics helps him tackle this head on.

## PART THREE: MAINTAINING THE METHODOLOGY

## 8 Emerald Tablet

All entrepreneurs convene at a workshop to learn how to identify and document their business processes into a Business Process Manual. They each receive a coveted Emerald Tablet containing a signpost that at first seems cryptic, but toward the end of the workshop, they realize its clarity in revealing the keys to maintaining their business infrastructure.

## 9 Sankofa

Building a business infrastructure is a dynamic, not static, endeavor. Moving forward and upward requires reflection on the past in order to maintain the methodology's results and stay true to a company's purpose, as evidenced by several examples of well-known companies.

## APPENDICES

# ACKNOWLEDGMENTS

I n the fall of 1996, I failed an exam in my Heat and Mass Transfer course — a course offered to chemical engineering students in their junior year at Louisiana State University.

I remember it as though it were yesterday. There were only two problems on the exam. The first problem involved calculating the flow of blood through an artery as a heart pumped it. I recall being baffled, panic-stricken and angry; angry because I was an engineering student, not a medical student! I had grown accustomed to calculating the rate of a fluid flowing through pipelines either by gravity or by force (a pump). Turns out, the blood vessels are the pipelines, the blood is the fluid flowing through them and the heart is the pump.

I learned a lesson that day that forever changed the way I absorbed and comprehended information; the best way to know you understand something complex is if you can apply its concepts to different scenarios and situations. Danny Reible, Ph.D., thank you for this most impressionable lesson. Though painful at the time, I've never forgotten it, and I attribute it as the compass that guides me when communicating with non-technical audiences.

****

I credit my career's foundation to my family, teachers and mentors. Growing up, I was fortunate to be surrounded by grandparents, aunts and uncles who all worked hard and instilled in me that if I wanted something, *anything*, I would have to work for it. To my parents, Shelia and Sidney Butler, thank you for instilling in me an incredible work ethic that has served me well. You taught me that there are no handouts and indeed no shortcuts on the path to long-lasting success. It was in that spirit that my sister, Renita Butler Varghese, M.D., and I grew up challenging each other to excel at whatever we pursued. It seems to have paid off!

To my husband, Chris, thank you for your support during the countless nights when I either never slept or slept restlessly. I'm sure it drove you mad, but you never complained, and I could not imagine being on this journey without you.

My high school chemistry teacher, Vita Keblys, first noticed my scientific aptitude and introduced me to chemical engineering. Mrs. Keblys, you set me on a trajectory that would not have been possible had you not taken the time to prepare me for my future career.

To John Elstrott, Ph.D., my entrepreneurship professor at Tulane University and former chairman of the board at Whole Foods, it was during your classes that I first conceived what would eventually become the Kasennu methodology. Thank you for stressing the importance of interpreting financial statements, for giving me access to founders and owners of companies with household names and for providing a safe space to express and test business ideas without fear of rejection. Your counsel has left an indelible mark.

A special and heartfelt thank you to Theresa & William Blount and Carolyn Malbrue, all of whom have known me since I was a child. They taught me, by example, how to leverage skills, talents and abilities to build businesses. Joseph Wink, P.E. gave me the chance to work in his engineering consulting firm, effectively giving me a front-row seat of how to run a successful small business and what one looks like.

I cannot imagine where I would be if not for the mentorship and guidance of people who, of their own accord, invested their time to help me achieve my goals. To my mentors over the years: Essie Escobedo, Clarence Francis, Phillip Kneiper, George Lottier, Randy Meadoux, Stephanie Naquin, Roland Neville, Liviu Sofian and Patricia Thibou, M.D., thank you!

\*\*\*\*

*Synergy* is defined as the whole being greater than the sum of its individual parts. My success is truly the sum of the people I know and have worked with as well as the experiences I've had. An amazing team of people in the early years of my consulting business helped in bringing the concepts of this book to light. Like puzzle pieces, their work helped form the outer edges around the center of the Kasennu methodology.

Louisa Kamau challenged me to package my services as you will read about in Chapter 1. Jill Pullen helped coin the phrase *business infrastructure*. It was the first time the term would ever be used in the marketplace, which, as I would later discover, was a wonderful challenge in and of itself. Charles S. Finch III, M.D shared his Egyptology expertise to give me words that what would ultimately form *Kasennu*. Vernell Mosley designed the original logo. Elizabeth Gordon helped lay the groundwork for communicating value. Sherean Malekzadeh Allen insisted I capitalize on my process engineering background as a competitive advantage, and she was right! Sherry Heyl and Jim Stroud introduced me to the world of online community building, and Kimberly Fennell developed a plan of action for continuous community engagement. Michelle Frizell developed the business infrastructure software prototype. And Santiago Prada, Carlyon Christian, Ankit Patel and Nicole & Gerald Carter, each painstakingly took my concepts and designed iterations of the website as the business evolved.

I believe a major part of most people's success is based merely on knowing who they are and what they want. As the age old adage says, "Know thyself." Olatunji Lumumba, thank you for providing the stepping stone on my journey to self-awareness through a historical lens.

Another part of success is surrounding yourself with people who will be candid with you. Kemba Margulski, thank you for being my sounding board and never leaving my side. Maegan Lane, my insightful goddaughter, thank you for showing me that truth can come from anyone, even the mouth of a babe. When she was eight-years-old, Maegan, unprompted, searched for my business online, critiqued it and gave me invaluable advice. And Keith Finger has stopped me numerous times from marketing blunders. Thanks, Keith!

****

Around the third year of my consulting business, I started having reservations about whether I should keep the doors open. It would be the first of many times when I've wanted to call it quits. Entrepreneurship is not for the faint of heart! I once confided in a neighbor, Larry O. Johnson, who told me that my business idea was like a boomerang — if it were meant to be, it would come back to me. Larry, thank you for that sage advice. Had I not heeded it, this book would not be possible.

Never in a million years did I think I would, or could, write a book. Robert D. Brown III and Derek Caffe saw otherwise and were actually the first two people to encourage me to do so. It was Bro. Bedford who not only supported me in writing this book but actually kickstarted my efforts to commit pen to paper to write what he referred to as "my life's work." Gentlemen, I am humbled by your belief in my abilities as well as your insights.

Figuring out *what* to write was not difficult, but *how* to write it was. Were it not for Greta Counts, who first discovered my knack for storytelling, I may not have incorporated this art form into this book. Toastmasters International gave me the platform on which I began practicing my storytelling. The positive feedback from all of my speeches let me know that I did, in fact, possess a unique way of educating people.

It took me seven weeks to write the manuscript, and Chandra L. Thomas was the first person who read it. Chandra, our friendship spans close to three decades. Thank you for not only being a true friend but for also giving me boosts of confidence to continue forward.

There was also an incredible team of people who enthusiastically jumped at the chance to help this book become a reality. Terrance Durousseau, my cousin, fact-checked my economic diagrams and Ron Durousseau, my uncle, fact-checked my military references. Though an ocean separates us, Milena Vitorovic was able to take my vision of each character and bring them to life with her beautiful illustrations. My patent attorney, Steve Wigmore, Esq., ensured the book's content contained appropriate intellectual property protection. Steve and I have worked together for years, and, like Rhonda Lynch, he believed in and saw the potential for Kasennu since its inception. Steve, I appreciate you more than you may realize. In true entrepreneur fashion, I took some editorial risks in the formatting and style of this book. When editors Jeffrey Shoap, Ph.D. and Lynn Suruma each returned the manuscript back to me with the stories all intact, I knew that they too felt it was a risk worth pursuing. Jeffrey and Lynn, thank you!

When it came to seeking book reviewers, some people stepped up to the challenge without hesitation. They completed an almost impossible task — they read a 400-page digital manuscript in the summer, a time when most people vacation. I was overwhelmed by their level of commitment. John Kamp was recovering from a concussion while still juggling his client work and preparing the syllabus for his next round of training courses. Kelly Burton, Ph.D. launched a significant application in her own company and took my manuscript with her on vacation. She conducted research to provide supportive statistics in her review. Charles Green was also vacationing and felt so strongly about the manuscript's content that he took time to call me upon his return home to personally connect me with his literary agent. These reviewers were unpaid, yet they paid me in full with their feedback. John, Kelly, Charles, I'm not sure if it's possible for me ever to repay you. There are no words to express my gratitude adequately.

Writing the manuscript was relatively easy. Prepping the actual manuscript for publication was not. In preparing for the book's release, I reached out to three professors who, to my surprise, were more than gracious, each giving me more time than I anticipated as they shared their experiences and advice as accomplished authors. Dennis Kimbro, Ph.D. (bestselling author of *The Wealth Choice*) charged me with using my book not just to build my business, but to build a movement. Frank Lee Harper Jr., Ph.D. (renowned author of *A.G.I.L.E. L.E.A.D.E.R.S.H.I.P. with a G.R.I.P.*) told me to trust my instinct regarding my message delivery. Jeffrey Liker, Ph.D. (international bestselling author of *The Toyota Way*) reminded me of the importance of stressing continuous improvement in executing process-related methodologies.

Before the manuscript-turned-book was published, there was a group of women who, also without compensation, went out of their way to promote the book to their respective networks: Dianne Dawson, Marie Fratoni, Latarsha Horne, Erika Jefferson and Andrea D. Smith. A world of thanks to each of you!

I would be remiss if I did not thank the following people, my cheering squad, who, along this book writing journey, reached out to check on me and make sure I was still sane: Alton Brinja, Sharon Durousseau, Kamaria Goggins, Shanta Harrison Proctor, Ph.D., Jay Jemal, Frank Jones,

Byron Minor, Corey Moore, Mark Pegues, Victoria Pinzon, Delores Price, Nelli Sarkuchikova, Sylvie Soudin, Gary Vause II, Tim Walter and Dee Williams.

People are already asking how I came up with the stories in this book. It was partly my imagination and partly inspired by experiences with clients I've been fortunate to work with over the years. Thank you to everyone who enlisted my services and read, listened to or watched my online content. As I mention in Chapter 1, my "research" for this book is mostly rooted in 13 years of working with clients and interacting online with entrepreneurs around the world. I am grateful for every project, blog and video comment, content download and newsletter and podcast subscription. Although customary to keep client names anonymous, there are some with whom my relationship has transcended the formal client/consultant one, for they have become like family to me. Sindy Schneider, Charles DeBaptiste and Adam Walker, thank you for being the big sister and brothers I never had.

I also must mention Gwendolyn Keyes Fleming, Esq. (former District Attorney), Donna Frazier and Kim Farmer, PMP (The Coca-Cola Company) for being the first group of people to extend the opportunity for me to apply my methodology on enterprise-level projects.

And last, but certainly not least, I must thank Dilsa Saunders Bailey. Dilsa, you guided me throughout this entire process. Those walks in the park, lunch meetings and on-the-spot phone calls kept me motivated. Thank you...for everything!

****

As you will discover in the stories contained in this book, none of us is an island unto ourselves. Whenever one attempts to thank those who played an instrumental role in completing a body of work, it can be a mission impossible for you will most assuredly and inadvertently leave someone out. If I have done that, please blame my head and not my heart.

BEHIND THE FAÇADE

# INTRODUCTION

"A Peacock, puffed up with vanity, met a Crane one day, and to impress him spread his gorgeous tail in the sun. 'Look,' he said. 'What have you to compare with this? I am dressed in all the glory of the rainbow, while your feathers are gray as dust!' The Crane spread his broad wings and flew up toward the sun. 'Follow me if you can,' he said. But the Peacock stood where he was among the birds of the barnyard, while the Crane soared in freedom far up into the sky.

**Moral:** The useful is of much more importance and value, than the ornamental."[1]

Is your fast-growing small business like the peacock or the crane? Be honest. Chances are, if this book piqued your interest, your small business is like the peacock. Although comparatively larger than cranes, peacocks cannot sustain flight time, distance or height. In fact, the peacock's beautiful tail that he bragged about in the above fable is nothing more than a façade — externally beautiful but anatomically inept for flight.

Similarly, the *peacock* small business does not have the operational structure to support surges in customer demand (flight) for extended periods of time. Conversely, the *crane* small business is svelte and built with an anatomy that lends itself to soaring for extended periods of time.

## The Business Façade

In the context of this book, a façade is nothing more than an illusion describing the imbalance between perception and reality. Have you ever walked into a business based strictly on its appearance only to be disappointed by the shoddy customer service? If so, then you can attest to the dangers of the façade (perception) of a business not matching your actual experience (reality) as a customer.

Admittedly, it is tempting to choose form *(the ornamental)* over function *(the useful)* in the early stages of a business. Façade is not necessarily a bad thing as long as you identify it and plan eventually to match the function to the form. Unfortunately, the function usually gets ignored until chaotic periods of fast growth make it necessary to address.

There are some who argue that CEOs must choose between form and function. However, I believe it is possible to have both. Think of a luxury hotel where it not only looks inviting from the outside (form), but the décor, amenities and services are equally as inviting on the inside (function).

For the past 13 years, I have studied what it takes to have the back-office operations match the façade of a well-branded business. I now recognize how fortunate I am in being exposed to companies of all sizes and how that exposure led to my discovery of a key ingredient in the elixir for sustainable fast growth, that thing that enables small businesses to become large enterprises: business infrastructure.

## What is Business Infrastructure?

Business infrastructure links together all operational activity to ensure things don't fall apart during fast growth. Once in place, it provides a foundation to scale and sustain a small business, operationally, during growth spurts. It enables you, as a small business owner, to make better decisions as you can easily see and analyze the impact that a change in one area of your business has on all others.

## A Different Kind of Business Book

At first glance, you may be wondering, *Why is this book so thick and why are the chapters so long?* Short answer: it is a how-to book. And no ordinary how-to book for sure, as the bulk of its structure is in the form of storytelling and is primarily intended for owners of fast-growing small businesses and the people who advise them (consultants).

I constructed the stories intentionally to be three-dimensional to show the physiology of the business itself, the psychology of its owners and the sociology in which the consultants apply the Kasennu methodology to help both the business and its owners.

Normally, such discourse is presented in the form of a case study but case studies are, at best, one, maybe two-dimensional in their description. The traditional case study focuses on a problem-action-solution format that leaves readers without the ability to know what the business owner was actually thinking and feeling, in real time, and the role those senses played in creating the problem, taking action, and implementing the solution.

Because of the secrecy of the façade, it was critical that I developed stories that you could either directly relate to or, at the very least, chalk up as cautionary tales. Therefore, I chose to play on the five senses and incorporate the use of character dialogue in the stories, giving you a front row seat to an otherwise stealth problem.

As a result, you will be able to see how the chaos manifested in the small businesses profiled were not just the result of fast growth in and of itself. The chaos is also a manifestation of the specific actions and decisions of the business owners. Those actions and decisions stemmed from unchecked, sometimes self-destructive behavior that led to the institutionalized mess in which they found themselves and their businesses.

## The Entrepreneur as the Hero

I went to great lengths to determine the best way to share the methodology I created for business infrastructure. From past experience, I knew better than to provide a dry, step-by-step instructional book. Although such a book would have been significantly shorter, it would have lacked depth, context of use and, honestly, it would have been flat out boring!

What better way, I thought, to not only introduce the methodology but to also demonstrate its use than using characters that represent composites of past clients I have worked with? In doing so, I was inspired by Rabbi Daniel Lapin's book *Thou Shall Prosper* to highlight the entrepreneur and consultant characters as heroes, not villains.

A recurring theme you will notice throughout each story is that there are, in fact, two types of heroes: the entrepreneur and the consultant. The consultants have the task of not only fixing the business on the inside, but also playing the role of investigator, scientist and therapist to the entrepreneurs in ensuring that the solutions they recommend will *stick*. This *stickiness* is what leads to the sustainability of the methodology, as it is industry-agnostic.

## Beyond the Problem-Action-Result Approach

In drawing from my experiences in implementing the methodology for building business infrastructure, each story is divided into five main parts based on the scientific method for problem-solving:

| Scientific Method | Description | Business Infrastructure Application |
|---|---|---|
| 1. Identify Problem | 1. State the problem to solve. | 1. The Fast Growth Predicament |
| 2. Conduct Research | 2. Ask questions to determine root causes of problem. | 2. The Research |
| 3. Form a Hypothesis | 3. Propose a solution based on research. | 3. The Hypothesis |
| 4. Experiment & Observe | 4. Implement the solution. | 4. The Experiment |
| 5. Draw a Conclusion | 5. Determine if the solution was successful. | 5. The Result |

This book is less on motivation and more on action. Transformative action to be exact. Specifically, it gives you, the reader, insight into how different consultants introduce business infrastructure as a compass to help entrepreneurs navigate the intersection of their businesses with media, politics, law and banking as they work through their growth spurts.

## How to Read this Book

Because this book is written with the busy CEO of a fast-growing small business in mind, it is structured such that most of the chapters can be read in isolation of the others. Chapter 1 introduces the methodology for business infrastructure while Chapters 2-7 include independent short stories in applying the methodology.

The methodology's application varies, as you will read, depending on the circumstances. In Chapter 8, all of the entrepreneurs featured in Chapters 2-7 convene at a workshop to learn how to apply the final and most time-consuming element of the methodology. Chapter 9, the last chapter, offers inspiration for maintaining the results of the methodology using examples of well-known people and brands.

The fastest track for reading this book is: *Introduction, Chapter 1, Chapter 2, Chapter 8* and *Chapter 9*. After reading Chapter 1, you may want to scan the Table of Contents to determine which of Chapters 3-7 you may want to skip.

For the most part, I aimed to keep the content jargon-free; however, there are instances where I felt the need to explain or reference the use of certain terms for context in relation to the methodology and the industry in which it might be applied in a particular story. Such terms are located in the Notes. Further, you should note that the words *small business, company* and *organization* are used interchangeably. The same is true of *CEO* and *business owner*.

## There Is Hope

In writing this book, I am well aware of how important it can be to keep up appearances. It can be risky to let others see our businesses as they really are. No one wants to be seen as a loser; rather, we all want to appear as winners and, therefore, be in the company or flock of other perceived winners. One simply has to look no further than at the types of braggadocios posts uploaded by the second on social media channels to understand the instinctive nature of humans to want to appear as winners.

The desire to keep secret failures, struggles and losses forces many entrepreneurs to suffer in silence, all in the attempt to keep up the façade that all is well with their companies. One thing's for sure: if you are struggling to keep up with customer demand, what got your company here to this point, will not necessarily get your company where you want it to be in the future. Are you content to continue maintaining the façade? Or do you want to see your business, like the crane, spread its wings and soar to greater heights?

It's something to ponder on your journey to mega success.

Alicia Butler Pierre
Atlanta, April, 2018

# PART ONE
## INTRODUCING THE METHODOLOGY

*"Great minds discuss ideas; average minds discuss events; small minds discuss people."*

~ Eleanor Roosevelt

# CHAPTER 1

# EMERALD CITY

Over 100 years ago, L. Frank Baum wrote *The Wonderful Wizard of Oz*. He introduced us to a now-beloved character Dorothy, a young girl who awakened from a tornado only to find that her home landed in a strange, yet beautiful place far away. Grateful for her arrival, Munchkins greeted her and summoned the Good Witch of the North to thank Dorothy properly. In landing, her home accidentally killed the Wicked Witch of the East and the people in this land were most appreciative.

As beautiful as the land was, its inhabitants were strangers and, being an orphan, Dorothy was eager to return home to her aunt and uncle — the people who loved and took care of her. The only reminder of home she currently had was her faithful dog. Seeing she was distraught, the Good Witch of the North told Dorothy about the Wizard of Oz. He could help her return home. All Dorothy had to do was wear the silver shoes (incorrectly represented as ruby shoes in many film and play adaptations) that belonged to the Wicked Witch of the East and follow the paved, yellow brick road to Emerald City. There, she would find the Wizard.

Dorothy set out on her journey to Emerald City with a single mission: to return home to Kansas. Along the way, she met an assortment of friendly people and talking creatures, three of whom asked to join her in exchange for protection. They too wanted to visit the Wizard. Together, this team of five (including Dorothy's dog) encountered many obstacles but, once they reached Emerald City, its beauty instantly struck them. Eager anticipation replaced all fears and apprehension. Upon entering the City's gates, they received instructions to wear mandatory glasses, less they become blind. As they walked toward the Wizard's palace, they took note of all the precious gems, rare stones and advanced architecture, all radiating brilliant hues of green. Even the residents had a greenish tint to their skin. By all appearances, Emerald City was just as magical as they had imagined.

Once Dorothy and her team actually made it to the Wizard's palace, they learned that no one, in fact, had ever physically seen the Wizard. To their dismay, the Wizard refused to see them, not once but twice. Their initial disappointment turned into anger. After all, they paid their dues and *deserved* an audience with the Wizard. In the midst of a heated exchange with him, Dorothy's dog accidentally knocked over a screen, thereby revealing not a god-like figure as they anticipated but "a little, old man, with a bald head and a wrinkled face, who seemed to be as much surprised as they were."[2] There was no Wizard after all. Emerald City was simply a façade, a cruel illusion masked with pomp and grandeur.

Upon interrogation, the man explained that, like Dorothy, he accidentally landed in this magical place, except in his hot air balloon. Because he descended from the sky, people assumed he was a Wizard. Relishing the attention, he never corrected anyone but, instead, had them build Emerald City. Once the city was built, he had the residents wear green-tinted glasses permanently as part of the masquerade's buy-in. For fear of being outed, he secluded himself into his palace, making himself appear mysterious. As he explained it, Emerald City really is a marvelous city even if it is not actually green.

As consolation, the Wizard offered to take Dorothy home via his hot air balloon. Upon departure, Dorothy made a fateful decision to run after her dog just as the balloon took off without her. Inconsolable, Dorothy's last gleam of hope came when she learned that Glinda, the Good Witch of the South, actually had the power to get her home. Once she met Glinda, the witch revealed that Dorothy, in fact, possessed the power to go home all along. All she had to do was click her silver shoes together three times. Voilà! Dorothy made it safely home to Kansas.

If only life and business were this simple.

## Building Emerald City

Unfortunately, putting on a magical pair of shoes does not solve the problems we face in life and business. However, one thing that we do have in common with Dorothy is that in our quest to make it to the proverbial Emerald City, we also face obstacles in the form of trickery, bad decisions, thieves and natural forces completely out of our control.

Yet, where others give up, there are those of us who continue to fight our way through, fueled by sheer determination and tenacity. We understand the difference between an expense and an investment and steadfastly build our businesses to provide products and services that meet customer needs. Initially, these heavy investments in building the business start with a laser focus on branding and promoting, all with the hope of attracting more customers. As you attract more customers, you re-invest profits earned back into the business until, before you know it, you have built your Emerald City!

The Emerald City is symbolic of us *making it*. It represents external success, whatever that looks like to you. Your Emerald City, that is, the storefront of your business, could be a website, a booth at a market or a brick-and-mortar location. Regardless of what the storefront is, customers come because they like what they see and hear. Of course, they only see what is on the surface (as a result of your marketing efforts). They have no idea what is going on behind the scenes (the operations necessary to provide products and services). Our job is similar to that of the Wizard: to make sure they never find out. There is no need to air any dirty laundry unnecessarily.

So the cycle continues: invest in marketing, realize a return on that investment in the form of more customers and re-invest the profits back into the business. With each re-investment comes new and improved ways to attract more customers, in essence, creating a path for customer acquisition.

## The Road to Emerald City – Increased Exposure

The path of customer acquisition that you create is similar to the yellow brick road that led to Emerald City. An educated guess leads me to think that people started creating a buzz upon Emerald City's completion. Its sheer size and shimmer alone were enough to cause intrigue and, naturally, make people want to find out more about it. For those who did not already live within the city's gates, it was next to impossible to reach Emerald City. This led to the construction of the yellow brick road.

Now, with a path to ensure that passersby, aspiring residents and those seeking help had a way to get to Emerald City, there was little need for a full-blown marketing campaign as word-of-mouth proved to be very effective. It was no wonder; after all, the city glowed in green the color representative of balance, abundance and prosperity. However, the yellow brick road, although paved in most parts, was not an easy one to traverse, a reminder that even Emerald City needed to loop through the marketing cycle and make continuous improvements so that more *customers* could reach them.

As a *customer*, Dorothy found certain parts of the yellow brick road treacherous. It is not a stretch to think this could be by design, a ploy to support the illusion that the Wizard must be powerful; otherwise, it would be easier to get to him. Imagine if the entire road was paved. Once news traveled about the Wizard granting Dorothy her wish, surely demand for his services would surge. A surge in demand would require not only more of the Wizard's time but also more staff to support the growing demand. Likely, he knew this and for years intentionally stifled demand for his services through a combination of mystique, scary disguises and denied requests. However, it would only be a matter of time before people would rebel and his strategy backfire, threatening the very existence of Emerald City.

## Maintaining Emerald City – the Transition from Entrepreneur to CEO

Emerald City, in all its glory, hides a secret. Until Dorothy and her team arrived, the only person who knew the secret was the Wizard himself. What started as a harmless attempt to protect his identity developed into a full-fledged gated city that eventually he admitted he could not maintain.

This is how the façade begins. You may argue that, with your small business, you never intended to build an Emerald City. Whether you intentionally built it or not, or even if you inherited Emerald City, it requires maintenance in the form of streamlined operations. Else, you can expect either to do as the Wizard and walk away from Emerald City altogether or watch the business implode.

Façade is the idea of keeping up appearances for the sake of drawing a continuous stream of customers when in fact the reality is your business lacks structure and therefore struggles to keep up operationally. The problem is your customers/clients, vendors and colleagues only see the surface of your business (the projected image due to marketing). They do not know the mess that lurks behind the veil of your operations until they have a bad experience with your company. When your customers approach you about a bad experience, they will have little interest in learning about your sleepless nights, strained relationships or the constant threat of a nervous breakdown as you work to try to keep up the façade. They simply will not care.

The Wizard found this out when, even after hearing the rationale behind his façade, Dorothy accused him of fraud. At best, your customers will only be interested in your *story* once you prove you can build and maintain an Emerald City.

Ensuring the proper care and maintenance of your Emerald City requires a mental shift. You must transition from being a roll-up-your-sleeves-and-get-it-done entrepreneur to being a true CEO/business owner who sees the business holistically, delegates effectively and knows that every decision has an impact on all aspects of the business.

## The Fast Growth Predicament

As the Founder and CEO of a fast growing business, you will find that maintaining the thing that makes your business so special is a constant struggle. You may have found that things were simpler when your business was in the start-up phase, but now that your business is the beneficiary of excellent marketing, customer demand is rising and the stakes are much higher.

How do you know when your company is in trouble? Symptoms of unmanageable fast growth include increases in the following areas:

- Inconsistent quality
- Failed audits and inspections
- High customer and employee turnover
- Task redundancy and/or task avoidance
- Increase in customer and/or vendor complaints

It is no wonder that people say, "More money, more problems." To be more precise, *more growth, more problems*. Even with the best operational foundation, there will be moments of chaos during growth spurts. However, the effects of an Emerald City-like façade primarily becomes a problem when the inability to match it with solid operations becomes the norm and not the exception. The goal is not to ever experience chaos; rather, to have a standard or foundation to revert to once things calm down.

Whether the growth is acute or chronic, or whether it happens organically or via acquisitions, the faster your company grows, the more people you will need to add to your team. Without clarity on what should be done, who should do the work and when, where, why and how, your business is guaranteed to miss the mark in customer, employee and vendor satisfaction. Surely, you need no reminder that dissatisfied people are rarely quiet. Bad news always travels faster than good news.

Left unchecked, chronic inconsistencies in quality, value and product or service delivery can lead to irreparable damage, the most severe being a shutdown. Shifting blame is an easy defense mechanism as it is easy to believe that if you had better people around you, everything will improve. That is only part of the solution.

### The Search for a Cure

I set out on a quest to find a cure for the fast growth predicament and realized, I first needed to determine the root causes of the predicament. My research led me to the violation of three laws that are the primary root causes of the chaos associated with fast growth: The law of supply and demand, the law of conservation and the law of polarity.

### Law #1: The Law of Supply and Demand

The law of supply and demand is an economic law. Its most basic definition describes the relationship between customers and suppliers and its affect on determining a price for a product or service in a competitive market. The onus is on the supplier (or small business in this case) to respond to fluctuations in customer demand. Figure 1.1 below illustrates a simplified representation of the law of supply and demand.

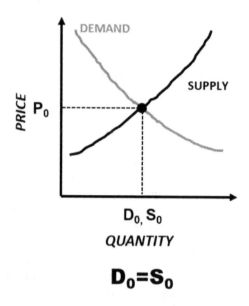

DEMAND

SUPPLY

PRICE

$P_0$

$D_0, S_0$

QUANTITY

$D_0 = S_0$

**Figure 1.1** Graph Illustrating Equilibrium in the Law of Supply and Demand

In Figure 1.1, the vertical axis represents *price* and the horizontal axis represents *quantity*, either supplied or demanded, at a particular price. While the quantity supplied has a direct relationship with price, the quantity demanded has an inverse relationship with price. Using Emerald City as an example, the number of people wanting to visit the Wizard per week represents the quantity demanded, $D_0$, on the graph in Figure 1.1. The quantity supplied, $S_0$, represents the number of people the Wizard is willing (and able) to see.

If the number of people who want to see the Wizard per week equals the number of people that he is willing and able to see, then a point of equilibrium is achieved, $D_0=S_0$. Suppose the number representing this intersection of $D_0$ and $S_0$ is five people as represented by $P_0$. What happens if the number of people wanting to see the Wizard is more than five? What if the average number of people wanting to see the Wizard per week doubled to 10 with no signs of ever reverting to five? This scenario describes a shortage as shown in Figure 1.2.

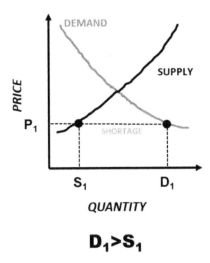

PRICE

DEMAND

SUPPLY

$P_1$

SHORTAGE

$S_1$  $D_1$

QUANTITY

$D_1 > S_1$

**Figure 1.2** Graph Illustrating a Shortage in the Law of Supply and Demand

In Figure 1.2, the number of people demanding to see the Wizard doubled, $D_1$. However, the Wizard is only willing and able to see five people per week, $S_1$. This creates a shortage, $P_1$, as the Wizard simply does not have the bandwidth, $S_1$, to accommodate the rise in demand, $D_1$. The only way for him to reach a point of equilibrium again is to stifle demand by either placing people onto a waiting list, charging a premium for his services or refusing to see people altogether.

Consider another scenario. What happens if the average number of people wanting to see the Wizard per week decreases to two? This was sure to happen if people found out his secret. This scenario describes a surplus as shown in Figure 1.3.

In Figure 1.3, the number of people demanding to see the Wizard decreased, $D_2$. The Wizard is dismayed because he has the bandwidth or capacity to see five people per week, $S_2$. This creates a surplus, $P_2$, as the Wizard has more idle time on his hands. Now, the challenge for the people of Emerald City is to figure out why demand is so low. Have they figured out the façade of Emerald City? Are people complaining about the Wizard's services? Is the effort to follow the path to get to the Wizard not worth it? The way to reach a point of equilibrium again is to implement a solid marketing plan guaranteed to get more people eager to visit Emerald City and visit the Wizard.

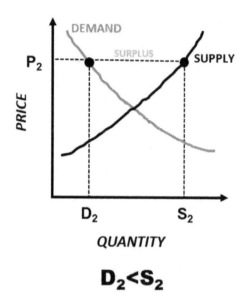

**Figure 1.3** Graph Illustrating a Surplus in the Law of Supply and Demand

Now let's put the law of supply and demand in the context of your fast growing business. Look at Figure 1.4.

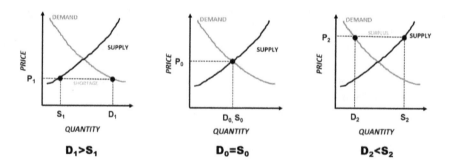

**Figure 1.4** Graph Illustrating the Law of Supply and Demand

As word spreads about how good your product or service is, the quantity demanded increases ($D_1$) as shown in the far left of Figure 1.4. However, you may not have the resources required to supply ($S_1$) or meet the surge in demand. When demand is greater than what your business can handle ($D_1 > S_1$), a resource **shortage** occurs. **This is what unmanageable fast growth looks like**. The violation occurs when there is an imbalance in your company's labor supply and customer demand.

One quick solution is to raise the price. This stifles the demand, biding time for you to hire more staff, secure larger space or upgrade equipment to increase speed and capacity. Another solution is to automate the processes used to make your product or deliver your service.

Raising the price, hopefully, gets you to the point where supply and demand meet or balance each other ($P_0$). This is known as the **point of equilibrium** (as shown in the middle of Figure 1.4): the price that represents the intersection where customers are willing to buy and you can provide the product or service without resource constraints ($D_0=S_0$).

Warning! Your supply constraints may only lift temporarily during a price hike. If you raise the price too high, you may lose customers who will never come back. This could cause a **surplus** in your resources ($D_2<S_2$) as shown in the far right of Figure 1.4. In this situation, you will either need to offer more value at the new price or scale back on your resources. Implementation of the Just-in-Time[3] approach for resource use is one approach to consider. Balancing what your customer desires with what you can actually provide is no small feat and can be a constant juggling act.

### Law #2: The Law of Conservation

The law of conservation is a scientific law. In its most basic definition, it states that energy is neither created nor destroyed. It is merely transformed. That is, a loss, whether perceived or real, is a gain somewhere else. This is perhaps one of the most difficult truths for people, not just CEOs, to accept. Before delving into this from a business perspective, let's first look at this law from a scientific perspective. Below is a chemical equation:

$$H_2 + O_2 \rightarrow H_2O^-$$

The letter $H$ symbolizes Hydrogen and the letter $O$ symbolizes Oxygen. When you combine chemicals, reactions are considered stable once they reach a **point of equilibrium**. In the above case, we are attempting to make water by mixing one Hydrogen molecule ($H_2$) and one Oxygen molecule ($O_2$). However, this 1:1 combination yields an unstable reaction since there is one Oxygen atom leftover. Not having anywhere to go, this lone atom becomes unstable as shown by the negative charge emitted ($H_2O^-$).

Like the law of supply and demand, the law of conservation centers around the idea of balance and any disturbance to that balance can cause undesirable conditions. With that in mind, consider what happens when two Hydrogen molecules ($2H_2$) mix with one Oxygen molecule ($O_2$).

$$2H_2 + O_2 \rightarrow 2H_2O$$

This 2:1 combination produces a balanced, stable reaction as the number of atoms on both sides of the equation (the left and right sides of the arrow) are equal a total of four Hydrogen atoms and two Oxygen atoms on both sides.[4] What may appear as the loss of Hydrogen and Oxygen as individual molecules actually transforms into water.

Back to Emerald City. Once the Wizard realized the jig was up, he decided to leave Emerald City altogether. The residents were upset, after all, they were losing their leader. However, the Wizard did something very important before he left; in a final act of redeeming his image, he left one of Dorothy's teammates in charge of Emerald City. The residents lost the Wizard as their leader, but gained someone better qualified as their new leader. In transferring his power, the Wizard actually freed himself of the pressures in keeping up the façade.

Now let's put the law of conservation in the context of your fast-growing business. Fast growth usually means you will have to invest in hiring more people. Remember, this is a hallmark of the transition from entrepreneur to CEO. The violation of this law keeps many business owners from allowing their businesses to soar. Try replacing the phrase *give up* with *delegate* and watch the effect it will have. By delegating, you actually gain more time to focus on value-added tasks that produce income for your business.

**Law #3: The Law of Polarity**
The law of polarity is a universal law. The law of polarity simply states that opposites attract. This law has probably existed since the beginning of time as evidenced by the myriad of symbols used by different ancient civilizations describing its context. The ancient Chinese represented polarity as a yin-yang.

**Figure 1.5** The Yin-Yang Symbol of Polarity

As shown in Figure 1.5, the yin-yang is a circle with one side predominantly white and the other side predominantly black, with the understanding that both sides exist at all times in order to form a whole circle. The white side, yang, is symbolic of the sun and is akin to masculinity, light, heat and logic. Conversely, the black side, yin, is symbolic of the moon and is akin to femininity, darkness, cold and emotion. Both **harmoniously co-exist** with the idea that one is not necessarily better than the other and that each serves a distinct purpose.

One might equate this idea of polarity as the cancelling out of both elements that co-exist but quite the opposite is true. If nothing else, the yin-yang is a visual reminder of the duality of existence. In order to know or appreciate one side, you must have knowledge or experience of the other side. Some conceptual examples of this dual existence in your business include: the concepts of scarcity/abundance, dilution/concentration, abstraction/concreteness, and digital/analog.

Think of your brain: there is a left side and a right side. The left side represents analytical abilities and the right side represents creativity. The two sides of your brain do not cancel each other; rather, they work together in providing cognition. Even batteries do not provide electrical current until a positive charge pairs with a negative charge.

In business, the primary violation of this law comes in the form of emphasizing the importance of marketing over operations, or vice versa, when in fact both must co-exist in relatively equal parts in order for a company to thrive.

**Figure 1.6** The Polarity of Marketing and Operations Represented by the Yin-Yang

By marketing, I am referring to the activities that fall under the umbrella of the traditional 4Ps — Product, Price, Place (the way you distribute your products and services) and Promotion, that is, activities that include branding, communications, social engagement, sponsorships and pricing strategies. Marketing represents those activities that create the *face* or *front* of your company — what your customers see that attracts them to your company.

Operations refers to the *back office* of your company. It's the grease needed to keep the marketing engine running. It represents those activities that include administration, bookkeeping, logistics, production and order fulfillment — things your customers may not see, but experience.

The Wizard spent the majority of his resources on maintaining the façade of Emerald City (the marketing). As stated earlier in the law of supply and demand, when it came time to actually service customers (the operations), he was inept.

I propose that one is not necessarily better than the other; rather, we need this duality in order to keep things in perspective. Toeing the line (or staying in the middle) often gives the balance needed to keep activities aligned with goals.

Think of a scale. The more you place on the marketing side of the scale, the lighter the operations side becomes and soon you are unable to deliver the operations (supply) required to meet the marketing (demand) of your customers and clients. I advocate staying as close to the center of the alignment of marketing and operations as much as possible. Returning to your *center* might mean saying *no* to certain things. Too much marketing may expose the fact that you cannot supply the demand. Too much focus on operations may mean you create a great product or service with little demand because no one knows about it.

****

Whether speaking in terms of economic, scientific or universal law, one thing is for sure: balance is critical to combating the fast growth predicament and ensuring longevity, scalability and sustainability.

## Developing the Cure

Once I analyzed these three laws and their violation as causes for the fast growth predicament and the reason the façade develops in the first place, I then set out to find a cure.

The quest for the cure happened to coincide with my own struggle in my business. The year was 2007. Unlike the name of my company, Equilibria, I had no balance in my life or my business. By that point, I had appeared on a local television show and had done enough networking to where a good bit of my business was referral-based. I had reached the first of what would be many *tipping points*.[5] In my attempt to keep up the façade of having it all together, I was spreading myself thin, taking on all kinds of projects with little to no discretion.

After confiding in a friend, she suggested that I find a way to package my services. Otherwise, I'd run the risk of falling victim to burnout. You know how it is. When you first start your business there is no shortage of people reminding you of how many small businesses fail in their first three years and, God forbid, if you survive the three-year mark, you'll probably fail within the next two years due to burnout. Well, I claimed victory and decided to play the entrepreneurial game to win!

So I put on my engineering hat and made a trip to the mountains of North Georgia where I barricaded myself in a cabin for a few days. I decided to use the Pareto Principle (80/20 rule) to figure out which projects accounted for 80% or more of my company's revenue in its first two years. This was my initial step in figuring out how to package my services.

Up to that point, I had worked on about 70 different projects for clients. After applying the 80/20 rule, I not only figured out which of those projects were most profitable but, in the process, I also discovered interesting trends and patterns that seemed to hold true across all projects.

One major trend I uncovered was the fact that the majority of my clients were past the startup phase in their businesses. Their issues were less about marketing and cash flow and more about operations. They each suffered from fast growth because of violating one or more of the aforementioned laws. I also noticed an attribute I shared with my clients: we were both visual and tactile learners and my sales cycle was significantly shorter whenever I divided projects into shorter periods of time, guaranteeing incremental improvements. With this client profile in tow, I analyzed the patterns of the projects I worked on and I noticed that the roughly 20% that accounted for 80% or more of revenue boiled down to seven key areas, as you will learn later in this chapter.

By the time I emerged from the cabin, I had seven *packaged* services. There it was — the solution! *But what do I call it?* I remembered thinking to myself. I hypothesized that if I could link those seven services together it could become a methodology, especially if I could duplicate the results with each application. I needed to experiment to confirm the results.

My clients and their businesses became my laboratory. I continued working over the next couple of years, hammering out additional details and refining the methodology along the way until I became certain that it worked with each application. Some clients implemented the whole methodology while others implemented certain elements of it, but one thing was for sure, gone was the chaos!

I hired a team of marketing consultants who helped me realize that the result of applying the methodology was more than just having a better-organized business. The result was more permanent, more foundational. The result was *business infrastructure.*

By narrowing down my services to an all-encompassing methodology, I was able to charge a higher price which, temporarily, allowed me to supply the growing demand I faced at the time. By the following year, the growth became a good problem to have all over again as it forced me to automate my methodology via proprietary software. This enabled me to keep the same price point while maintaining the ability to supply the demand.

Next, I needed to name the methodology. The original name I chose was *klonos,* which is Greek for *clone,* the premise being that with this methodology you can replicate or clone your success. However, the name was too close to a time-management software already on the market called *Kro-*

*nos*, aptly named after the Greek god of time.

After consulting with an Egyptologist, I later settled on *Kasennu*, (pronounced, ka-sen-nu). In Ancient Egyptian, *ka* means *spirit* and *sennu* means *twin* or *clone*. Therefore, the purpose of the Kasennu methodology is to clone the spirit or essence of what makes your small business so great that it has more business than it can handle.

This methodology, rooted in cognitive psychology, physics and engineering principles, provides a formulaic approach to calming the chaos of fast growth while allowing your business to continue growing in a sustainable and repeatable manner – something the Wizard could have benefited greatly from in maintaining the façade of Emerald City.

As you will learn in subsequent chapters, this methodology is not rocket science, though it may take time to absorb some of its principles. It is also industry-agnostic. Both the novelty and the paradigm shift lie in the linking of activities that are normally done in isolation, a common attribute in large enterprises. To date, thousands of small business owners around the world know and use this methodology. Let's now take a closer look at it.

## Business Infrastructure – A Closer Look

Business infrastructure is the systematic linking of a company's organizational goals with the people, processes and tools necessary to support those goals in a scalable, repeatable and sustainable manner. It helps identify *what* needs to be done, *who* should do it, and *how* the work should be done so that the product and service delivery remains consistent, regardless of who performs the work. Most importantly, business infrastructure provides a framework with which to clone the best parts of your business while matching your company's operations to its façade. Further, business infrastructure provides businesses with:

- A solid foundation for future growth,
- A model that makes each time you do something easier than the time before,
- Consistency in your delivery of customer value, and
- Economies of scale.

Meeting customer demand without compromising quality assures not only your customers but also your staff that you effectively know what you are doing and that you have an organized and efficient way of doing it. This translates into positive customer experiences resulting in continued sales; only this time you have a way to supply or manage operations better.

The Kasennu methodology for business infrastructure encompasses seven areas. In order to properly market and share this methodology with others, I needed not only a name but also a symbol. I realized that by splitting the yin-yang symbol of Figure 1.6 into separate yet conjoined circles, business infrastructure serves as the point of intersection between marketing and operations as shown in Figure 1.7.

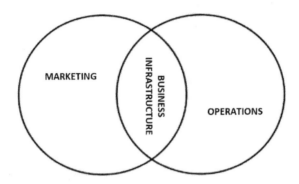

**Figure 1.7** Business Infrastructure Representing the Intersection of Marketing and Operations

However, the symbol in Figure 1.7 was still insufficient in visually illustrating what business infrastructure actually is. By focusing exclusively on what business infrastructure involves, I replaced *Marketing, Business Infrastructure,* and *Operations* in Figure 1.7 with *People, Processes* and *Tools.* I chose *tools* instead of *technology* intentionally, as I found technology, as a word, to be improperly used and grossly misunderstood. In this digital age, many people equate technology with software or digital assets when in fact technology can also describe advances in furniture, material goods and equipment among other things.

A slight rearrangement of the three circles in Figure 1.7 produced a Venn Diagram as shown in Figure 1.8.

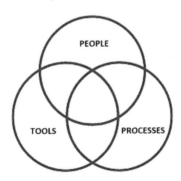

**Figure 1.8** Business Infrastructure is the Linking of People, Processes and Tools

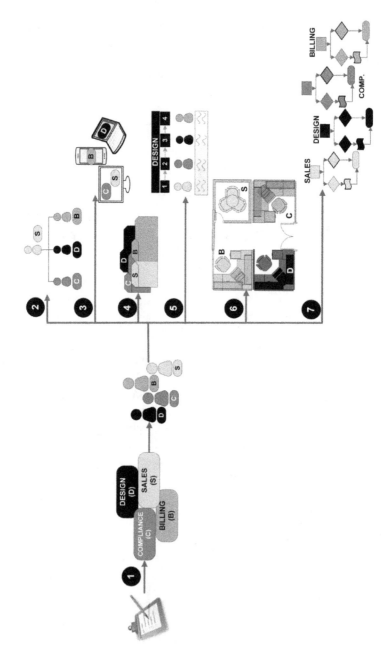

**Figure 1.9** Conceptual (Flowchart) Illustration of Business Infrastructure Methodology with Seven Elements

Careful examination of the Venn Diagram of Figure 1.8 shows seven unique sections, which was fitting since each of these seven sections could represent an element of the Kasennu methodology.

Figure 1.9 illustrates the first element of the methodology which is the listing of tasks to perform in your company. These tasks are then categorized into departments. Next, roles are assigned to each task within a department. This exercise of identifying tasks, departments and roles is critical since it serves as the foundation for the structure and organization of the remaining elements, two through seven. For instance, the second element shows how the identified roles and departments are structurally laid out in your organizational chart. Then, those same department names are used as a basis for organizing your electronic and paper records as shown in elements three and four. The fifth element documents the workflow of your company's core department (i.e., Design Department) and element 6 shows how to organize your workspace based on that workflow and key roles. Last, the tasks previously categorized per department are further grouped into processes and procedures to document, as shown in element seven.

Combining the Venn Diagram of Figure 1.8 with the flowchart illustration of Figure 1.9 led to the development of the logo that now represents Kasennu.

**Figure 1.10** The Logo for the Kasennu Business Infrastructure Methodology (with Numbers)

A detailed description of each element of the Kasennu methodology for business infrastructure follows.

1. **Business Parts Analysis** defines *what* tasks to perform, *how* to organize those tasks into departments and *who* should perform those tasks based on competency and experience. *Why is this important?* Fast growth requires delegation to ensure critical tasks do not fall through the cracks. Hiring the wrong people for the wrong jobs is costly. With strategic task allocation, you will be prepared to lure and retain top talent. *The Business Parts Analysis is a prerequisite for the remaining six elements.*

2. **Business Design Blueprint** defines *how* to manage the business via a reporting structure based on the departments and roles identified in the Business Parts Analysis. *Why is this important?* Fast growth requires an intelligent business design that does not slow down progress. Having the right management structure is critical to maintaining profitability and illustrating your company's maturity and ability to scale.

3. **Electronic Records Management** defines *where* to find digital information to perform the tasks identified in the Business Parts Analysis. The departments identified in the Business Parts Analysis provide a basis for organizing electronic records, while the roles identified provide context for record ownership. It also identifies the optimal tools to store digital records. *Why is this important?* Fast growth requires quick and easy access to a reliable repository for electronic records. Having the right electronic records management system is critical to managing disaster recovery and facilitating mobile/virtual communications.

4. **Paper Records Management** defines *where*, physically, to locate information to perform the tasks identified in the Business Parts Analysis. Like its electronic equivalent, the departments identified in the Business Parts Analysis provide a basis for organizing paper records while the roles identified provide context for record ownership. It also identifies the optimal tools to store paper records. *Why is this important?* Fast growth requires a compliant recordkeeping system that makes mandated paperwork easy to find. Ideally, the organizational structure of the electronic and paper records management systems should mirror each other where applicable.

5. **Service Delivery Blueprint** defines *how* you deliver your core ser-

vice or product to your customers. This is a specialized process based on the department associated with the core service or product and documents *who, how* and *when* all roles identified in the Business Parts Analysis ultimately play a part in delivering value to customers. It also identifies the tools used in delivering value. *Why is this important?* Fast growth requires a consistent quality and delivery of services and products. Documenting the way your team creates an excellent customer experience is critical to maintaining operational consistency and keeping the momentum of increasing value and revenue through happy customers.

6. **Work Space Logistics** defines *how* to organize workspace for maximum productivity regardless of the size of the space. The departments and roles identified in the Business Parts Analysis serve as a starting point for understanding the optimal arrangement of people and tools to yield maximum productivity, workflow and information flow. *Why is this important?* Fast growth requires a clutter- and hazard-free work environment. Having the right workspace layout is critical to demonstrating scale, productivity, competence and satisfied employees.

7. **Business Process Manual** defines *how* and *when* to perform the tasks identified in the Business Parts Analysis. These tasks, further grouped by likeness within each department, become the basis for processes. The Business Process Manual is a collection of documented processes, procedures and tools deemed necessary to ensure consistent operations that yield high quality services and products. *Why is this important?* Fast growth requires a culture of information sharing. Documenting processes and procedures is critical to capturing business intelligence, building equity and cloning your business.

****

Methodologies articulate specific steps in their application and Kasennu is no different. Appendix A contains an abbreviated listing of such steps. What makes Kasennu different is not necessarily the elements themselves; rather, it is the linking of these elements to show how changes permeate throughout the business. That is, it shows how a gain or loss in one area can transform another part of the business (law of conservation). Moreover, Kasennu accounts for the people, processes and tools used across marketing and operations (law of polarity), showing the equal importance of both. Last, its application provides a course of action when imbalances occur in the law of supply and demand.

As previously described, the elements of Kasennu not only answers *who, what, when, where* and *why* to perform certain activities in a specified manner but also answers *how* to perform certain activities, thereby eliminating ambiguity. Empowering you as the CEO with the *how* factor gives you the ability to implement strategic plans and organize people, processes and tools effectively and efficiently, all while staying true to your company's core competencies.

The identification and organization of people is tantamount to an *effective* business infrastructure design, that is, a design that ensures that your company and everyone who does work for you is engaging in the *right activities*. The *right activities* include those activities necessary to: 1) prevent errors or defective services and products, 2) yield profitable results and 3) assure a positive customer experience.

Streamlined processes are critical to ensuring an *efficient* business infrastructure design; that is, a design that ensures that you and everyone who does work for you are doing things the *right way*. Performing the *right activities* the *right way* means using tools and processes in such a way as to minimize waste and deliver services and products on time, within budget and according to specification.

## Silver Shoes = Silver Bullet?

Regardless of your access to knowledge and information, if you do not apply it, it is useless. Unlike Dorothy's silver shoes that, once clicked three times, transported her home safely, the Kasennu methodology is not a silver bullet that will magically fix your fast growth woes overnight. No methodology will for that matter. In fact, you should question any methodology that purports to offer these kinds of speedy results.

This might explain why the Wizard chose to fly off in his hot air balloon to escape the challenges of maintaining Emerald City. Had the Wizard been more patient, he could have overseen the development of a business infrastructure that capitalized on his cleverness and ingenuity without having to out himself at all. Emerald City could have remained intact and perhaps grown even larger.

While there is no silver bullet, the good news is that the fast growth predicament is fixable! You can implement the various elements of Kasennu, as you will learn in later chapters, in 30- to 60-day increments, with the exception of the Business Process Manual. The entire methodology can take anywhere from six to 18 months to execute; however, this can vary according to the size (number of employees), age and complexity of your business.

Kasennu is neither a silver bullet nor a band-aid solution to stop the bleeding caused by fast, unmanageable growth. Replacing habits that no longer serve you take time. You should allow yourself time to absorb the principles of each element so that they will *stick*.

Whether you do a full implementation of the methodology or only use certain parts of it, one thing is certain: what got you here in the present, won't necessarily get you where you want to be in the future.

### Applying Kasennu – Meet the Entrepreneurs Turned CEOs

The skills it took to build Emerald City are not the same as the skills needed to maintain it and take it to the next level. This is an important lesson that spans across the stories of the entrepreneurs you are about to read.

Because of the pre-requisite nature of the Business Parts Analysis, you should read Chapter 2 next. Feel free to skip around when reading Chapters 3 through 7 before returning to Chapter 8 because, like the profiled business owners, you may have a different starting point.

****

**Get ready to revolutionize the way your Emerald City operates.**

# PART TWO
## APPLYING THE
## METHODOLOGY

"...a stuffed memory does not make an educated man or woman. There's a huge difference between absorbing knowledge and transmuting that information into working capital and power.
In short, knowledge only becomes powerful *if* and *when* it is applied." [6]

~ Dennis Kimbro, Ph.D.

# CHAPTER 2

## IDENTITY CRISIS

**Kasennu™**
Business Parts Analysis™

Emily Miller is in jeopardy of losing her position as executive director of the non-profit she founded. The company seemed to grow overnight thanks in part to her appearance on a popular daytime TV show. Though appreciative of Emily's hard work and dedication in building the non-profit, the board of directors recognizes she is ill-equipped to handle the organization's burgeoning growth. Her replacement is inevitable. Unbeknownst to the board, Emily is aware of their plans to replace her. In a proactive move to salvage her reputation, she hires a consultant who introduces her to the first element of the Kasennu methodology — the Business Parts Analysis.

"I'm crying everyone's tears
"I have already paid for all my future sins
"There's nothing anyone can say to take this away
"It's just another day
"And nothing's any good.
"I'm the King of sorrow
"King of sorrow
~ Sade Adu. *"King of Sorrow"* [7]

*O*h *my goodness*, she thought. *She's singing this song about me!* On what should have been one of the happiest days of her life, Emily Miller found herself sobbing uncontrollably as her favorite artist, along with 50,000 concertgoers, sang with the band harmoniously playing along. Emily's friends had surprised her with a trip to London, England, to see Sade perform.

January 10, 2015, marked her 55th birthday and, considering her recent divorce, Emily needed a mood lifter and her friends knew it. Yet she could not help but feel an overwhelming sense of sorrow. Emily's cheeks were beginning to burn from the tears now flowing from her eyes. Her only redemption was the fact that it was dark inside the arena and her friends were too distracted to notice her. Quickly, she reached into her purse and grabbed a tissue to wipe away the evidence. She was sure her makeup was a mess by now.

As the next song played, Emily began reflecting on the past 10 years of her life. *How could this be?* In the blink of an eye, her life turned from a merry-go-round of good fortune to a roller coaster of unpredictable peaks and valleys. This trip to England was also to celebrate her non-profit's 10-year anniversary. Little did her friends, yet alone most people, know that her board was planning a coup to dethrone her as executive director.

You see, Emily was good at keeping up appearances. Her adolescent years spent in charm school taught her that masking public emotion was proper etiquette. Before the concert ended, she had already re-applied her makeup and further garnished her face with her trademark smile — a quality known for being a key ingredient in getting her way. Friends and family alike always joked that Emily would make an excellent salesperson or attorney. She was good at persuading people to give her what she wanted.

However, that all seemed to be changing; her charm was fading. After 32 years of marriage, her husband asked for a divorce and now she was in jeopardy of losing control of her non-profit — an organization she had built and nurtured from inception. These painful reminders overshadowed the remainder of her London trip and, sadly, she still had no viable solution for the board's plans to replace her. *Hopefully the answer will present itself on the flight home* is what she convinced herself.

The eight-hour flight from Heathrow to Dulles was a blur. Emily needed more time to ponder her next move. *Play chess, not checkers* is what she kept telling herself. It was a phrase her father often told her whenever she pondered a decision as strategic thinking was never her strong suit. *But how?* she wondered, *I don't even own a chess set. I don't even know the rules for playing chess! All I've ever known is how to play checkers.* No sooner did she have that thought when she remembered a book her oldest son gave her as a birthday gift. So far, he was the only one who knew what she was going through and, in his gentle, indirect way, he inserted into the book the business card of someone he believed could help his mother.

As Emily examined the card, she managed to draw a smile. She recognized the name on the business card as belonging to her son's best childhood friend, Timothy McKiver. Though apprehensive, she decided she would take her son's advice and call Tim the next day. Just then, the pilot announced that the plane would descend in Washington, D.C. in 20 minutes.

****

Emily arrived in D.C. with mixed emotions. On one hand, she was glad to be home but, on the other, she dreaded what lay ahead. To her dismay, the lines in customs were also surprisingly short and, before she knew it, she secured her luggage and was inside a cab on her way home in less than 30 minutes. Ironically, she wished she had arrived later. It would have given her more time to think.

As the cab turned onto her street, she reflected again. This time, the past 20 years of her life quickly flashed before her. On this very street, she had lived as a teacher, wife, mom, daughter and entrepreneur. In those same 20 years, she had lost her job as a teacher, got divorced and was about to lose her non-profit. *Who am I?* she asked herself. She was so consumed with her feelings of lost identity that she did not hear the cab driver confirm her home address.

"3408. Right ma'am?" the burly cab driver said in a louder, more stern voice.

"Yes, yes, 3408. I'm sorry. I was daydreaming," Emily told him. She was always aware of how important it was to show good manners no matter the circumstance.

When she arrived on the doorstep of her three-story brick rowhouse, she took a deep breath, inserted the key into the doorknob and turned it as if in slow motion. Once inside, she de-activated the alarm, left her luggage near the door, walked into the kitchen and retrieved from her purse a beautifully packaged set of green tea bags she bought while in London. Emily appreciated the therapeutic nature of tea and could not wait to drink her first cup. When the tea was ready, she walked upstairs to her bedroom, drew a bath and placed her teacup on the side of the tub. She did not get past her first sip of tea before, hunched over, her head in her hands, she sobbed uncontrollably.

About an hour later, she managed to pull herself out of the bathtub. She was completely numb and her body felt heavy. She left her teacup on the bathtub and walked to her bedroom. The sound of her feet against the hardwood floor sounded as though someone were sliding heavy furniture across it. The fact that she is the only one living in the house now made the echo of her movements more noticeable.

Once inside her bedroom, she pulled back the covers on her large, California-King sized bed and got in. The bed seemed to swallow her thin, 5'6" frame, especially since she no longer shared the bed with her ex-husband. The sheets felt amazingly soft against her skin. Then she leaned over to grab the remote control on her nightstand and scanned different channels in search of something funny. She landed on a channel that specialized in airing comedies from the '70s. "Good! This is perfect. The '70s were a good time in my life," she said aloud. An hour later, she was sound asleep.

## The Fast Growth Predicament

The next day saw Emily feeling better. When she turned on her cell phone, she learned that her voice mailbox was full. Her top priority was to call her parents as well as her sons. They all needed to know she was okay and that she had arrived home safely. Her conversation with her parents was the usual heartbreak; her dad seemed to lose memory of her as each day passed. The dementia progressed faster than her family anticipated.

The next phone call was to her youngest son, Michael, a freshman at Arizona State University. He always managed to make her feel better with each conversation. Emily's last call was to her oldest son, Brian, a real estate attorney and freshly minted entrepreneur living in New York City. When he answered, her mother's intuition told her that something was wrong.

"Are you okay, son?" she inquired. "What's wrong? You sound down. How's the business coming along?"

"I'm okay, Mom. I don't want to bother you with my troubles. You have enough stressing you out. Hey, have you called Tim yet?" Brian was trying to deflect attention back to his mother.

"No, not yet. I plan on calling him this afternoon."

"Don't wait, Mom. I don't like what the board is up to. We need to jump on this right away. I've already talked to Tim and he's expecting your call."

After ending her call with Brian, Emily held her cell phone in one hand, picked up Tim's business card with the other and headed toward the staircase leading to her basement. For the past 10 years, this basement had served as the headquarters for her fast growing non-profit. The board argued that it was time to relocate to a "more suitable location conducive to business." Deep down, Emily knew they were right, but she liked the coziness of her space and worried that a new location would change the culture of her non-profit.

She sat down at the head of a long, oblong-shaped wooden table that rested in the center of the basement and then dialed the number on the business card.

**** 

Tim knew the reason Emily was calling and, out of respect for their mother/son-like relationship, waited for her to bring it up first. After a few more minutes of small talk, Emily said, "Tim, Brian gave me your card and said you could help me. I really don't know where to start.

"Shortly after you boys finished high school, about a month before the start of school the following fall, I received notification that my services were no longer needed at the middle school where I taught."

Tim was shocked. In past conversations over the years, Brian had omitted that detail. He replied, "Oh Mrs. Miller, I'm so sorry."

"Ah, don't be," Emily said. "Sure, I was upset at first but that waned once I started my non-profit, which I was inspired to start as a result of meeting with so many people my age who were also displaced from work. We were all too young to retire legally, yet too old to hire. Their stories were all so heartbreaking. I decided to channel my anger and frustration into creating an organization that would empower us to convert these obstacles into opportunities through the power of relationships.

"I am a firm believer in the idea of six degrees of separation. The concept took off, too! With the help of my garden and tennis clubs and the scores of contacts through my husband's, I mean *ex*-husband's real estate law practice, I had a strong pool of employers eager to attend my matchmaking events. My events are a far cry from a career fair. I work hard to create an environment that encourages genuine conversation and networking. Before I knew it, people were getting jobs! And word about my events spread faster than fire."

Emily straightened her posture as she became nostalgic over her nonprofit's humble beginnings. She continued, "The next thing we knew, we were helping dozens of people throughout D.C., Maryland and Virginia with quality connections that landed them jobs. Mikey had already taken Brian's room when he graduated and left for college. So I used a vacated bedroom as my new office. I quickly outgrew that space and moved down to the basement. I had more room to spread out and things really took off. Eventually, I hired an assistant, started adding more people to the board and..." Emily stopped abruptly.

Thinking about the board and the recent anguish they had caused her almost made Emily cut the story short.

"The board. The board. The current bane of my existence!" Emily did not want to leave the wrong impression and immediately regretted saying that. Instead of going down a path of negativity, she continued talking about what led to her latest fast growth predicament.

"Just when I didn't think things could get any better, I had the opportunity to appear as a subject matter expert on that daytime talk show. I was only on the air for about five minutes but that was enough to see my non-profit's popularity go through the roof. We were gaining momentum and fast!

"Turns out, that was their concern, that it was happening *too* fast. The board said that my being 'the face' of my non-profit was an issue. 'What if something should happen to you?' they'd always ask. Meanwhile, with each new donor, each new client, each new event, my time was no longer mine. It belonged to my organization. This meant more time away from Dan, the boys, my parents…pretty much everyone. I justified it by saying that I was saving people's livelihood. Dan would say, 'Yeah, while destroying your own.'"

"Sounds like you lost work/life balance in the midst of the growth. Is that an accurate statement?" Tim asked.

"In retrospect, yes, that's exactly what happened. Before I knew it, Dan filed for divorce, my dad was diagnosed with dementia and one of the board members, who I still consider to be a very good friend and a reliable source, told me about the board's plans to replace me."

Looking at his watch, Tim realized that 30 minutes had passed and he needed to leave for a meeting across town. This would require a longer conversation and they agreed to meet for dinner.

Once she hung up the phone, Emily decided to take a walk. It was cold but she needed fresh air. An hour later, she returned home, checked her phone and noticed an email from Tim's assistant, Rhonda. Emily and Tim would meet next Monday at 7:00 pm at a seafood restaurant in Baltimore.

*Baltimore?! Well, at least I'll get a good crab cake.*

## The Research

As a native Washingtonian, Emily grew up with a natural aversion to Baltimore, Maryland, a city relatively close in proximity that seemed worlds apart. Although she was apprehensive about traveling to Baltimore to meet Tim, she knew she would have to put that aside and focus on the issue at hand — rescuing her non-profit.

When Emily arrived at the restaurant situated on the Inner Harbor, Tim stood up from the table where he was sitting and held his arms open.

Emily was just as he remembered her — an attractive lady with short, neatly cropped blond hair always wearing a dress suit and her signature pearl necklace and earrings.

"Mrs. Miller, you look stunning!"

"Well, you don't look so bad yourself, Tim." Emily could not deny being flattered.

After several minutes of small talk, they realized they needed to place their order as the waiter stood patiently waiting.

"So, Mrs., I mean, *Ms.* Miller. I understand you've been blessed with a problem recently."

"I beg your pardon?"

"The situation at your non-profit."

"You call that a blessing? It's for sure a curse!" Emily proclaimed. "If you knew the whole story…"

"Well, why don't you tell me that story?" Tim said, hoping that he did not come across as condescending. He wanted to be careful not to offend Emily but he also realized he needed to be in consulting mode.

"As I mentioned during our last call, things were going well until the board grew larger. It was important to me to have an odd number of people so that we'd never run into a split vote situation. I also knew it was important to have a diverse board that included men and women, all with different backgrounds. Don't get me wrong. All of them are exceptionally bright and talented but, for about the past year, I've bumped heads with one board member in particular. Unlike the other members, I did not hand-select her. One of our members resigned due to retirement and the board seized that moment as an opportunity to try something different."

"Something different?" Tim interjected.

"Yes, something different," Emily continued. "They told me that they had developed some criteria, a sort of checklist for what would make a good board member. They actually wanted to implement a recruitment and interview process, you know, to make everything more formal. I thought it was absurd. Why fix something that isn't broken?

"So, they went on this quest to find a replacement for the member who had retired. I suggested that they start with the very people that we service: baby boomers displaced from their jobs before they can legally retire and collect benefits. They agreed that was a good idea. Wouldn't you know it? The person they voted to add to the board was none other than a client that I highly recommended, Clara Dixon!"

"Is that a bad thing?" Tim asked, somewhat confused.

"Oh, you don't know the half of it!" Emily answered. "From day one of joining the board, I noticed Clara making sly remarks, wanting to change things here and there. It seemed harmless, at first, but progressively got worse. She has since been like a virus spreading her poison and influencing the board that, mind you, I originally assembled for a non-profit that I had created! She has been plotting a coup to have me removed, saying I'm not qualified to be executive director, that I lack the vision to truly lead the non-profit to the next level. My source tells me she even accused me of merely being a 'school teacher with a hobby' as a way of further discrediting me.

"Clara argues that I can't have intelligent conversations about budgeting and forecasting. All I know is that I bring in the money and lots of it! Through my events, we raised $2 million alone in the past year for a total of $2.5 million in revenue! That has to count for something." Emily noticed her voice rising in pitch. It was unlike her to show such outward displays of emotion.

"May I?" Tim asked Emily as a signal to respond. Emily nodded. "Do you know this hearsay to be fact?"

"Yes," Emily said, "it sounds like something she would say. I'm sorry, I get so mad every time I think about it because this woman has cried on my shoulder, she's eaten at my home, we've had many late night conversations. She's a former executive of a large non-profit and, truthfully, I think she wants my job. The time we spent together, I now believe, was merely her way of getting close so that she could take over."

Looking her directly in the eye, Tim said, "Ms. Miller, first, thank you for sharing your story with me. There is a lot to unpack here, but I'll start with something I noticed from our phone call last week. You say 'my non-profit' or 'my organization.' I think that's a symptom of the larger issue. It does not belong exclusively to you. You need to change your narrative from *owner* to *founder*."

Emily's raised eyebrows caused fine lines to appear across her forehead. Unmoved, Tim continued, "I have a hunch that you are a victim of the Peter Principle.[8] Do you know what the Peter Principle is?"

"No," she responded.

"It's the idea that, 'in a hierarchy, every employee tends to rise to his level of incompetence.'"

Before he could finish explaining, Emily interrupted, "But I'm not an employee! As you just pointed out, I am the Founder."

"Exactly," Tim replied. "When you started your non-profit you were keenly aware of the nuances of its legal structure. Aside from not paying taxes, you know that non-profits are governed by boards. By referring to yourself as the founder, it gives credit where credit is due, but it does not imply that you are ultimately the final decision maker in the same way that owner does. Does that make sense?" Emily nodded in agreement.

Tim continued, "The non-profit has a fast-growth problem, which, by the way, is a good problem to have! What you interpret as a 'coup' is really their way of saying that they need someone qualified to take the organization to the next level. By you founding the non-profit, you automatically assumed the title, executive director, and the original board went along with it, perhaps not knowing any better.

"But Clara is a former executive who knows firsthand the experience needed to operate on a higher level. Now that she has a bird's eye view of the organization, she can see the limitations of your skill set. I know it sounds insulting, but she's really pointing out that, unless the right people are placed in the right positions to manage the growth, the entire non-profit could implode."

"Implode?" Emily busted out loud. "Isn't that a little extreme, Tim?

"No ma'am," he answered. "Not at all. I've specialized in working with non-profits through my community activism for the past nine years and the ones that do well are operated by people who recognize when they may be getting in the way of success. One of the hardest things to do is to let go. But you have to let go in order to grow. In your case, this might mean letting go of your title, as a starting point."

Emily began squirming in her seat. She did not like where this conversation was going. Tim was supposed to be on her side.

At that moment, the waiter appeared to remove their plates from the table and asked if they would like to order dessert. Emily was too disgusted to respond. Tim could see she was upset and ordered a thick slice of cheesecake, thinking he could offer her half of it as a peace offering. He knew he needed to say more and so, without further hesitation, he resumed.

"Ms. Miller? I know this is a lot to process. By your own admission, you feel as though you've suffered enough loss: your beloved teaching job, Mr. Miller, your sons, and now this. Please be comforted in knowing that admitting when it is time for someone else to take over the reins is not an admission of failure; rather, its recognition of your maturity as a leader. You don't have to put out someone else's light in order to shine. You and Clara can shine together! You've accomplished so much! Just as you had to let go of your sons in order for them to grow into independent adults, so you must do with this non-profit."

Emily mustered the courage to speak, "Tim, I don't like what you're saying. It's hard to hear the truth when it stares you in the face. I realize you have no reason to hurt me so I want to believe that you are genuine in your remarks. It reminds me of what I used to tell my students and my own children: 'I'm not telling you what you *want* to hear; I'm telling you what you *need* to hear.' What can I do about this?"

"It may not seem like it Ms. Miller, but there is a win-win solution in this. I can help you."

"How?" Emily asked.

Tim leaned forward in his chair and told her, "You are in an amazing position to leverage your network to secure jobs for a targeted group of people! We just need to get a business infrastructure in place that can sustain the growth and ensure its viability."

"But we're not a tech company," Emily contested.

Realizing she misunderstood what he meant by business infrastructure, Tim further explained. "No ma'am. You're right. The non-profit is not a tech company. I'm talking about *business* infrastructure, an infrastructure that shows how the non-profit is structured operationally. You, as well as the board, are experiencing growing pains right now. This is compounded by the fact that there is no solid foundation upon which to keep growing. It's like trying to build a house on sand without a concrete foundation. This is what I meant earlier when I said that this non-profit runs the risk of implosion or, in this case, it can collapse."

Emily leaned forward in her chair. This was a good sign. They were talking about solutions and Tim, feeling encouraged by the change in her non-verbal cues, continued, "I've been around and worked in dozens of non-profit organizations at this point. The biggest difference I've noticed is that the more successful ones have this business infrastructure, whether they refer to it as that or not, in place where the others don't. The others are in a perpetual hamster-in-the-wheel state, spinning round and round yet never moving forward or upward.

"I learned this methodology for creating business infrastructure called Kasennu and realized that I could apply this to the political, legal and non-profit organizations that I work with. Once utilized, I've personally witnessed the turnaround within those organizations: it's amazing what people can accomplish when they have greater clarity about what they are supposed to be doing, why they are doing it and how they should be doing it."

By now, the waiter returned with the check. They had been at this restaurant for almost three hours! Tim paid the tab and then looked at Emily. "Would you like to move forward?"

"Yes," Emily answered, but I have one major concern. The board will meet again in about 45 days to discuss our 10-year anniversary celebration. I'm assuming they'll also use that as a time to discuss my potential dethroning. What can we accomplish before then?"

"Leave that up to me Ms. Miller."

With that, Tim then asked if he could speak with the one board member Emily described as a reliable source who had warned her of the coup. She agreed to pass along her contact information but stated that she needed to speak with that board member first. Emily knew this was risky, but she was desperate to fix this problem. Tim asked that she make the call as soon as possible since he wanted to submit a proposal to her before the end of the week.

As they walked toward the front door of the restaurant, Tim assured Emily that she was taking a step in the right direction. Once she arrived home, she called Kathy, the board member whom she trusted, and gave her a recap of her conversation with Tim. Knowing the urgency of the situation, Kathy agreed to speak with Tim.

****

The next day, Tim called Kathy Jacobs, the entrusted board member. Their conversation was amazingly efficient, lasting no longer than about 15 minutes. In that time Tim learned that Clara Dixon, the new addition to the board, has a background in forensic accounting. Clara suggested that the board start making decisions backed by numbers, as opposed to educated guesses and hunches. The board complied and, in doing so, they learned that, although fundraising dollars and number of active clients were up, the number of complaints by the clients was also on the rise.

Their clients felt neglected. The board addressed Emily and knew that she had a knack for working one-on-one with the clients but, with more of them coming through, it was simply too much for her to handle by herself. She had a choice to make: spend more time with the clients or focus more time on fundraising. One thing the board was clear on was that Emily could not remain as executive director.

Clara showed them the danger in Emily not knowing how to interpret financial statements and have meaningful dialogue about them. Apparently, Emily thought it unnecessary but Clara argued that, although they had a tax-exempt status, they still had a duty to be fiscally responsible and accountable to their donors and clients. Kathy offered to share some figures with Tim and he happily accepted knowing it would add more context to his proposal. Their conversation ended with Tim asking Kathy if she would keep their conversation confidential.

As Tim conducted more research on the non-profit and prepared the proposal, Emily thought about how she would spend the remainder of the week. Thankfully, she had the foresight to take this week off too when she made her trip to London last week. In that time, she called her son Brian and told him about her meeting with Tim. Brian strongly encouraged her to work with Tim and mentioned that he wished Tim was available to help him with his own real estate business in New York.

Emily bought and read a copy of the book about the Peter Principle. Similar to the epiphany she had at the Sade concert, she took a shower thinking to herself, *Oh my gosh, Tim is right! I'm a victim of the Peter Principle!* Her eyes welled with tears. She had to stop feeling sorry for herself. This was not the end of the world and, as Tim said, she had the power to fix it. She went to bed that night and, for the first time in a long time, felt hopeful.

## The Hypothesis

Tim's proposal arrived by email Friday morning. At first glance, the proposal seemed to be a repeat of their conversation. As Emily read more, she realized it included financial information she knew she did not disclose to Tim. *That must've come from Kathy*, she thought. She continued reading and came to a diagram that explained the Kasennu methodology Tim previously mentioned. According to the diagram, the first step to take in defining and building the business infrastructure was the Business Parts Analysis (BPA) exercise. The proposal described the benefits of the BPA:

> Fast growth requires delegation. As the executive director, you are responsible for maintaining the financial health of the non-profit, as well as its good name. Hiring the wrong people can result in poor performance, procrastination or, worse, loss of control. The Business Parts Analysis can rescue an organization from task redundancy, improper work distribution and angry clients.
>
> By going through the process of defining what tasks to perform, organizing those tasks into departments and identifying who should perform those tasks based on competency and experience, you can:
>
> • Delineate roles and responsibilities to eliminate task redundancy, maximize talent, reduce waste and save money;
>
> • Stay in charge by effectively delegating office support tasks to others without compromising service quality;
>
> • Increase productivity through synchronization across all departments and tasks and effectively cross-train current and/or future employees; and,
>
> • Attract and retain top talent through job descriptions that communicate responsibilities, expectations and organizational culture.

As she continued reading, she learned that the output of the BPA would produce task, role and department identification, as well as succinct job descriptions with a prioritized hiring strategy. This work would take place over a four-week period, with one meeting session taking place each week.

A final statement in the proposal gave Emily pause. It read, "Like the founder, the non-profit is suffering from an identity crisis. It has the opportunity to evolve into something much bigger but requires proper guidance." Those were piercing words and, for a split second, Emily had a mind to call Tim and scold him the way only a mother could. However, she didn't. After all, it was the truth.

****

Instead, Emily waited a couple of hours before calling Tim. Once she did, she told him she read his proposal and, although she had many questions, she first asked, "When can we start?"

Tim was glad to hear that she was eager to begin working together. However, Emily mentioned concern regarding the payment. "I trust that this will work, Tim. But there's one major problem. The board will never approve of this. Can you do this work pro bono?"

Rather than provide an answer, Tim responded with a question, "What is the maximum amount of money you can spend without their approval?" Emily told him the amount and Tim told her he could split this one project into four mini-projects, according to the weekly sessions. "That way, you can avoid getting the board's approval for the lump sum. I can send you an invoice upon the completion of each phase."

Emily agreed knowing that, if they could do most of this work before the board convenes in 45 days, then she would have the results to show her proactiveness in addressing their leadership concerns.

## The Experiment

The next week, Tim and his assistant, Rhonda, arrived to Emily's home at 8:00 am sharp on a frigid Tuesday morning. He was on her turf now and he hoped he could keep her focused for what was sure to be a long and intense day. This was their first session of the BPA — a brainstorming exercise. Emily escorted them into the basement. Tim could not help but survey the room in amazement. It was very different from the basement he remembered playing video games and shooting pool in as a child. The once kid-friendly basement was transformed into an adult's office adorned in lapis lazuli suede wallpaper, live plants and vases filled with fresh white lilies.

In the center was a freshly polished mahogany table and lapis lazuli dining room side chairs. Sitting in one of the chairs was another woman who appeared to be the same age as Emily.

"Wow, Ms. Miller you've really spruced things up!" Tim exclaimed.

"Do you now understand why I don't want to relocate the office?" Emily asked, beaming with pride. "Oh goodness, where are my manners? Tim, this is Julia. She's *my*, I mean, *the* office manager. She's my right hand. She'll be helping us today."

Tim and Rhonda began setting up. Tim also looked around the room for a bare wall.

"May I ask why you need a bare wall?" Emily inquired.

"Because I need a place to secure large pieces of paper from the easel pad," he responded.

Tim then handed Emily and Julia each an 11" x 17" laminated sheet of paper with the words *Task Identifier* in big bold letters across the top. Underneath it was seven columns of topics. The topics covered the areas of marketing, operations, legal compliance, accounting & finance, information technology, human resources and management. Tim explained he would use this as a guide in facilitating the brainstorming session.

He noticed the puzzled looks on their faces. He walked over to the easel pad, and chose a topic randomly from the Task Identifier — *business license*. Looking at Emily, Tim directed his first question of the brainstorming session, "Ms. Miller, tell me, who renews the business license?"

Emily replied, "Well, I receive the email prompting me when it's time for the business license to be renewed. From there I make sure I go online to renew the license. After that, we receive a bill confirming the amount owed, and then I ask Julia to either cut a check and mail payment or pay online. Then we wait for the new license to arrive."

As Emily talked, Tim wrote the following tasks onto the easel pad in black marker:

1) *Receive notification to renew business license*
2) *Renew business license online*
3) *Receive clearance to pay the business license renewal fee*
4) *Save an electronic copy of the receipt*
5) *Send receipt to bookkeeper*

Before Emily or Julia could ask a question, Tim beat them to it. "How do you know the gross revenue information to report when renewing your business license?"

Julia blurted out, "I get that information from the tax return that the CPA prepares for us." With that, Tim added another task to the easel pad:

6) *Receive prepared tax return from CPA*

Emily was already impressed; Tim generated a list of six tasks from just a few sentences spoken about that one topic. She was starting to understand the significance of this brainstorming session.

Tim then began going through the listing of topics on the Task Identifier, diligently writing each task starting with an action verb onto the easel pad. As he ran out of space on a sheet of paper, he would remove it from the easel and secure its adhesive backing to the blank wall. With each task identified, Rhonda recorded the task into the business infrastructure software on her laptop.

Four hours later, there were 20 sheets of paper covering the wall. It was time to take a lunch break and Emily offered to order carryout, but Tim and Rhonda instead chose to walk down the street to a deli. He told Emily to be prepared to resume the session in about an hour.

When Emily escorted Tim and Rhonda out of her home, Julia stood behind her. She turned to face Julia and, almost as if communicating telepathically, they both started laughing and high-fived each other.

"Oh my God, Emily! Can you imagine the board's reaction when they learn just how much stuff you and I do together? We should take a picture of the walls downstairs."

"Great idea!" Emily said, equally enthused.

The hour seemed to fly by because no sooner than they finished their lunch, Emily's doorbell rang.

Everyone settled back into their seats at the table while Tim remained standing at the easel. "Up to this point, we've identified everything that you all currently do in making sure the non-profit stays afloat and operates in a compliant manner. Now, I'm going to challenge you on certain topics that we skipped over and ask you about tasks that are not currently being performed, but that you recognize and agree need to be done. For example, the hiring and recruiting process for board members. Do you have a similar process in place for actual employees and event volunteers?"

Emily looked up and said, "No, we don't have a process for that."

"Exactly," Tim said. He began recording in red marker tasks not currently performed to make a visual distinction from those currently performed, which were written in black marker on the large sheets of paper.

Another two hours passed and, confident they had exhausted all task identification possibilities, Tim called the session to a close. Emily felt as though her head was about to explode. She was now surrounded by 22 large sheets of paper taped across not one but three walls. Julia took more photos of the basement.

Tim dismantled the easel and then began removing the sheets of paper from the wall, but Emily asked that he leave them up.

"As much as I love an organized space, this is inspirational for me." It was not a problem to leave the papers there, as Rhonda had inputted each task carefully into the business infrastructure software. Tim asked if there were any board documents he could look at from which he and Rhonda would be able to extract more job tasks. Julia offered to email them copies of the board's bylaws and agreements that each member signed highlighting his or her duties.

As Emily escorted Tim and Rhonda out of her home, she assured them that, if she and Julia thought of any additional tasks, they would share that information before their next session on the following Tuesday.

****

The second session was different mainly because Tim insisted that they meet at an offsite location near Union Station which was convenient for everyone involved since it was accessible via the Metro rail system. Initially, Emily rejected the idea of working outside of her basement, but Julia convinced her that Tim made a good point. "This really will be a first step toward getting used to the idea of working on the non-profit *outside* of your basement. Think of how many brownie points you'll score when the board finds that out."

Emily and Julia arrived at 8:00 am and Tim and Rhonda already had the room setup, ready to work. Tim greeted them and asked that they take a seat on the same side of the conference room table, across from a large, dry erase board. Then, he stood next to the board to address Emily and Julia. "Before we start with today's exercise, and to help keep things in perspective, I'd like to remind you of why we're here. This will segue nicely into the role identification exercise we'll do today."

He turned toward the board and began sketching a Supply and Demand diagram.

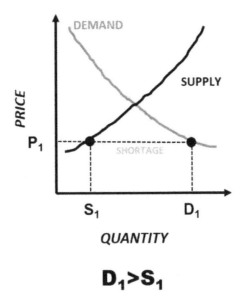

$$D_1 > S_1$$

Tim explained that, as long as people in their target market continued to be laid off and the non-profit continued its marketing winning streak (all other things constant or *ceteris paribus*), they could reasonably expect a shortage in their supply of one-on-one client relationship programs.

"Ms. Miller, your current capacity is 15 clients per week. You'll either have to shorten the amount of time you spend in these one-on-one sessions so you can accommodate more clients each week, or you'll have to hire more people to assist in supplying the growing client demand. This explains why client complaints are on the rise. Unbeknownst to them, the backlog for these one-on-one sessions is growing by the day all because there's really only one person who can currently facilitate these sessions — you! The façade of the non-profit being bigger than it actually is was cemented when you appeared on that TV show; now it's killing you and poor Julia to try to maintain it!

"This non-profit is becoming bigger than what the two of you can handle. It has the potential to evolve into a nationwide program, but you have to have the business infrastructure in place to support that. The board recognizes this and, though they may not have articulated it in the same way, this explains why they want to bring in someone with the experience of running a larger nonprofit organization.

"Ms. Miller, I know you see this as a loss, but I need for you to see it as a gain. Your biggest fear right now is that you will lose what you worked so hard to build. But that's the farthest thing from the truth. By delegating, you free up more of your time to focus on the things you are the best at —

fundraising and client relationships. Think about it. We're in the nation's capital. Even the President of the United States has a cabinet. Why? Because it's impossible for the President to know everything. This is why cabinet advisors exist. They are the subject matter experts who inform the President. Does this make sense?"

"Yes!" Emily and Julia collectively replied.

"Great," Tim said. "I want both of you to keep this in mind as we start assigning tasks to the specific roles you identified last week."

Rhonda directed their attention toward the end of the table. There lay several stacks of what appeared to be small white index cards. Printed on each index card was a specific task they had identified last week. The cards also included tasks he and Rhonda extracted from the board's bylaws and agreements information Julia provided.

Tim asked that Emily and Julia stand. At that point, Rhonda presented Emily with a small stack of cards. Tim instructed Emily to spread the cards out across the table and, in the process, group cards together that described similar tasks. Rhonda also handed a small stack of cards to Julia to help the process go a little quicker, as there were close to 450 tasks to begin grouping.

As they began distributing the cards on the table, Tim suggested that they create no more than nine groupings of tasks. The reason, he explained, was because of the Attention Intensity factor.

"What's that?" Emily asked.

"It refers to the amount of information people can process at a particular moment.[9] Cognitive psychologists believe that the average person can easily recall seven (plus or minus two) bits of information at a time.[10] Your ability to recall information about a certain thing is what they and marketers refer to as the *consumer consideration set*. It's the reason why phone numbers, aside from the area codes, have seven digits. I'll give you an example. Julia, in 20 seconds, I want you to name different types of fruit."

Julia looked up from the table, puzzled. "What?"

"Don't think hard about it. List the fruits that immediately come to mind in 20 seconds," Tim requested again. He set the stopwatch on his cell phone. "Go!"

Julia stopped what she was doing, looked up at the ceiling and began to rattle off a list, "Um, okay…apples, oranges, bananas, plums, kiwi, pineapple, grapes, mango…"

"Stop!" Tim yelled. "In 20 seconds, Julia named eight fruits. That fell within the five to nine units of information a person can recall and/or process at a given time. Now, what if we were selling pomegranates? Pomegranates are not a part of Julia's consumer consideration set, meaning they are not on the top of her mind. If Julia represents the average customer, then we would be in trouble and would have a serious marketing problem on our hands.

"This is why I ask that you not create more than nine groupings. When you articulate the new business infrastructure to the board and other constituents, you need to be able to do so succinctly, without hesitation and in such a way that makes it easy for them to recall also."

With all of the cards distributed on the table, there emerged seven groupings. Then, Rhonda placed a larger blank index card above each grouping and Tim instructed Emily and Julia to assign a department name to each grouping of tasks. They were confused and asked for an example.

Tim pointed to some of the tasks grouped together on the far left. He read a few them aloud, "*Confirm meeting venue, Secure photographer, Print registration list*...what do these tasks describe?"

Emily replied, "Those tasks refer to things that we do in preparation for any of our events."

Tim asked, "Would you agree that this is the core of the non-profit?"

Emily looked at Julia and answered, "Yes, but our client relationship programs are also core to what we do."

"Well, some people refer to their core department simply as *Operations*," said Tim.

Emily frowned, "That sounds so corporate. It doesn't fit with our culture."

Julia made a suggestion, "What about *Events & Programs*?" They all agreed that was a more suitable name. Rhonda handed a black marker to Emily so that she could write *Events & Programs* onto the large index card above the grouping of tasks they were currently looking at.

It took Emily and Julia about 30 minutes to name the remaining departments as: *Executive Management, Marketing Communication, Human Resources, Finance, Office Administration* and *Legal*. Tim then had them assign a color to each department, saying the reason would become more evident as they progressed through the remaining elements of the Kasennu methodology. For now, all they needed to know, he told them, was that color assignment would help increase their ability to recall important operational information in the future.

It was now 10:30 am. Tim suggested they take a 15-minute break, so Emily, Julia and Rhonda excused themselves from the room.

When Emily and Julia returned to the conference room, they noticed that only one department and its associated tasks remained on the table. The other groupings of tasks were carefully rubberbanded together, resting on the far corner of the table. Tim explained that they would now assign roles to all of the tasks within each department, starting

**Name of Role Goes Here**

with the newly identified Events & Programs Department. Rhonda then placed what appeared to be laminated stick figures holding a sign onto the table. This amused Emily as it reminded her of the creative things she used to do when she worked as an educator.

Tim instructed Emily and Julia to spread out the index cards associated with the Events & Programs Department and to write onto each stick figure the name of the role that ideally should perform certain tasks. "Do not," he warned, "write the names of actual people. I want you to think, *in a perfect world if I had a full staff of people, who would perform this task?*"

Rhonda handed black, red and blue dry erase markers to Emily. If the role represented a resource already in place, she was to write that name in black marker. Conversely, if the role represented a resource to hire, she was to write that role in red marker onto the stick figure. Current resources to whom work was outsourced were indicated by the blue marker.

One of the first roles they identified was event planner. Emily wrote the name of this role in red marker on one of the stick figures. She then wrote the name of her role, *Executive Director*, on another stick figure. When Tim noticed the types of tasks she assigned to this role, he decided it was time to have a very important discussion.

"Ms. Miller, I'm going to challenge you on this particular role assignment. Are those really the tasks of an executive director? They seem more in line with someone who would manage the Events & Programs Department."

Emily did not budge. Tim went on to say, "The executive director is like the CEO of a for-profit company." He asked Rhonda to look up the *Dictionary of Occupational Titles* online. She searched for *Chief Executive Officer*, read the definition and then compared it to the description of an executive director. Just as Tim had said, the responsibilities described were similar. Emily realized that neither description entailed getting involved on the ground-level of the organization (as she had been doing); rather, it involved setting the overarching direction from which the company operated.

Emily realized the point that Tim was trying to make. She thought about their conversation over dinner and his mentioning the Peter Principle. No matter what title she ultimately held, she was still the founder, a title that no one else could hold. She wiped off the original title she wrote on that particular stick figure and replaced it with *Director of Events & Programs*. Tim grinned from ear to ear. Unlike many clients in the past, he did not have to drill home his point. Emily self-identified it.

As they identified all roles for the Events & Programs Department, Rhonda diligently entered this information into the business infrastructure software. Then, she carefully picked up all of the stick figures and index cards and spread out the next department and its associated tasks. Emily and Julia went through the role identification exercise until they completed all departments. By this time, it was noon. Though mentally exhausted all over again, Emily and Julia thought the session was life changing and told Tim and Rhonda they looked forward to their next session, which would take place remotely.

In just two weeks, Emily and Julia could both easily articulate the names of the new departments of the non-profit, the work associated with each department and the names of the roles of the people who would perform the work within those departments.

Emily spent the remainder of that week facilitating client programs and reflecting on the Peter Principle. She decided to make a trip to the Library of Congress and do some more research on occupational titles, among other things. She emailed Tim with a few changes to make to some of the names of the roles she and Julia previously identified. Tim made the updates gladly, as long as she no longer insisted on remaining the executive director.

****

Emily was now into the third week of the BPA and had paid two invoices to cover the first two weeks of work. Tim had emailed a document to her the previous Friday summarizing the work completed so far. On separate pages was the name of each department identified, in the assigned color, along with a listing of all of the associated tasks and the roles identified to perform those tasks. Following this first set of pages were 17 job descriptions, one for each role identified. Each job description contained the following sections: Title and Type of the Role or Position, a brief Company Background, Qualifications and Skills, Job Requirements, Duties and Responsibilities, Proposed Hours and a Disclaimer.

Emily printed the entire document and reviewed it over the weekend in preparation for her third session with Tim. She noticed that the Duties and Responsibilities section was pre-populated with the information that came directly from the first set of pages. Certain roles had responsibilities that spanned across multiple departments and that was all organized and captured succinctly in those particular job descriptions. *Amazing!* she thought. *All of this work just to be able to define who we actually need to support our growth.*

Only Emily and Tim were on the online conference call for the third session. Emily told him she did not object to any of the information presented. The next step, Tim told her, was to start filling in the blanks on the job descriptions. He would kick start this effort, but she should work with Julia to fill in the others; in particular, they should include a brief description of the non-profit, and explain how it is fast growing and that the nature of the role can change due to business demands and environmental factors (the Disclaimer section).

Tim opened the first job description and asked Emily to identify whether each role was full-time or part-time. Then, they discussed each role's classification as outsourced, volunteer or internship. As they talked through each role's job description, Tim filled in the information. Next, he asked her to start thinking about opportunities for advancement for each role, if applicable. He explained that it would be important to think through this ahead of time because, during the recruiting and interviewing process, people would want to know this information.

This two-hour session was their shortest. Before ending the session, Tim emailed an updated version of all the job descriptions to Emily and told her to have Julia help her research a competitive salary or hourly rate for each position, even for those outsourced positions; the exception was the volunteer positions.

After the call, Emily showed Julia the job descriptions. She, too, could not believe the results. Emily shared Tim's instructions to review the job descriptions and fill in the blanks with information about pay rates and opportunities for advancement. They spent two to three hours each day for the remainder of the week completing this assignment.

****

Finally, the fourth and final session of the BPA arrived. Emily, Julia and Tim met at the conference room near Union Station where the second session had taken place. Tim presented Emily with a brief report that included attached copies of all the job descriptions, completely filled. He told her, "Ms. Miller, you should be very proud of yourself. In a proactive move, you are setting in motion actions not only to secure your position within the organization you've worked so hard to build, but also to ensure the future viability of the non-profit."

Emily smiled, "Would you describe it as a chess move?"

Tim looked at her, bewildered, "I'm sorry?"

"Whenever I needed to think through a challenge as a child, my father would tell me to 'play chess, not checkers. Chess is a game for thinkers,' he would say."

"Yes, Ms. Miller, you are now playing chess!" Tim told her confidently. He then pointed Emily and Julia to a specific area on the first page of the report and asked them to read it to themselves. Emily placed the report between them so that they could both read it. It was a short paragraph followed by a chart:

A major purpose of the BPA was to identify all roles and responsibilities for the non-profit with the intent of matching the right employee to the right job. Currently, Emily and Julia are collectively working the jobs of six different positions (executive director, director of events & programs, marketing director, bookkeeper, H.R. & volunteer coordinator, and administrative assistant). By identifying additional key personnel needed to foster the non-profit's growth, you are positioned to re-allocate the management team's time from being office and administrative-driven to executive management and client development-driven. Note the recommended 18-month hiring strategy in the chart below: (listed in priority)

| 18-month Hiring Priority | | Number of Tasks to Delegate | % Task reduction of Emily |
|---|---|---|---|
| 1. | Executive Director | 50 | 26% |
| 2. | H.R./Volunteer Co-ordinator | 7 | 4% |
| 3. | Bookkeeper | 5 | 3% |
| 4. | Marketing Director | 24 | 13% |
| | **TOTAL** | **86** | **46%** |

After reading this information, Emily looked up at Tim and asked, "How did you calculate these numbers?"

"Do you remember the first two exercises where you identified tasks, departments and roles?" Tim asked her. Emily nodded. "Remember," Tim continued, "the total number of tasks identified after the first session was 446. Of those, you and Julia identified 189 tasks that you alone perform! Out of those 189 tasks, you assigned 86 of those tasks to other roles. This represents a combined 46% task reduction giving you more time for executive management and client development activities.

"Keep in mind that although these are rough estimates, they illustrate the importance of what can be accomplished through hiring the right people in the right order, delegating tasks and empowering staff through well documented processes. What better way to promote the non-profit than by bragging about job creation? If we actually computed an average time assigned to performing each task, you'd have an even better idea of just how much of your time you can devote to the things you do well. This strategic task allocation allows you to concentrate your efforts as opposed to dilute them. Concentrated efforts are far more effective than diluted efforts.

"Ms. Miller, by your own admission, you're not a fan of budgeting and forecasting activities." Emily started to lower her head. "But I think I have an idea for you. What if your new position became founder & managing director instead of director of events & programs? Such a title could potentially put you on equal footing as the executive director. As directors, you both would be in charge of overseeing the entire organization, but the executive director would focus more on board relations while the managing director would focus more on client relations, with the understanding that there would be shared focus on donor relations."

Emily grinned like a Cheshire cat. "This makes so much sense! I wish I had thought of this. Thank you so much for giving me an out."

"Let's not think of this as a way out as much as it is a new beginning," Tim said. "This non-profit is going to run like a well-oiled machine. This is just the first step in establishing the foundation on which to design all other operational activities. If my math is correct, you will meet with the board in about two weeks. I'd like to attend that meeting with you. Do you foresee any objections to that?"

"No." Emily replied. "Our meetings are pretty informal. We usually meet at a member's house, but I will need to give them advanced notice. Julia, can you send an email later today letting them know that I will invite a guest, Tim McKiver? Tell them he wants to give a 10-15 minute presentation on business infrastructure. I don't foresee any issues with adding his name to the meeting's agenda, given Tim's background in non-profit consulting."

Tim resumed, "Have you saved all of the job descriptions in a safe location?"

"Yeah, I saved all of them on our cloud drive and password-protected them," Julia answered.

Tim then told Emily and Julia to continue looking at the newly defined departments identified because, now, they serve as the basis for how they should organize their paper and electronic records. They would also have a better idea of how to set up future workspace once they make the inevitable move outside of Emily's basement. Most importantly, these departments and the tasks assigned to them gave Emily and Julia a starting point in defining the processes and procedures needed to ensure consistency in service delivery as they hire new people. "You will be able to show the board that you are making some real, tangible efforts to scale in a sustainable and repeatable way."

Tim persuaded Emily that she could (and should) retain her office at home and use it as a satellite location. That was a good compromise. She had an even greater appreciation for the law of conservation — she was not losing anything she did not need to lose, but gaining everything she wanted.

**The Result**

Two weeks later, the much-anticipated board of directors meeting took place. Emily arranged with Tim to reimburse him for use of the conference room they had used in two previous sessions. If it had had the intended effect on her and Julia, it would likely make a good impression on the board too. Emily arrived an hour early, giving herself enough time to set up for the presentations. She wore her signature pearl necklace and a two-piece suit the same shade as her sapphire pendant earrings. Not a single hair was out of place. She was here to leave an impression today and every detail counted. Emily felt as confident as she looked.

The board of directors arrived one by one, including Kathy, the one member she trusted. Upon confirmation that everyone was present, the president of the board called the meeting to order. The first 15 minutes included a follow-up on action items generated during the last board meeting. The next item on the agenda was Tim's presentation. Before Tim stood up to speak, Emily introduced him. Up to this point, the board was under the impression that Tim would be giving a sales pitch of some sort. Imagine their shock when Emily projected a graph displaying the financial figures from Tim's original proposal.

Emily began to speak. She had practiced this introduction for the past two weeks, figuring out the best way to convey the message without letting on that Kathy had already revealed their plans to replace her. "As we all know, we've experienced double-digit growth over the past four years. This growth, while exciting, brings challenges as we struggle to keep up with the demands and expectations of our clients and donors. I'll be the first to admit that I failed to ask for help and that refusal may have jeopardized *our* amazing organization!

"I was in denial and it first became apparent when I was at a Sade concert while in London. As I watched Sade sing, I found myself drawn to her band. Without the band, there would be no Sade and without Sade, there would be no band. Then I started thinking about all of the people it probably took to put the concert together. I know from experience what it takes to plan an event and our events pale in comparison to that concert. I thought about all of the people, the equipment, the promotions, and the logistics that it takes for Sade's team to replicate this concert consistently with each city they visit on the tour. When I returned home, I mentioned this to my oldest son, Brian. He strongly suggested I contact Tim.

"I've known Tim most of his life, but saw less of him over the past several years. I honestly had forgotten about his background in working with some of the largest non-profits in the area. I was elated to hear that he started his own consulting firm. We met and Tim constructed a plan of course correction for us. For four weeks, Julia and I worked with him in some of the most tedious meetings I've ever participated in! Tim will now summarize the work we accomplished together and present his recommendations for moving forward."

Before anyone from the board could ask a question, Emily said, "Please welcome Tim McKiver!" As the board members clapped, some struggled not to display any sign of emotion; they didn't know whether to be proud of or furious with Emily for not discussing this with them prior to working with Tim.

Tim walked toward the front of the room. With the click of a button, he projected his presentation onto the white board behind him. Standing to the side of the white board to allow room for others to see, he first thanked Emily for her introduction of him. On the white board was a picture of a charter bus and a mini-van.

"Every organization, regardless of its size, industry and maturity, needs business infrastructure as it answers the following questions:

- What work needs to be done?
- Who is supposed to do the work?
- How do we do the work?
- What is the contingency plan just in case things don't go accordingly?
- How do we profitably replicate our business model?

"What Ms. Miller described in her introduction can be summed as supply not meeting demand. The issue here is that, although there are many people sitting in the proverbial van, some are not sitting in the right seat. Ms. Miller has been in the van's driver's seat for the past 10 years. But now the roads you all are traveling on require a stronger, bigger vehicle that can also accommodate more people. Unfortunately, Ms. Miller knows how to drive the van, not a bus."

Tim then clicked forward to the next slide. "My research and observations proved there was a lack of transparency in the day-to-day operations. This may have led many of you to question how Emily and Julia spend their time, especially as the rate of client complaints escalated. I recommended we implement the Business Parts Analysis element of the Kasennu methodology for business infrastructure. Together, Ms. Miller and Julia went through a rigorous four weeks to formalize a structure that supports the non-profit's growth as well as promotes transparency. These sessions were intentionally spread out over a four-week period, allowing them time to absorb the information. We also made sure that Ms. Miller was still able to meet all client appointments during this time."

Tim progressed to the next slide. It contained an infographic that summarized the total number of sessions, the number of tasks identified, the names of the new departments, a listing of all positions identified and an image of a sample job description. He ended his presentation by recommending that the board review carefully the work done during the BPA.

He also suggested that they heed the prioritized hiring strategy and strongly consider developing a personality, work and communication style profile for each position. They could leverage assessment tools like Kolbe™, Myers Briggs® and DiSC® to help them match the right person to each position. Their current pool of volunteers and clients seeking employment was an excellent place to start.

Tim's 15 minutes was up. Any anger the board members may have felt waned when Tim left the final slide of his presentation on the white board. It showed one of the pictures Julia took of Emily's basement when most of the walls were covered in papers full of tasks.

Before moving to the next item on the agenda, the president said, "Emily and Tim, thank you for that informative presentation. I'm sure many of us have questions, but we must move on to other business, in particular the planning of our big 10-year anniversary celebration. But, really quickly, I'm curious, how soon can this be implemented? What are the next steps?"

"Thanks to Ms. Miller, you've already started," Tim answered. "Now that we know the tasks, roles and departments, this information will provide the framework for developing an organization chart, paper and electronic records management systems, the organization of the new headquarters and business processes.

"In fact, there's a business process workshop coming up in Atlanta. We didn't have time to discuss this, but Ms. Miller self-identified the fact that she should no longer be the executive director; rather, her title should be managing director. She and the new executive director can share responsibility for donor relations. I strongly recommend getting these processes documented sooner rather than later so that all new hires will know the proper way to perform certain tasks."

The president thanked Tim again for his time. Shortly before adjourning the meeting, the president turned to Emily and asked, "Why didn't you tell us about this? We had no idea how much you were struggling to keep up. You always gave us the impression that you had it all together."

Emily stood up in front of the room to address everyone. "Yes, I know. It was just a façade. I don't like admitting failure. Tim helped me realize that my only failure was in not seeking help. He also helped me realize that my strength is in fundraising and helping the clients and I should remain in this capacity. Being the executive director requires more than just being able to raise money. It requires skillful coordination of the entire organization, including financial management, and I hate getting bogged down in details. This was something my ex-husband often complained about.

"I now have a better appreciation for some of the things he used to tell me about his law practice. For instance, I never understood why he always delegated to the paralegals and junior attorneys. Now I know. When it comes to our financials, I only look at the bottom line to determine whether our total donations and expenses are trending up or down. The truth of the matter is I don't know how to read financial statements and have no clue about how to look for signs of trouble, aside from the obvious.

"A couple of weeks ago, I spent several days in the Library of Congress, poring over all kinds of business books. I've even signed up for some online classes to help me better understand certain business basics. I never thought any of this was necessary since we are a non-profit, but I know better now. We still have to remain in compliance and show responsible use of all monies raised."

Emily took the fact that they were now 30 minutes past the allotted meeting time as a good sign. It showed there was interest. She just had to convince the board to let her continue. As they walked out of the conference room, Clara Dixon, Emily's arch nemesis, asked if she could speak with her. To her surprise, Clara gave her a big hug and told her how proud she was. It took courage to do what Emily did and that was the hallmark of

a true leader. Emily masked her suspicion with a smile. It would be a while before Clara could earn her trust again.

****

With a renewed sense of purpose, Emily realized she was not losing her identity; rather, she was strengthening and re-defining it into something even more spectacular! This was Emily 2.0. If she had had this kind of awakening in just a short time, she could not imagine what would happen after this process workshop in Atlanta.

All she needed was the board's approval. Would they continue or would they halt her progress?

# CHAPTER 3

# CHILD'S PLAY

**Kasennu™**
Business Design Blueprint™

Albert Andoh has a golden opportunity to take his young application software development company to the next level. Investors are currently courting him to help make that possible. His company's growth is steady and is predicted to skyrocket once he appears at a popular technology conference. With all his success, there is just one problem. He is still in high school. While his parents do not want him to miss out on these opportunities, they also want him to finish high school and, preferably, college. The investors are concerned about his age — they need assurance that: 1) they are not placing over a half million dollars into the hands of a child, 2) there is a sustainable growth plan in place and, 3) experienced, capable adults are running the company. A chance encounter at the conference leads him to working with a consultant who introduces him to another element of the Kasennu methodology — the Business Design Blueprint.

It was 11:15 am. Not even drawn shades could prevent the sun's rays from beaming throughout the classroom. The stillness in the room was only broken occasionally with the sounds of birds tweeting; a welcomed reminder that in two more weeks, spring would officially arrive. The proctor almost lost herself in daydreaming. She was already thinking about her plans for the weekend. As soon as she had that thought, she checked herself and began another round of room scanning.

For the past three hours, she sat in the back of the classroom performing these periodic room scans, searching for potential cheating or other nefarious activities. The students were sitting in desks lined up in four rows, all facing the front of the classroom. As she continued scanning, her eagle eyes noticed something different. Normally, she saw a sea of 19 students looking at white computer screens with black font; but one of the computers now had a black screen with white font. Admittedly, she was still adjusting to the idea of computerized standardized tests; however, she knew she needed to investigate this black-screened computer.

The proctor stood up slowly so as not to draw attention to herself and, like a lioness sneaking up on her prey, she approached the student facing the black screen from behind. She realized right away that this student was not taking the standardized test at all. He was typing what appeared to be gibberish; a strange sequencing of numbers, letters and symbols. Careful not to cause a scene, she whispered in the student's ear, "Young man, just what do you think you are doing?"

Startled, the student froze and stared at his screen wide-eyed. He quickly saved his information onto his USB drive and turned, almost in slow motion, to face the proctor. With his eyebrows still raised, he muttered, "Uh, nothing really. I'm just uh…" Some of the other students looked up from their computers and started snickering. They knew exactly what he was doing. In fact, everyone seemed to be in on this except the proctor.

But the proctor was not amused. "Young man, you are here to take a very important, standardized test. This test will help determine how well this school is teaching, not to mention whether or not you are college material."

The students' snickering turned into full out, discernible laughter. The proctor was furious. She stood up straight, walked to the front of the classroom and said, "Excuse me! You may not realize it now, but this is the beginning of your future!"

She knew she needed to restore order quickly. She walked over to the startled student again and asked him to follow her to the back of the classroom near the desk where she sat. She maintained her composure as well as her hushed tone.

"What's your name?"

"Albert."

"Albert what?"

"Albert Andoh."

"Well, Mr. Andoh, we're going to take a trip to the Principal's Office. Need I remind you that you are in the top high school in the state of Texas? You should take this test seriously."

"Ma'am, if I may," Albert said, in an equally hushed tone. He needed to defend himself.

"What? What? If you may, what?" The proctor's voice now oscillated between a whisper and a normal tone. She realized that she had indeed caused a scene and did the very thing she hoped would not happen. By raising her voice with Albert, she disrupted the exam process and now all eyes were on the two of them.

"Ma'am..." Albert could not remember the proctor's name. "I actually finished the test about an hour ago."

"Are you being sarcastic with me young man?" Her voice got as fiery as her red hair.

"No ma'am. I really did finish it. Here, look at this confirmation screen." Albert walked over to his desk and the proctor followed. He reduced the size of the black screen he was working on to show her the date and time-stamped screen from the test. He had indeed finished the exam.

For a split second, the proctor almost forgot that she was a substitute. She needed to remain poised less she never be asked to sub again. She looked at Albert. "Why didn't you say something? What on earth were you doing anyway?"

"I was writing some last minute code for my demo." Albert was still whispering. "I'm preparing for the big South by Southwest conference this weekend. I'm one of the presenters."

The proctor's scornful look began to soften. Unbeknownst to her, she had just reprimanded one of the top students in the junior class. She did not know whether to be angry or amazed. She knew that the South by Southwest (SXSW) conference was a large, global conference that brought together people representing a diverse array of industries including technology, film and music.

"Well, I, I..."

Albert interjected, "I'm sorry if I appeared to be rude. I just thought of some code that might improve upon a web-based app I plan to demonstrate at this conference."

Still bewildered, the proctor looked Albert up and down. He was polite and well-groomed and, as he spoke, she realized he no longer fit her initial stereotype. She had thought he was an ungrateful teenager. However, his humility threw her off-course.

"Well, we have about 30 minutes left. Go back to your desk, but please keep it quiet."

"Oh, yes ma'am. Not a problem. Thank you so much."

"I'm still going to mention this to your teacher, and the principal."

"Yes, I understand." Albert had been through this before. The son of Ghanaian parents, he knew the importance of respecting his elders and sometimes struggled to reconcile his West African upbringing with American culture.

The school bell rang, coinciding with the final hour of the four-hour standardized test. As the students powered down the computers at their respective desks and walked out of the classroom, the proctor wished each of them well. She noticed Albert walking toward her. When the classroom was cleared of all students, she motioned for him to walk alongside her.

As they walked down the hallway on their way to the principal's office, the proctor couldn't help but notice the school's magnificent interior. There were no cinder blocks as seen in many high schools; rather, the bottom half of the walls were covered in real wood paneling. All of the floors were freshly buffed and polished, so much so that the proctor could actually see her reflection on them! *How can kids take this for granted?* she wondered. She tried, unsuccessfully, to get her own daughter into this school.

When they reached the waiting area of the principal's office, they were greeted by the secretary, Linda Calandro. Her face lit up. "Hi Albert! How are you doing today? How was the test? Wait, let me guess. You finished in, like, an hour."

Albert smiled. "I finished it in two hours."

The proctor locked eyes with Linda. "So, you know about this? Is this the norm for him?"

Linda motioned for the proctor to step behind the counter that separated her work area from the waiting area. Albert remained seated in the waiting area. "Yes. This is the norm. You see, Albert is one of our brightest students. He usually aces all his standardized tests and completes them early. If I were to guess, I'd say you brought him here because he finished the test early and started working on something else."

The proctor nodded.

"We allow him to do that so that he won't get bored sitting there with nothing to do. The students, faculty and staff, we all love him! He's even scored points with the so-called cool kids. He's developed all kinds of phone apps for different sports teams and clubs here at school. We're fortunate to have him here. He could have easily skipped a grade or two, but his parents refused. They feel it's important for him to remain grounded. But I gotta tell you, Al is light-years ahead of his peers."

The proctor struggled to reconcile her preconceived notions about Albert with what Linda told her. "Well, I brought him here because…because he appeared to be doodling. I was concerned that he would disturb the other students."

"Weren't they all wearing headphones?" Linda asked.

"Yes."

"Well, how was he disturbing the other students? I'm asking because I need to know what to report to the principal before he sees both of you in his office."

Clearing her throat, the proctor answered. "Well, it's clear to me now that I've made a mistake. The teacher I'm substituting for did not include anything about Albert in the proctoring instructions she left for me."

The proctor apologized to Linda for wasting her time and then turned to face Albert who was now sitting in the waiting area writing more code on a small notepad. She walked up to him. "Albert, I owe you an apology, sweetheart. Your teacher did not give me advanced notification about you and your *gift*. Will your demo be recorded?"

This was truly a first for the proctor; she had never apologized to a teenager before.

"Yes ma'am. I believe much of it will be live-streamed, too."

"Can I ask a favor then? Can you send me a link to your recorded demo?" The proctor handed Albert her business card which contained her email address.

"Sure."

"Perfect!" the proctor forced a smile. "Where's your next class?"

"In A.P. Tureaud Hall, but it's time for lunch now."

She felt bad for cutting into his lunch time. "I'll walk with you to the cafeteria. Again, I apologize." As they walked to the cafeteria, Albert knew he dodged another bullet. After so many repeat offenses, he still had not become accustomed to the unwanted attention he received by first-time and substitute teachers.

## The Fast Growth Predicament

With just two days left before the conference, Albert still had much work to do. As soon as he got home from school that day, he rushed to his bedroom, locked the door and buried himself into his world of coding. At 16-years-old, he not only excelled in academics but in business as well, or so he thought.

In fact, he already had investors waiting to infuse additional capital into his business to support its fast growth and help take it to the next level. This is why the stakes were so high: not only would the investors be at the SXSW conference, but there would be other potential investors and business partners there too. Up to this point, he generated business primarily via word-of-mouth. He predicted this would all change after the conference.

Specifically, the investors were prepared to invest $600,000 USD over a three-year period for 10% ownership in Albert's company, based on a current valuation of $1.5 million USD (double the revenue last year). Albert's company turned a profit since its inception. Therefore, the investors had no doubt about his company's proof of concept, potential market size or proposed customer acquisition strategy. Their biggest concern was, and frankly always had been, Albert's ability to manage the business while still in high school.

Though they were aware of Albert's Uncle Selom's contributions, he was thousands of miles away in Ghana. To add to their concern was the fact that Albert's parents also had demanding jobs. For these reasons, they had recommended a small business development incubator, a place where Albert could receive the face-to-face support needed to grow his business responsibly.

By the time his mother arrived home from work, she had already heard what happened to Albert earlier that day at school. She ignored the *Please Do Not Disturb* sign hanging around his bedroom doorknob and knocked on the door anyway.

"Albert! Are you in trouble? How was the test? Did the substitute teacher scold you? Are you hungry? Have you eaten yet?"

Albert unlocked his door. "Everything's fine."

His short, two-worded response let his mother know that she had probably interrupted him while he was in the midst of something. She felt badly and told him to join her and his father in the dining room at 6:30 pm for dinner. Until then, she would leave him be in his cocoon of coding.

Albert put the finishing touches on the demo portion of his presentation just in time for dinner. Pushing his chair away from the desk in his room, he took a deep breath and let out a sigh of relief. *Whew! Just in time for food!* Similar to his homework assignments, he liked finishing anything related to his business at least one day before the scheduled due date. This allowed him time to mull over the details and, if necessary, make additional changes.

After dinner, his father asked Albert if he was ready to practice his presentation, including the demo, in front of them. He synchronized his computer to the television in the living room. It provided a screen large enough to simulate what the screens at the conference might actually look like. His parents, also both detail-oriented in nature, asked tough questions that allowed Albert to realize where he needed to add more context to his presentation. By the time he went to bed later that night, he felt confident that he was ready for what would be the biggest event of his life.

\*\*\*\*

The next day at school seemed to go agonizingly slow. Albert was so anxious to get on the road to Austin that he could barely contain himself.

Thankfully, his misery did not last long since he only attended school for a half day. His mother picked him up from school around noon so that she could drive to Austin and get there the night before the conference.

When he arrived home from school, he took his time to pack everything he would need for the conference. He also made sure he saved several copies of his presentation in multiple locations, including his laptop's hard-drive, three different USB drives, an external hard drive and a few different cloud-based locations.

Albert ate lunch and then loaded their luggage into the trunk of the car. Their goal was to be on the road no later than 1:30 pm, ensuring that their estimated three-hour drive from Dallas to Austin would not double due to heavy traffic.

Thankfully, the drive to Austin was uneventful and they arrived at their hotel without a hitch. By now it was 4:00 pm. As soon as they had checked into their hotel room, Mrs. Andoh suggested they find the exact room in the hotel where his presentation would take place. "We should go to the room to see if they will allow you inside. The sooner you get an idea of the size and layout of the room, the better prepared you will be."

The theater-style arrangement would seat 125 people comfortably. Albert walked onto the stage facing the chairs. As his father had taught him for years, he used the power of suggestion and closed his eyes to imagine himself giving his presentation.

When he opened his eyes, he walked over to the lectern. He checked the projector connections to make sure he knew which devices to bring and he plugged a USB drive into the laptop resting inside the lectern. He asked his mother to sit in the audience to critique the clarity, sound and color.

Closing his eyes again, he projected in a loud, confident voice, "Thank you so much for this opportunity!" He opened his eyes, this time imagining he was receiving a standing ovation as he exited the stage. He even dusted off his shoulders, one at a time. *Yep, I got this!*

Albert felt confident that he had seen everything he needed to see. Once they returned to the hotel after eating dinner, Albert asked if he could practice his presentation again using the television in the hotel room and if his mother would critique him one last time.

After he concluded the last practice run, Mrs. Andoh looked at the conference's schedule, specifically the *Code & Programming* track, to double-check the time of his presentation. It was scheduled for the next day at 1:00 pm. She worried about this time of day. "This is too soon after lunch! People will be sleepy. Al, you'll have to make sure you keep your presentation lively. Remember to work on your transitions so that everything you say flows nicely. And be animated! Tap into your youthful energy. Make it a presentation they'll be glad to cut their lunch break short for."

\*\*\*\*

Finally, the big day! Albert and Mrs. Andoh arrived at the conference early. Each wore a bright orange, long-sleeved shirt with his company's logo and website address on the back. The color was a nice contrast to their mocha complexions. They figured they could serve as walking billboards while at the conference.

They perused the agenda and circled those presentations they wanted to attend. As tempted as Mrs. Andoh was to attend separate presentations, ultimately she opted not to, as there were thousands of people at this conference and it was best that they stick together.

At 12:30 pm, Albert and Mrs. Andoh cut their attendance at the keynote speaker's presentation short to allow themselves time to go to the room where his presentation would take place. Once there, he began setting up.

As 1:00 pm approached, people began to fill the chairs until it became standing room only. Albert fought desperately to calm his nerves, but the excitement was almost more than he could handle. *Why are you worried? These are your people. They "get you" and what you do.*

Like clockwork, at exactly 1:00 pm, a conference facilitator introduced him. Albert walked onto the stage. There he noticed his mother sitting proudly in the front row. Her wide smile was all he needed to assure him that everything would go well.

*It's showtime!* he thought. He proceeded to give his presentation, just as he had practiced countless times, except there was one major twist. On completion, Albert displayed a blank, black screen to ensure everyone paid attention to him and only him. He walked to the center of the stage and stood there until the room became completely silent.

Mrs. Andoh watched in agony. *What is he doing? This is unscripted!*

At that moment, Albert looked ahead and saw a large timer display that showed he had five minutes left. He spent those last five minutes telling his personal story, highlighting his upbringing and sharing how his parents instilled the values of hard work, ethics and morals in him. He connected his upbringing to the quality of the application software that he develops and the power they have in connecting people as well as systems together. He ended with a powerful question, "Do you want to work with companies who build bridges or build walls? We build application software that builds bridges."

He pressed the button on his clicker to display a *Thank You* slide and graciously ended his presentation. As he walked to exit the stage, he noticed, in his periphery, that the crowd was standing. *Sweet! Just as I imagined it…a standing ovation!* He looked up and noticed his mother's eyes glistening. He hated to see her cry, but he knew they were tears of joy.

By the time Albert exited the stage, Mrs. Andoh was already there to greet him. She gave him a big hug and kissed him on the cheek. "You nearly gave me a heart attack! But you executed flawlessly…and kept everyone awake! I'm so proud of you."

He was embarrassed by the public display of affection but his mother didn't care. "You must be starved honey. Let's grab a bite to eat.

She was right. Albert's stomach was beginning to tie into knots. What started as butterflies developed into full-blown stomach pains by the time he finished his presentation.

They walked to one of the many café areas. Along the way, they received a barrage of compliments. Many people stopped Albert to shake his hand, congratulate him and hand him their business cards. Wanting to make the most out of this conference, Albert gulped down his food despite his mother's repeated requests that he slow down and make sure he chewed before he swallowed.

Then, they walked to the next presentation. While Albert walked toward the center of the room to grab a seat, Mrs. Andoh stayed outside of the room to make a quick phone call to her husband. "Oh honey, you would be so proud! Our son did it! He even received a standing ovation!"

As she continued gloating about Albert, she noticed a young woman walking toward her. She paid the woman no mind until she realized that the woman was waiting to speak with her. "Honey, I better go. I think there's someone waiting to talk to me. We'll see you at the hotel. I love you."

Mrs. Andoh put her cell phone into her purse as the young woman walked closer toward her.

"Hello. That was quite a show that young man put on. Are you his…"

"I am his mother!" Mrs. Andoh boasted before the young woman could finish.

"You must be so proud!"

"Yes, I am!"

The young woman extended her hand for Mrs. Andoh to shake. "I'm Victoria Villareal. I couldn't help notice the *Thank You* slide of Albert's presentation. I'm familiar with the venture capital firm he cited. Many of my clients have worked with them."

"Really?" Mrs. Andoh asked, intrigued. "And what do you do?"

"Well, I'm a project manager. I used to work as a software developer but eventually I decided to do consulting instead. I burned out on coding and decided I wanted to still work in the field but help other rising stars. It keeps me connected to the development community without the late night coding jamborees and poor dietary habits."

Victoria and Mrs. Andoh chuckled in harmony. "Lucky for Albert, he has me as his personal chef to make sure he doesn't gorge on junk food."

Victoria continued, "I now do a lot of project management for software development projects. I've done the gamut from design and development to client engagement and account management. It looks like Albert already has a company in place."

"Yes, that's right. He's officially going into his third year of business. It's really taken off, too, thanks to the incubator he started working with."

"Incubator?

"Yes, that was at the suggestion of the venture capital firm."

"Hmm, I'm surprised they didn't recommend me to you. I have a good relationship with them and they should know that Albert would be an ideal client for me."

"Well, it's probably because we don't have a current need for project management. Albert and my brother-in-law are both well-versed in Scrum."[11]

"If you don't mind me asking, Mrs. Andoh, how long will you all be here in Austin?"

"Until tomorrow morning."

"Same for me. Can we set aside some time to talk more before you leave? Do you have plans this evening?'"

"'We're expecting my husband to land this evening so that we can meet with some of the investors of the venture capital firm." Mrs. Andoh hoped she was not divulging too much information. Her husband constantly warned her about the industry vultures looking to prey on less experienced and more impressionable developers.

"Is it possible for us to meet before or after that meeting?"

Mrs. Andoh looked at Victoria with suspicion. *What does she really want?* "I suppose so. May I ask, what do you want to discuss? We meet many people who say they can help us. Being in this industry, I'm sure you can appreciate that many of them have ill intentions. That's why my husband and I keep close guard over everything. Albert is still a child, you know."

Though currently single and childless, Victoria empathized. "I think, excuse me, I *know* I can help Albert. With that phenomenal presentation, he's about to come into even more money and notoriety. With that comes much responsibility. I have seen this scenario play out a thousand times. These young, energetic and talented developers work hard to bring attention to their creation. Once they get funding to back it, it starts gaining traction. Because these companies are started by developers and not necessarily businesspeople, they tend to struggle to get their operations to a point where they can meet the rising demand for their product.

"Before they know it, things start nosediving and the VCs [Venture Capitalists] step in to replace them with people better qualified to grow the company. With so much going on, it's easy for things to fall through the cracks. Quality gets diminished and deadlines aren't met. I'm sure you can appreciate that most techies aren't known for being savvy entrepreneurs. Development is one thing; the *business* of development is another.

"This is why I was so excited when I found out about this methodology called Kasennu. It helps companies like Albert's to put into place a business infrastructure that, among other things, ensures he will have the right people on his team as he scales up. It takes a look at what needs to be done, who should do it, as well as where and how the work should be done.

"Non-tech startups tend to place a heavy focus on marketing and sales initially, but funded tech startups are expected to scale quickly and therefore are also expected to have a structure in place to support anticipated fast growth. VCs require they have a solid marketing *and* operational strategy to execute in addition to an attractive ROI."

"Hmm…" Mrs. Andoh responded. "Before I give you an answer, I'd like for my husband to be in on this conversation. He is expected to arrive shortly before dinner with the investors. We won't have time to meet with you before then and I'm not sure how long we'll be out at dinner. Besides, we'll all have had a long day by then. Pending our decision, we can try to meet for breakfast. What time is your flight?"

"I'm scheduled to fly out at 11:30 am tomorrow. Here's my business card."

Mrs. Andoh accepted Victoria's business card but was careful not to give her own contact information. Instead, she told Victoria she would send her a text message if she and her husband decided to entertain a meeting with her. After saying good-bye to each other, they went in opposite directions.

Victoria attended a couple more presentations that day, meeting several people along the way, but none of them stood out like Albert. He's special and she wanted to help him grow, successfully, to the next level. She hoped his parents would agree to a meeting before she headed home to California.

Meanwhile, Mrs. Andoh was also thinking about her conversation with Victoria. She was right, they are barely balancing school with the demands of the business. Something has to give. More people are starting to take notice of her son and his talents. She remembered a framed quote from Dr. Jonas Salk that she kept on her desk at work: "The reward for good work is the opportunity to do more." *How do you handle more work once you get it?* she asked herself.

She could not imagine what life would be like if she and her husband had more children. There is no way they would be able to keep up. She was eager to tell her husband about Victoria. She sent him a text message before joining Albert in the room of the presentation they agreed to attend, *More great developments. Will fill you in when you arrive. Safe travels* ♥.

****

When Albert's father arrived to the hotel in the late afternoon, the room was peppered with conference swag, including tee shirts, notepads, pens and assorted mechanical gadgets. Mrs. Andoh handed him a booklet from the conference displaying all of the presentations. She had grabbed an extra copy as a keepsake for her husband.

Dr. Andoh had tried his best to be at his son's presentation, but duty called and he had to perform surgery earlier that day. As he perused the booklet, he struggled to keep up with Albert and his wife — they were both so excited that, simultaneously, they gave him a rundown of the day's events. Their mouths seemed to move a mile a minute. Dr. Andoh enjoyed seeing them so happy. Suddenly, his cell phone made a choo choo sound. That was his signal to keep a phone appointment with his brother, Selom.

Selom played an integral role in setting up and now helping to run Albert's software development business. "Shush! Quiet, please!" he jokingly begged of his wife and son. "We need to get Selom on the line to confirm certain things before tonight's dinner."

He dialed Selom on his cell phone and turned on the speaker. Albert and his parents sat tightly together around the phone, eagerly waiting for Selom to pick up.

"Hello?" a groggy voice answered. It was in the wee hours of the morning for Selom and, though he expected this phone call, he still struggled for consciousness.

"How did my nephew do today? I was at the mechanic for most of the day and was unable to watch it on the live stream."

"Your nephew received a standing ovation!" Mrs. Andoh exclaimed.

"Congratulations, Al! You make your parents and your uncle very proud!"

Dr. Andoh knew that they only had 30 minutes before it was time to meet the investors for dinner, so their conversation with Selom needed to be brief. He asked Selom to share any potential new developments they needed to be aware of prior to the dinner meeting. Selom confirmed there were none and wished them good luck.

A few minutes later, they got into their family car and made the short trip to a steakhouse on Austin's infamous 6th Street. Albert's father had hoped they would arrive before the investors and they did. Soon afterwards, three investors representing the venture capital firm showed up. One of them they had never met before.

Once everyone was seated, the investors spared no time in asking a barrage of questions. "How many projects do you currently have in queue?" the new investor asked.

Albert answered, "I'm currently working on four different projects for two customers. I've had to turn away some business recently."

Each investor's eyebrows shot up.

Albert continued, "I'd like to explain. It's because I spent a lot of time preparing for this presentation. Now that it's done, I can get back to focusing on my customers."

"Well, first Albert," one of the investors said, "congratulations on your presentation! Each of us was there and, from the reactions we personally witnessed, you are on to something that is much bigger than you, your parents and your uncle. Expect your voicemail and email inboxes to overload soon!"

Albert smiled.

The investor continued, "That's what concerns us. We need to be assured that you can handle this surge in demand."

Before Albert could say anything, Dr. Andoh responded, "Yes, we are aware of that and are putting the finishing touches on assembling our offshore development team."

"Yes, about that," the new investor replied, "I'll admit I don't know much about offshoring work to Africa, though I know many of the bigger tech companies have a presence there. It'll be interesting to see what you all come up with."

"I can assure you we are working through all of those details and we look forward to presenting this to you at our next meeting in April. By then we will have these details completely fleshed out. We've already made a significant amount of progress and I would say we are about 75% complete with the strategic growth plan," Dr. Andoh said with confidence.

"Just keep in mind, our concern is not Albert's capabilities, it's his *capacity.*"

Out of nowhere, Mrs. Andoh blurted out, "You might be happy to hear that we're actually going to meet tomorrow morning with a young lady who says that she knows some of you. Her name is Victoria Villareal." Albert's mother shot a quick glance at both him and his father.

Even though she knew it was a risk to bring this up without having first confirmed with Victoria or her husband, Mrs. Andoh was relieved when the investors responded collectively, "Yes, we know Victoria! How did you meet her?"

"I met her earlier today at the conference. She recognized the name of your firm on the last slide of Al's presentation and said that you've funded many of her clients."

One of the investors confirmed, "Yes, that's true. I've known Victoria for a few years now. Great gal. Hard worker. We didn't refer her to you because one, you're too small and, two, you're in Texas and she lives in California. She works for one of the Big Four consulting firms, you know."

"Yes, but I don't think she would have approached me unless she thought she could work with us. She mentioned she would be able to help us out with structuring the business, from an organizational perspective, for success. I got the impression that she does consulting work for smaller companies on the side. We might attain quicker results working with her as opposed to the incubator at this time. With our work schedules and Albert's schooling, we find it nearly impossible to get over to the incubator during its office hours."

"I do remember her mentioning that. It'll be interesting to see how this plays out." At that moment, one of the investors gave a cue to the waiter that he was ready for the check and shortly after placed his napkin onto the table — a sign the dinner meeting was officially over. As they walked out of the restaurant, all three investors bid them farewell.

Albert and his parents returned to their hotel room completely exhausted. It had been a whirlwind of a day. Before falling asleep, his mother made it a point to send Victoria a text message, *This is Mrs. Andoh. It's a go. Let's meet at 8:00 am at the café at the hotel. We can talk up to two hours. Hopefully, that gives you enough time to get to the airport. Thanks!*

**The Research**

The bright sunshine of the morning made the alarm clock invalid, as Albert had awakened an hour before it was set to go off. He could not wait to meet Victoria. In less than 30 minutes, he was dressed and packed. He walked outside with his father to help load the luggage into their car while his mother went into the café.

Victoria noticed Mrs. Andoh right away and walked up to her. "Good morning, Mrs. Andoh! It's good to see you. May I get you a cup of coffee or tea?"

"It's nice to see you too Victoria. My husband and Albert should be here soon. We should be treating *you* to coffee or tea." Mrs. Andoh smiled as Victoria led her to the table she reserved.

When Albert and Dr. Andoh entered the café, they noticed his mother sitting down with a younger woman. She appeared to be in her mid-to-late thirties and was dressed similar to Albert in blue jeans and a long-sleeved tee shirt, the only exception being her snazzy blazer.

Mrs. Andoh introduced Victoria. "This is the person we raved about last night!"

Victoria appreciated the compliment and introduced herself, "Hello! You must be Dr. Andoh. And I know you, you're Albert! Congratulations! That was one of the most impressive and heartfelt presentations I've ever seen at a technology conference."

"Thank you," Albert replied shyly.

"Ms. Villareal, may I get you something to eat or drink?" Dr. Andoh requested.

"No, thank you. I've actually eaten already."

Dr. Andoh walked over to the café's counter to place his family's order. Mrs. Andoh took advantage of that opportunity to brief Victoria on their meeting with the investors. "Our meeting went well last night. The investors are excited about the direction the business is headed in and they echoed your sentiments about fast growth and capacity. I told them I met you and they were thrilled to hear that we might work together!"

Dr. Andoh returned to the table. "Ms. Villareal…"

"Please, call me Victoria," she responded.

"Very well, Victoria. My wife and the investors told me great things about you. Tell us a little more about your background."

Looking for another common characteristic to jumpstart the conversation, Victoria replied, "From your accent, I'm assuming you emigrated to the U.S."

"Yes, my wife and I both came here to the States from Ghana about 33 years ago to attend college. And we stayed."

"Well, like you, I also emigrated here but I came as a young child. I'm originally from Ecuador. I grew up in southern California but currently I live further north in Oakland. I made that my home after graduating from Stanford. San Francisco is just too expensive. I work at a top consulting firm as a project manager on enterprise-level software development projects. But I have a passion for working with smaller companies, too. At one time, I worked for several startups but, as I explained to your wife, I wore thin of the hustle and grind. I learned a lot from those experiences and, along the way, met some of the folks at the venture capital firm you're working with."

Victoria realized that she hadn't yet heard from Albert; so far, his parents had done most of the talking. "How about you Albert? Tell me a little more about yourself."

In a soft tone, he replied, "As you know I'm a software developer. I'm in 11th grade at a private high school in Dallas. I've been coding since I was nine and began developing phone apps when I was 11. It comes easy to me. To me, coding is like child's play."

Victoria smiled. She could barely hear Albert over the coffee bean grinding machines. *A typical teenager*, she thought. Albert seemed to walk that fine line between cockiness and confidence. Regardless of whether he is cocky or confident, she is sure he still had a certain naivety, which is why no investor with sound mind would entrust the full oversight and management of a company in his care.

"So, tell me about school."

"What do you want to know?"

"What are your plans once you graduate from high school?"

This was a point of contention in Albert's household. Before answering, he looked over at his parents. His African home upbringing suggested he should mask the true answer out of respect for his parents' wishes; however, his American lifestyle suggested he exercise his first amendment rights by telling the truth, unfiltered.

"Can I be very honest with you? Who needs college?"

Mrs. Andoh bit her bottom lip to prevent an outburst while his father gently patted the arm she had resting on the table.

"I'm a coder. I live to program. If I play my cards right, I'll probably be a millionaire before I even make it to college. Attending a university to teach me what I already know seems like a grossly inefficient use of my time, time that I could devote to growing my company. I see no point in going to college for four years only to get a degree that, once I finish, might be obsolete. But that's not what my parents want. They really value higher education. I wish we could reach a compromise because the last thing I want to do is disappoint them."

Victoria probed further and asked Albert more personal questions. This helped her gain a better understanding of his goals as well as his management style. This would be key to designing a solution for him and his company. "Considering how you feel about college, do you find it difficult being in high school?"

"Not really. Things have gotten a lot better since I was a freshman. Back then, I was an introvert, a 'nerd,' but when the amount of money I made leaked, I became 'cool.' I started creating different phone apps for my classmates. While they were so consumed with winning popularity contests, I was building a business. It's funny how they invest more of their time in social currency than actual currency. I ask a lot of them, 'what good does it do you to have 100,000 followers online if you have $0 in your bank account?' But that always falls on deaf ears because most of my classmates come from affluent families. One thing I know for sure is that wealthy people respect money. That's the real reason why I think they like me."

"How did your business start?"

Before Albert could answer, Dr. Andoh chimed in. "I'm sure you can tell that my son is very gifted. My wife and I have always encouraged him to engage in activities that stretch his mind. When he began expressing an interest in coding, I didn't think much of it. It seemed like just another hobby. But then, one day, Albert was sitting in the break room at the hospital where I work. He overheard some of my colleagues complaining about a new database. It didn't communicate with our other legacy systems. It lowered our productivity rather than increased it. Albert told me about it and asked if he could take a look at the different systems.

"I discussed it with some of the other doctors and, once they agreed, Albert started coming to the hospital straight after school. In two months, he had developed application software that allowed information to flow seamlessly among the different systems. Word spread fast and, before we knew it, more doctors requested his help. My brother, Selom, is also in computer technology. He suggested we start an actual business. And the rest is history."

Mrs. Andoh added, "Albert and Selom are currently working on a strategic growth plan to present to the venture capital firm in early April. As you predicted when we met yesterday, they want to know that the business is structured and managed to handle the continuous growth. Their biggest concern is the fact that Albert has no work history and, therefore, does not know how to lead a company with employees."

The alarm on Victoria's watch sounded. As much as she hated to cut the conversation short, she needed to leave for the airport. Dr. Andoh offered to drive her, as it would be a relatively short distance and on their return route to Dallas. Plus, the ride would give them more time to chat. Victoria accepted.

****

Once inside their car, Dr. Andoh called his brother. Selom needed to hear what Victoria had to say. It was not yet nighttime in Accra, the capital city of Ghana, so he should answer. When Selom answered the phone, Victoria was surprised by his deep, baritone voice. It was much deeper than his brother's.

Dr. Andoh gave a recap of the dinner with the investors and their conversation with Victoria. Upon request, Victoria leaned toward the car's speakers and recited her full name, website and social media handles. Her website, she explained, contained more information about the Kasennu methodology for business infrastructure. In particular, she pointed out the Business Design Blueprint element.

Based on his tone, Selom did not seem enthused by the idea of working with Victoria. He tried his best to mask his frustration. They had less than a month to complete the strategic growth plan. The last thing they needed was to add someone new; this could set back their progress significantly. Nevertheless, he agreed to entertain the idea of possibly working together. Before the call ended, Selom asked Victoria if she would sign a non-disclosure agreement. She agreed.

Knowing they needed a quick turnaround, Victoria promised to email a proposal to everyone within the next three days. They arrived at the airport a few minutes later. She thanked the Andohs for the ride and bid them farewell.

"What do you make of all of that?" Albert's mother asked his father.

"She seems like a nice young lady. Definitely very knowledgeable. But the real test will be getting past Selom." All three of them chuckled.

**** 

Three hours later, Victoria arrived at Oakland's International Airport. While en route, she used her tablet to begin conducting more research on Albert. By the time her plane landed, she was familiar with many of Albert's publicized accomplishments over the years. She also had a better understanding of why he referred to his coding skills as "child's play." He had won a string of hack-a-thons throughout the Southwest. She learned he even participated on a robotics team that won second place at a competition at the esteemed Massachusetts Institute of Technology. Forget basketball and football, coding was definitely Albert's sport.

When Victoria arrived home, she knew she wanted to take a deeper dive into researching Albert's company, as well as Ghana as an emerging country. His company's website appeared as sleek and clean as any other larger tech company. The main difference was the orange logo which set it apart from the traditional blue that many people came to associate with software companies. She noticed there was no mention of Albert on the website and that their locations were listed as Dallas and Accra. Other business references online cited Albert as the CEO and Selom as the president of the company.

Victoria jotted down notes about Ghana to serve as potential talking points; things that could potentially affect the organizational design of the business, as well as affect service delivery and overall management. Specifically, she wanted to ask Selom more about electricity outage concerns, the five-hour time difference, the potential language barrier and the country's overall stability. These were the things she was sure any investor would question. Culture differences were less of a concern considering the proliferation of offshoring to the Asian market over the past 20 years.

## The Hypothesis

Selom noticed an email from Victoria not three, but two days after their phone conversation. The email included a signed Non-Disclosure Agreement as well as a proposal. He also texted his brother and sister-in-law to confirm their receipt of the proposal. Though intrigued, he was still concerned about the timing. They now had less than a month to finalize the details of the Three-Year Strategic Growth Plan.

As he had expected, based on his review of Victoria's background as well as the Kasennu methodology, her proposal included a statement of work for creating a Business Design Blueprint (BDB).

> The BDB is a blueprint, in the form of an organizational chart, that illustrates how the company is designed. Reviewed properly, it not only shows management structure, but also opportunities for advancement over time. Management or reporting structures are best represented by organizational charts. Taking the time to define the proper flow of communication can save the business owners a great deal of time and potential grief in handling day-to-day staff and customer issues during growth spurts.
>
> The BDB links the departments and resources of the Business Parts Analysis (which contains role and department identification) and arranges them into a visual chain of command that also highlights future growth opportunities. By visually communicating your company's operational scope and business design, you can:
>
> - Illustrate opportunities for internal staff promotions and organizational scalability;
> - Add staff quickly but in a logical, structured manner;
> - Improve current response rate to customers, investors and colleagues through reduced layers of management; and,
> - Showcase your ability to handle increases in workload through a well-documented internal and external resource network.

Strategic business development should involve the input and coordination of management, programmers and other back office personnel. Knowing who to hire and when is critical to managing rapid growth as well as maintaining order and effectively disseminating workloads. Breakdowns in communication can cost you valuable customers as well as employees and has the potential to ruin your reputation. This is especially crucial since the majority of the development team is in Accra.

Researchers have proven that most people learn best through visual aids. Therefore, I propose creating two of these BDBs. Collectively, they will work in tandem with the Strategic Growth Plan and will demonstrate the projected changes in management over a three-year period. Using this as a supplement to the Strategic Growth Plan will help address the investors' concerns.

This work can be completed in three weeks, with one remote session scheduled each week.

Dr. Andoh made a quick call to his brother. "Is it really this simple?" he asked Selom. "An organizational chart can do all of this?"

Selom admitted that initially he was against the idea of working with Victoria but, after reading her proposal, he realized she was not trying to change anything in their Strategic Growth Plan. Rather, she was merely suggesting they add the BDB as a supplement. He also appreciated her request for copies of previous work with the incubator to prevent duplication.

"We should move forward," Selom told his brother. "Especially if we can get this done in three weeks. Going through this process might give us the clarity we need to work through details of other parts of the plan."

"Very well," Dr. Andoh said. He asked Selom to respond to Victoria and copy him, Albert and Mrs. Andoh on the email. Within a few hours, Selom emailed Victoria with an attached copy of the signed proposal and the latest draft of their Three-Year Strategic Growth Plan, along with copies of the job descriptions and organizational chart that the incubator previously helped construct.

Victoria was elated when she saw the email and its attachments. She replied with dates for the three sessions. Each session would occur remotely and on a Saturday so as to not interfere with Albert's school week.

## The Experiment
Victoria logged into the remote desktop sharing app about 15 minutes ahead of the scheduled time of her first session with the Andohs. She intentionally chose a time that would work well for both Selom and Albert. Eventually her computer beeped twice, a sign that they both joined the remote session. "Good morning and afternoon! Can you see my screen?"

Both confirmed they could.

"Great!" Victoria wasted no time and explained what appeared on her computer screen. On it was a table of 10 columns. The far left column, she told them, listed tasks she had extracted from the job descriptions Selom had previously emailed to her. There were 84 tasks in total. The remaining nine columns were blank with the top row appearing in a light gray. This served as a placeholder for the names of the departments they were going to identify.

"Albert, I'm going to give you remote access to my computer. As you look at each task, I want you to click and drag it over to the right into one of the columns. The goal is to begin grouping similar tasks together. The maximum number of groupings is nine. This ensures your future ability to retain and recall easily the organizational structure of your company. As an FYI, normally you would complete this particular exercise during the Business Parts Analysis element of the methodology. Just know that, in the future, you can always add to this list. Selom, this is a time for you and Albert to talk through the proper grouping of all tasks."

One by one, Albert clicked and dragged tasks into their appropriate column on the screen until he filled six distinct columns. When they grouped all tasks successfully, Victoria asked Albert to click on the top row shaded in light gray. "Now, I want you and Selom to think about the ideal name of the department that best describes each column of tasks."

Selom and Albert breezed through the department identification as they referenced the organizational chart the incubator had created for them a few months ago. Luckily, there were six departments on that chart too that they could easily assign each of those to a grouping of tasks on the screen. Those six departments were: *Design, Production & Testing, Sales, Billing & Compliance, Customer Experience* and *Human Resources*.

Victoria then asked Albert to right click on each cell containing the name of a department. A color chart appeared. She instructed them to assign a color to each and explained again the importance of doing this to aid in memory retention and recall.

Roughly 90 minutes later, they had completed the task grouping and department identification exercise and Victoria resumed control of the screen. She opened a new screen and explained that she would begin populating an organizational chart template with the names of the six departments and the positions previously identified in their existing job descriptions.

Selom was glad when Victoria returned control of the screen to Albert. There was so much he did not know about running a business and it was important he paid close attention during this part of the exercise. Albert noticed there were stick figures on the left side of the new screen, each representing a unique position in their company. Victoria asked him to begin moving the stick figures above or below the departments within the organizational chart. Placements above the department indicated management over that department and its associated positions and activities. Placements below the department indicated a subordinate role within a department.

Playing around with the organizational chart feature of the business infrastructure software, Albert realized he could insert layers of management above or below a department's name. Selom nearly popped a blood vessel at the sight of this. "No, Albert! You're creating a pyramid!"

Stunned by his uncle's reaction, Albert quickly deleted the extra layers. "I was just curious to see what it would look like, that's all."

Victoria thought it necessary to explain Selom's reaction. "A large part of what attracts bigger organizations to doing business with smaller companies is the fact that they are lean. So I agree with Selom, we want to show as few layers of management as possible, especially in the beginning stages of your company."

Albert was confused, but dared not say anything. *I have no clue what they're talking about. I just want to code.*

Sensing his confusion, Victoria asked Albert to search online for *government organizational charts*. A quick search led Albert to an organizational chart from the U.S. Housing and Urban Development's website. "Whoa!" Albert exclaimed. "This is massive! This chart has more layers than the Leaning Tower of Pisa!" Immediately, he understood what Uncle Selom and Victoria were trying to teach him.

Coincidentally, this happened to tie into what he was currently learning in his Civics class regarding the Executive, Judicial and Legislative branches of government. *Now it makes sense why some people say it takes forever to get a decision made and a law passed. It goes through so many hands!*

Victoria was amused by Albert's reaction. "Yeah, you see that?! This is what your uncle is warning you about. Do you see the different layers of management? They are top-heavy. Reduced layers of management communicates not only to the investors, but also to future customers, that your company is lean, agile, that it can easily adapt to changes and, most importantly, that you can get things done quicker than a bigger company can. More layers of management communicate a bureaucracy with longer decision-making times. Your company should be like a gazelle, light and nimble; not like a whale, big and slow to move or respond."

Selom chimed in, "Thank you so much for sharing this! I hope my nephew understands what we're talking about. But, I still object to the pyramidal structure."

"May I ask why?"

"The pyramidal structure represents a Western way of thinking: putting a few individuals before the collective. I envision a circular structure that shows how everything that we do in this company is interconnected and centered on our customer."

"Like a wheel and spoke structure?"

"Yes, exactly!"

"Okay, I think I know where you're going with this. I like that concept." Victoria found Selom's feedback rather interesting, especially considering that the chart from their incubator did not reflect the wheel and spoke structure.

She instructed Albert to return to the business infrastructure software and click on a button at the top menu of the screen. "Name and save this chart. Then, open a new chart. Select *Insert,* then *Wheel and Spoke.*"

At that, a wheel and spoke image appeared. Selom then told Albert to type *Customer Experience* at the center or hub as a visual indication of their competitive advantage. Albert typed the names of the remaining departments into the five areas on the wheel.

Visually, this was no doubt representative of their management style; however, Victoria pointed out a major flaw. "This representation does not allow for a chain of command or reporting structure. Even if we were to add additional spokes, it would consume a lot of real estate on the page and would be too cumbersome to understand. Why don't we save this as an illustration you can include in your Strategic Growth Plan to describe your management style? For now, we should go back to the original chart. It doesn't have to be a pyramid, per se. I agree, the structure should be as flat as possible but know that, over time, as the company continues to grow, additional layers of management will be necessary."

Suddenly, Selom lost his connection to the remote session. Five minutes later, he was online again. Victoria thought now was as good a time as any to bring up the issue of electricity outages in Ghana. Selom assured her that their power grid system was much more stable and reliable now and that the temporary outage he just experienced was an exception and not the norm. He also told her that, when outages do occur, they tend to happen in the daytime when the system works its hardest against the heat.

However, like many American programmers, Ghanaian programmers also prefer to work late at night when the weather is at its coolest and they can work with minimal distractions. He also told her about their plans to invest in state-of-the-art generators once they receive their first infusion of funds.

Victoria was glad to hear that Selom had already thought this through and suggested that he add this information in the Strategic Growth Plan as she was sure this would be a topic the investors would bring up.

They returned their attention to the organizational chart still on Albert's screen. He clicked on the stick figure labeled, "CEO" and dragged it to the top of the chart. He then placed the Chief Technology Officer (CTO) stick figure under the CEO and above the Design and Production & Testing Departments. For confirmation, Victoria asked who held each title. Based on her research, she knew that Selom referred to himself as the president and Albert as the CEO.

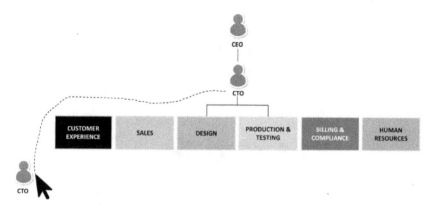

Without hesitation, Selom said authoritatively, "Nephew, I really should be the CEO." A brief moment of awkward silence passed. Selom continued, "Based on experience alone. Victoria, I have worked and moved up the ranks for some of Silicon Valley's giants in their Ghanaian, Kenyan and South African locations. I've even helped set up offices in Manila and parts of Indonesia. I have the know-how but, most important, I understand how business works. My nephew does not."

Victoria thought Selom's response, though accurate, was a bit harsh and attempted to soften the blow by asking, "Albert, how many languages do you speak?"

Albert thought this was an odd question, but answered anyway. "Five. English, Spanish, French, Twi and Fanti."

"Do you speak *Accounting*?"

"Huh?"

"When I was in graduate school, I had a professor who told me that Accounting is the 'language of business.' So, I'll ask you again, do you speak Accounting?"

"No."

In explaining the language of business, Victoria started by defining the difference between an executive and an entrepreneur. "The executive has more of the managerial skills necessary for running a large enterprise. The entrepreneur has the skills necessary to build a business from scratch," she said. "But, the higher you are in an organization, and the bigger your small company grows, the less it becomes about your technical skills and more about people and policy.

"In other words, you'll reach a point where you'll have to give up the coding and do more managing and leading, using your company's financial and accounting reports as one of many tools to guide your decisions. Your Uncle Selom has this experience and you do not. He also has existing contacts and corporate connections as part of his network. Executives tend to network with people on their level — other executives.

"This applies to all executive positions, not just CEO. Being fluent in the language of business means you can interpret profit and loss statements, balance sheets and cash flow statements and leverage that knowledge to manage risk. It also means you can handle an extreme amount of rejection and implies that you know how to network for business development and form strategic alliances. For now, I recommend you remove yourself as CEO until you've taken more business classes and become fluent in the language of business and not just coding.

"Candidly, this is why your parents are stressing the importance of a college education. It will at least give you more options. You're so young in your career. As a matter of fact, think about your vocation versus your career. Your career is what you do. Vocation comes from the Latin word *vocare* which means *to call*. Your vocation, therefore, is your calling. I want you to seriously ask yourself, *Is coding your career or your vocation*? I know this is a big decision for a 16-year-old but, hopefully, the answer will present itself sooner rather than later as you have at least another six to seven months before you start actively applying to college."

To Victoria's surprise, Albert listened attentively and offered no resistance to her demotion recommendation. Instead he replied, "I just want to code. I'm not interested in looking at financial reports every day. And I definitely don't want to spend my days sitting in meetings or getting on the phone talking to people all day."

As Albert spoke, Selom sent Victoria a text message to her phone, *Thank you!* ☺

"Good for you Albert!" Victoria encouraged him. "I'm glad you've come to that realization because so many people who are good at what they do think that they also have the skills to run the business when, in fact, they don't. It's good that you are mature enough to recognize that early on and not allow your ego to get in the way. I've seen far too many people suffer from 'Title Intoxication.'"

After further discussion, they all agreed that Albert's current title should be director of development. This was a more fitting title considering his current ability to delegate and oversee the work of the other programmers in Ghana. Over time, as experience and education dictate, he could elevate to a vice-president role and then, ultimately, become the CTO.

As Albert and Selom worked to assign the remaining roles in their proper position on the organizational chart, Victoria introduced the law of conservation. "As you configure the optimal placement of certain roles, keep in mind that what you think you are giving up in one area is actually a gain somewhere else. You'll need to balance out the technical positions with the sales positions as these are the people who will execute Selom's aggressive customer acquisition strategy detailed in the Strategic Growth Plan."

The session ended after three hours. Victoria said she would send them a draft of the chart and the wheel and spoke image they created during the session. She wanted them to have more discussions with Albert's parents and be prepared to share any potential changes during the second session on the following week.

Victoria also asked that they start thinking about resource management, in particular, filled versus vacant positions and part-time versus full-time positions. She also wanted them to think about what additional work they might outsource or offshore.

****

The following Saturday, Selom and Albert, feeling renewed, logged into the remote session with Victoria. She was pleased to learn that they had healthy dialogue with Albert's parents. Selom mentioned they wanted to add a new department, *Management.* He also mentioned wanting to change the wheel and spoke conceptual image to a hexagon. He justified the change after Albert mentioned something he learned in a geometry class — the hexagon is the strongest structure in nature.

Victoria corrected the logic by stating that the hexagon is considered the strongest natural structure only when tessellated. With that, she separated each department into its own hexagon and fitted, or tessellated, them together.

"From a manmade perspective," Victoria explained, "the pyramid is actually the strongest structure. Selom, I understand your need to explain the management style, but for the sake of time, I'm going to ask that we shift focus to the actual management structure."

Without further delay, Victoria shared her computer screen with Albert and Selom. This time they noticed a legend of symbols to the left of the organization chart they previously worked on. Victoria explained that they would place one or more of these symbols next to each role (or position) on the organizational chart. There were 13 unique roles identified in all and 17 in total, not including their advisory board.

"Let's start by first identifying the filled positions versus the vacant positions." Similar to the first session, she gave Albert remote access to her computer. He already knew which positions were filled and, as instructed, clicked on the filled and vacant position symbols and dragged them to the appropriate location on the organizational chart.

"Awesome!" Victoria said. "Now, I want the two of you to identify which of these positions will be outsourced versus offshored. Remember, *outsourced* refers to when a resource outside of your company does work for you. Your attorney, payroll advisor and CPA positions are good examples. *Offshored* refers to resources that work directly for your company but are located in another country. This applies to your programmers."

Albert began assigning the outsourced and offshored symbols to the appropriate location. To Selom's amazement, he was spot on in his assignments.

"Look at my nephew! What a difference a week makes!" They all laughed.

"Albert," Victoria said, "please save this version of the organizational chart. This time, add *Year 1* as part of the file's name. We are now going to create a *Year 3* version of the organizational chart. This version should include more positions as well as that additional layer of management Albert originally tried to add."

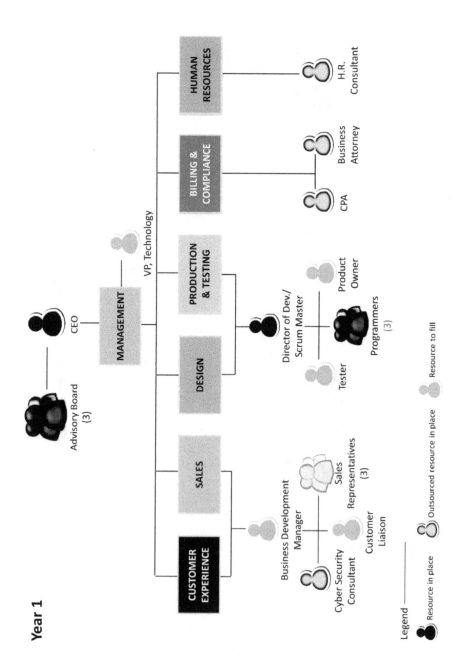

Year 1

*She's smart*, Selom thought. He recognized this new version of the organizational chart as an extension of the financial projections he tabulated for the Strategic Growth Plan. Those projections included line items that, via extrapolation, led Victoria to believe they were based on the assumption of more employees. One of those line items included the monthly expense of payroll.

Victoria broke Selom's deep thought when she said, "Selom, it's your turn to take control of the screen. I reviewed your financial projections and would like for you to add the additional resources you foresee having in place to accommodate the continued growth of your company."

Selom completed the exercise in record speed. The total number of people in the Year 3 version of the plan tripled from 17 to 51. It also included a board of directors in addition to the advisory board to which the CEO would report.

Albert was amazed at how differently the Year 3 chart looked in comparison to the Year 1 chart they created. In his mind, there was no doubt that his Uncle Selom knew what he was doing.

Victoria knew it was time to pivot. "Now, let's take a look at your job descriptions." She pulled up every single job description they previously shared with her. She asked them to start thinking about the promotional path for the lower level positions on the charts as well as their strategy for converting part-time employees to full-time over the next three years.

"I want you to be able to tell me where the growth opportunities are within this company," she told them. "Even though your company might still be classified as a startup because it's so young, you have a lot of money and exponential growth. That's exciting to certain people. They want to be a part of smaller companies with huge growth potential, but they also want to know that they can advance within that company. If they can't, they will leave and, trust me, you do not want high employee turnover. It's costly in more ways than one."

Before ending the session, Victoria asked Albert if he had given more thought to his vocation.

"Yes, I have," he replied. "I actually told my mother what you said during the session last week. My mom said her opinion would be biased so she told me to schedule some time with the guidance counselor at school. The guidance counselor helped me figure out that my vocation is helping to bridge communication gaps so that better informed decisions are made. It makes sense that my career, as of right now, happens to be developing software that enables systems to seamlessly integrate and communicate with each other. In turn, this helps the people using those systems to better communicate as well as make better-informed and quicker decisions. Communication is my calling."

"Wow Albert!" Victoria exclaimed. She was impressed by the maturity of his answer. "I'm not sure if you realize this, but you actually said something similar during the ending of your presentation at South by Southwest."

"Thank you," he responded, "but I don't really remember what I said at the end of the presentation. I also accepted the fact that my career can change over time but, as long as I stay true to my vocation, I'll be okay. Plus, we all know how fast computer technology evolves. This company is only as good as the latest technology. Either we innovate continuously or we die a quick death."

Victoria announced that she would send the draft of the Year 3 chart to Selom and Albert. This time, she asked that they review the Year 1 and Year 3 charts. Victoria promised to send a copy of her report summarizing their work together to Selom and Albert for their review at least three days before their third and final session next week.

## The Result

As promised, Victoria produced and emailed a final report to Selom, Albert and Albert's parents. It included a summary of their first two BDB sessions, followed by copies of the three versions of the organizational charts, associated recommendations, the hexagon management style diagram and the 13 job descriptions that now included a promotional path for each position.

Selom happened to read the report first. It was delivered during a time of day when Albert was still at school and his brother and sister-in-law were at work. The first page of the report contained a summary:

> The new, defined business management structure for the company can be described as a flat, line organization. A **flat organization** is one in which there are fewer layers of management resulting in less bureaucracy, more effective decision making and tighter management control.
>
> In a **line organization**, all authority and responsibility can be traced in a direct line from the top executive down to the lowest employee level in the organization. This delegation structure illustrates the chain of command and communicates each executive and director's span of control. **Span of control** represents the number of employees that any one executive or director supervises directly. The director who supervises too many people is overworked and unable to perform all duties effectively. On the other hand, valuable time is wasted if a director has too few people to supervise. For this reason, additional directors do not appear until the Year 3 organizational chart.
>
> Another principle of effective management structure is **unity of command**. Unity of command means that no employee reports to more than one supervisor at a time. Confusion and poor work relations can result when a person has work assigned by and is accountable to more

than one supervisor. It is important to determine and understand whose leadership takes precedence.

Attached are three copies of the organizational chart that illustrate the company's projected evolution over the next three years, labeled *Original*, *Year 1* and *Year 3*. The Original chart is the chart originally constructed by the incubator. It represents the current organizational structure. The Year 1 chart shows the proposed structure that includes off-shored programmers who can be hired full-time as early as May with the first round of funding. The Year 3 chart shows the projected structure that accounts for expected growth and the last round of funding.

Unlike the Original chart, the Business Design Blueprint exercise yielded Year 1 and Year 3 charts that clearly communicates how work is divided, who is responsible for that work, which resources are in place versus those that need to be hired or outsourced, and the relationships among all resources. It also included recommendations for managerial actions to take within each defined department, as well as recommendations for additional material to include in the Strategic Growth Plan.

Selom could hardly contain his excitement. *We did it! Never in a million years would I have thought that an organizational chart would be the missing link in finalizing our Strategic Growth Plan.*

In just three weeks, they had solidified their Strategic Growth Plan via these organizational charts. He prepared and, later, drank several cups of the strongest coffee he could make. He needed to stay up late so he could speak with Albert, his brother and sister-in-law about this report.

\*\*\*\*

Around 7:00 pm, Dr. Andoh called Selom on three-way, with his wife on the other line. It was midnight in Accra but he expected this call.

Selom answered the call without greeting them, "Have you read it?"

Albert's parents both laughed at his enthusiasm. It was amusing to see him, a man known as a straight-laced guy, sounding so upbeat. "Yes," they replied simultaneously.

"Do you think Victoria would be okay with us copying and pasting this information directly into the Strategic Growth Plan?" Selom wondered aloud.

"I don't see why not," Dr. Andoh replied. "After all, we've paid her for it and, as long as we give her credit, I don't foresee it being an issue. I think this will really impress the investors. It shows that we are proactively seeking and surrounding ourselves with experts who can guide us through our expansion journey. We'll discuss it with Albert tomorrow afternoon after school. He's at a girls' soccer game right now and you know he wouldn't miss that for the world!"

Selom released a hearty laugh. He recalled hearing that his nephew was popular with the girls at his school. "Very well then. I will start making adjustments to the Strategic Growth Plan in time for our last session with Victoria."

****

April showers ushered in the last session of the BDB. Mrs. Andoh interpreted the welcomed rain as a sign of starting anew. Unlike the first two sessions, she and her husband were logged into this last session. They wanted to thank Victoria personally.

As soon as Victoria confirmed that all participants had logged in, she wasted no time in starting. "Hello everyone! Looks like we have a full house! We're going to have a round-table discussion about the report I emailed a few days ago. Selom, we'll start with you. What feedback do you have?"

Selom cleared his throat. "I'm glad you asked. Victoria, I am very pleased with the work you have done for us. I was skeptical, but you've managed to help me see an organizational chart in a new light. It really is a blueprint for designing our business! You've helped close many gaps that existed in our Three-Year Strategic Growth Plan. With your permission, I'd like to embed that work into the plan."

He asked to share his computer's screen and then shared the latest version of the Strategic Growth Plan. As he scrolled through the various pages, Victoria noticed he had added a new section entitled, *Management Style and Structure*. She could see where he embedded an image of a pyramid with a hexagon base to illustrate, conceptually, their management style.

The management structure included, almost verbatim, information from her report, as well as the three versions of the organizational charts. She also noted that they converted the recommendations from her reports into action items, placed them into a Gantt Chart and assigned target due dates.

"Selom, this looks great!"

"So, you're okay with us using material from your report?"

"Yes, of course! That's what it's for. It's certainly not meant for decoration. You're supposed to leverage this as much as you can. Think of it as another management tool you have at your disposal."

"I've included your name as the source of the Year 1 and 3 drawings," Selom added.

"I see. Thank you for that." Victoria then directed her attention to Albert. "Albert, do you have any questions about or comments on the information in the report?"

"Actually I do," he answered. "On page three, under the recommendations you listed for both the Customer Experience and the Production &

Testing Departments, you mentioned enforcing English as the language to conduct all business in; we already do that."

"Oh, I apologize. I assumed you all communicate in a Ghanaian language. The reason I brought it up is because, through my job, I've worked on assignments where I sometimes interact with co-workers stationed throughout Central and South America. Although we all speak Spanish, we've been reprimanded for not speaking English since we all work for an American company."

"Oh, okay," Albert replied. "That makes sense. But FYI, English is actually the official language of Ghana. All of our programmers speak English clearly and fluently, in addition to tribal languages. And, as far as our Customer Experience Department is concerned, that will be managed exclusively in America."

"Out of curiosity, how many languages are spoken in Ghana?" Victoria inquired.

"Over 60."

"Over 60?"

"Yes," Albert replied.

Mrs. Andoh added, "And to think, Ghana is smaller in size than Texas!" They all laughed.

"Dr. and Mrs. Andoh, do you have any feedback?"

Mrs. Andoh simply said, "Ditto. Thank you so much, Victoria. You've had a tremendous impact on my family and on our son's company in such a short period of time."

Dr. Andoh followed, "Victoria, thank you! My only question is, are you available to help Albert practice presenting the Strategic Growth Plan?"

"Absolutely!" Victoria answered. "I'd be honored. Before we close, I want to congratulate you all. By enforcing this new organizational structure, you are closer to addressing the façade."

"The façade?" Selom asked.

"Yes, the façade of running a large company managed by seasoned adults," Victoria elaborated. "This was my presumption the first time I visited the company website before seeing Albert's presentation at South by Southwest. I could never have imagined that a 16-year-old was behind the core operations of the company. I guess that's where the 'child's play' comes in, right Albert?"

Albert giggled. He built the website with that very intent, to appear larger than they really are, else he knew they would be ignored.

Victoria continued, "With that kind of façade comes a certain expectation from both customers and investors, an expectation of experience and superior service delivery. I'm not suggesting you don't currently have those things, but you already have a customer waiting list and your current projects could become backlogged. You can only keep up the charade for so long before the lack of processes comes to bite you.

"You've made an important first step by going through this BDB exercise. Together, the Business Parts Analysis and the BDB provide the clarity and precision needed to project an efficiently structured, well-polished and professional image necessary to attract and retain more quality customers. Not to mention keeping your investors off your back. Now that you have defined your company's departments, associated roles and chain of command, you are ready to capture your records management systems and streamline your key business processes.

"You need processes to ensure service consistency and value, to prove scalability in a sustainable way and to show investors that there is a certain way work will flow in order to maintain quality. The best way to identify these processes is to attend a workshop coming up in Atlanta, Georgia in a couple of weeks."

As soon as the session ended, Selom arranged for him and Albert to attend the workshop.

****

Albert gazed out of the right side of the car's backseat window at the Dallas skyline as his father drove. He thought about the strategy he used in preparing for the demo at the SXSW conference, and imagined himself walking into the building where he and Selom would soon present their Three-Year Strategic Growth Plan. He foresaw ending the presentation with a signed funding contract from the investors. His mother and uncle, who had flown in the day before, were also in the car.

A beep on his phone broke Albert's gaze. It was a signal that a new email arrived. He checked his phone and chuckled.

"What? What is it? I want to laugh too!" his mother asked, inquisitively.

"You won't believe this. It's an email from Ms. Heather Mallory."

"Who's that?"

"Remember that proctor I almost got in trouble with? It's her. Apparently she looked up my demo at the South by Southwest conference online. With everything we had going on, I had forgotten to send her a link to it online. Anyway, she's attached her resume and wants to know if we're hiring."

"Ha! Go figure."

*Go figure is right*, Albert thought, *but the only thing I need to concentrate on is this presentation!* His father parked the car in a garage and they all walked over to the elevator. Albert's hands were too moist with perspiration to press the button inside the elevator. He was nervous, but his Uncle Selom kept his cool. In a matter of seconds, the doors to the elevator opened onto the 11th floor — the floor where the investors' offices were located. Once again, it was showtime!

# CHAPTER 4

# THE PRINCESS VS. THE POLITICIAN

**Kasennu™**
Electronic Records Management

Sarah Reuben is currently the COO of her family's 35-year-old furniture company. She really should be CEO and everyone seems to agree, or so she thinks. Everyone except her brother, Steve. Steve is the CMO and Sarah's nemesis. Their company thrives despite their tumultuous relationship; that is, until a virus attack and the abrupt loss of their I.T. manager left their operations vulnerable. Now they must band together to fix the problem and return to normalcy. News of the attack cannot leak to their customers. Their consultant introduces them to the Electronic Records Management element of the Kasennu methodology as a way to resolve this issue and ensure it never happens again.

Just one week into 2015, the year was already proving to be stressful. Upon doctor's orders, Sarah Reuben decided to take a weekend getaway. At 22°F, it was an unusually cold and bitter day in Dahlonega, Georgia. The mountains were capped with snow, making it the perfect environment to stay indoors, drink peppermint tea and read a good book near a fireplace.

That was what Sarah intended to do, but, despite the cold, she opted instead to take a walk along a nature trail to see the Amicalola Falls. She reasoned it would be the perfect place and the perfect weather to hopefully mask the smell of the freshly rolled joint she planned to smoke. Walking along the trail proved to be just as therapeutic as seeing the glorious waterfall itself. The stillness of the fresh air, along with the soothing sounds of the water rushing down the cliff and pounding against the rocks and into the creek below, made her forget about smoking altogether. *Nature is the best source of motivation and inspiration*, she thought. After basking in the wonderment of the waterfall for a couple of hours, Sarah decided to turn around and head back to the lodge where she was staying for the weekend. She had a massage appointment.

Instinctively, she pulled out her cell phone for a time check; however, she was in the middle of nowhere and there was no cellular service. So she decided to check the time the old-fashioned way; she stopped walking long enough to lift her left wrist and look at her watch. *Uh oh!* Her appointment was in 10 minutes. Jogging at a speed fast enough for a fallen tree branch across the trail to go unnoticed, she tripped and almost fell. *Slow down, Sarah! Take your time*, she told herself.

The spa was just as serene an environment as her walk outside. The warm, earth tone colors, the trickling sounds of water and the subtle flute music in the background helped Sarah maintain a sense of calm. She was escorted into a room where her massage would take place. She removed her clothing and lay on the massage table under the warm covers, making sure to place her face into the face cradle at the head of the table.

When the massage therapist entered the room, she asked Sarah what type of pressure to apply — light, medium or deep tissue — and where. Sarah replied, "Deep tissue, please! Over my entire body." The massage therapist began applying oil to Sarah's stressed body. Her neck and shoulders were especially tense. Sarah winced in pain several times during the massage, even when the massage therapist barely touched her.

As hard as she tried to relax, it was next to impossible. Her mind was racing as fast as a race horse. *How can I relax?* They were in the midst of their January White Sale while trying to recover from all hell breaking loose nearly two months ago. With her face still nestled in the face cradle, she practiced her breathing again, slowly inhaling and exhaling in a controlled fashion. Unfortunately, this did not quiet her mind. It had the opposite effect and Sarah felt like the controlled breathing opened a portal.

All of a sudden her life, post-college, flashed before her as though someone had pressed a rewind button at its highest speed. Her first job out of college was at a manufacturing facility in Ohio. She gained a wealth of knowledge during her four years there. She resigned and began working at her family's furniture store, applying manufacturing principles she learned while in Ohio. When the time was right, she approached her father about taking a lead role in the operations of the company. The timing seemed right because sales were down three years in a row and Sarah believed she knew the solution to stave off the fierce competition and reclaim their position as a formidable contender. She proposed shifting their business model from reseller to manufacturer.

Her father and her uncle, co-founders of the business, thought it was a great idea. However, they thought that the business model shift should take place gradually over an extended period of time, as opposed to the cold-turkey approach Sarah originally implied. She even pitched the idea to different employees and each one genuinely seemed to think it was the right decision. All cylinders were fired and Sarah was ready to execute. There was just one problem: her older brother, Steve.

Steve was in charge of marketing and, although he agreed that the shift could be good for business, he did not agree that Sarah, at that time a 25 year old, should be in charge of anything, let alone the lifeline of the company — its merchandise! To keep the peace, Sarah's dad placed her into an apprentice-type role by giving her a title, *Executive-in-Training*.

Sarah worked hard applying what she learned academically as well as professionally as an industrial engineer. Over the next five years, they successfully transitioned to providing custom furniture only and the company enjoyed exponential growth. Sarah received many awards in the local business community for her work. Everyone seemed to sing her praises. Everyone that is, except Steve. *Of course he didn't*, she thought. *He's too busy being a politician to notice.*

None of that mattered now. They were in trouble. A malicious virus recently threatened to undermine the entire company. The virus corrupted all of their customer data from last year, making it difficult to manage production schedules, answer client inquiries and reconcile payment information. In fact, more and more customers were successfully requesting chargebacks as they rightfully complained that their orders were either late or had no signs of being fulfilled. Despite Sarah's and Steve's best efforts to keep this information away from their dad, it was too late. He caught wind that the bank was threatening to freeze their account because of the chargebacks. Sarah and Steve were concerned that the bad news would cause their dad another heart attack. To top it all off, their I.T. manager bailed on them when they needed him most.

Sarah's mind race abruptly ended, as if the stop button was pressed, just as the massage therapist announced that the massage was over. Before she got up from the table to dress herself, she lifted her face from the face cradle and rested her chin on top of her clinched hands. *How did we get here?*

\*\*\*\*

Steve Reuben was born with the gift of gab, a natural salesman. His six-foot muscular frame, dark, curly hair and strikingly handsome good looks were usually enough to command attention before he even graced people with his baritone voice and poetic prose. His stubbornness was his only admitted flaw, but he chalked that up to being a Taurus. Talking to others was as easy as for him as breathing and he hoped today would be no exception.

Although it was cold out and he had a persistent cough, Steve made it a point to go to the exclusive golf club he had been a member of since he turned 21. He was on a mission. His family's business was in the midst of a crisis and, with a major sale going on, it would only compound the problem. He could not wait to discuss this with Alton.

Steve met Alton at the club several years ago and they connected instantly. He considered Alton to be not only a good friend, but also a trusted advisor with whom he happened to share many interests, golf being one of them.

It was Alton who helped clean their company's network following the virus attack. In the process, he discovered that their network was highly susceptible to attacks vis à vis its liberal Bring Your Own Device (BYOD) policy, a policy initiated by the now departed I.T. manager.

After eating a light breakfast, Steve and Alton walked outside of the café overlooking the golf course. Steve wasted no time. He brought up the virus debacle before they made it to the first hole. Alton was a little shocked. Normally, they waited until at least the ninth hole to talk business, if at all, but he knew his friend's situation was desperate. He told Steve about a partner at his firm, Gary Cornsilk who, like Alton, is also a cybersecurity consultant, but also has a strong background in risk management. "I can fix the problem once it happens," Alton told Steve, "but Gary can set up a system to minimize the risk altogether. That's what you guys really need: start being in prevention mode and not reaction mode."

They walked to the locker room after their round. Alton had to leave right away but Steve was not as pressed to leave so soon. He dreaded the thought of going to the store, but knew he had to. Once he had packed all of his things from his locker, he sat down on the wooden bench between the rows of lockers and looked up into the ceiling for a few minutes. Out of nowhere, he thought of his sister, Sarah. *So…the Princess isn't invincible after all. She claims she's the one always looking into the details. So why didn't she see through that piece-of-crap network we have?*

Suddenly, he broke out into a cold sweat and began coughing violently. Steve suppressed the cough by drinking some warm water from his sports bottle. Then, he leaned over and, with his elbows kneading into his thighs, placed his head into his cupped hands. *How did we get here?*

## The Fast Growth Predicament

While en route to his important meeting, Alton took advantage of an exceptionally long wait at a traffic light to send Gary Cornsilk a text message, *URGENT. Need to talk. I'll be at the office in 2 hrs.* Gary could not imagine what the urgency was. Everything seemed to be quiet around the office.

Later, when Alton arrived, he poked his head into Gary's office. "Hey, got a minute?"

"Sure, come on in," Gary answered. "What's the emergency? Everything okay?"

"For us, yes," Alton replied as he sat down in one of the chairs in Gary's office. "But not for my buddy. Have you rolled off that other project yet?"

"I closed everything out with the client last week. Why? You have something new for me to work on?" Gary asked. At this point, the suspense was driving him crazy.

"Actually, I do," Alton told him. "My buddy's dad owns that big furniture store up in Alpharetta. Recently, they had a major virus attack, but before I get into that…"

"Yeah, I remember you working on that. Is that the emergency?" Gary asked, still trying to figure out the urgent matter Alton texted him about.

"Yes. And I need your help. But before I tell you more about that, let me give you a little background so that you can decide if you have time to take on this challenge or assign it to one of our techs.

"My buddy's name is Steve Reuben. He's currently the CMO but he and his sister, Sarah, fight constantly over who should take their father's place as CEO. Their uncle retired a few years ago and now their dad is ready to retire, too. For years, I thought their contentious relationship was just normal sibling rivalry until I was actually onsite working there toward the end of last year. Dude, they really *hate* each other!"

Gary leaned forward in his chair as Alton continued. "From a person on the outside looking in, it seems to me they don't see the value that they each bring to the table; at least they pretend not to see. So they're both vying and jockeying for position to replace their dad. I shared all of that with you to put their virus attack situation into context. The attack happened last November. Turns out, like many organizations, they allowed their employees to bring their own devices."

"Yes, these BYOD policies can be problematic in both small and large organizations alike," Gary said.

"Exactly!" Alton agreed. "Not only do their design consultants bring their own smartphones, tablets and laptops to work, but so do the carpenters and the warehouse employees. Well, the day the attack happened, Steve called me, frantic. Man, it was bad. I could hear yelling in the background as we talked on the phone.

"I went over there as fast as I could and narrowed down the source of the virus to the laptop of one of the design consultants. His teenage son had used his computer the night before and…let's just say he went to a website he shouldn't have. That website installed a vicious virus that lay dormant in the background. It wasn't until that design consultant went into work the next day and logged into the store's network that the virus went into full attack mode. Once I isolated the source, I began the work of removing it from the network but, by that time, it had already spread throughout their network-based systems like a pandemic. It took about a week to remove it and another two weeks to add security protocol and a remote data backup system. I've been closely monitoring the situation ever since. I got one of our techs to help me install a VPN [Virtual Private Network] for them too. That way, they'd have a better, encrypted layer of security when accessing their company's private network remotely."

"Wait, they didn't already have a VPN?" Gary asked.

"No! Dude, turns out their system was wide open! Anybody could have logged into it and caused major damage. I'm amazed it didn't happen sooner. Anyway, I started asking their I.T. manager about the security, or lack thereof. I guess he felt undermined by my presence and my investigative questions. He resigned within a couple days of the attack. No offer to stick around and fix the problem or anything. The dude just left!"

"It's all coming back to me," Gary said as he leaned back in his chair. "I remember hearing you mentioning some of this during our weekly management meetings. Honestly, I didn't pay as much attention as I was fighting a fire at the time for my own client."

Alton continued, "I told Steve about you earlier this morning. I explained to him that, although I identified the source of the problem and removed the threat, all I did essentially was stop the bleeding. But you and I both know they need a mitigation or Disaster Recovery plan moving forward. Viruses are not the only way they can lose data.

"I'm gonna text you Steve's number." Alton reached into his front pants pocket and removed his phone. "I'm sure Steve is pacing back and forth waiting on your call. Poor guy. To further complicate things, they're in the middle of their January White Sale so the volume and velocity of sales is high. They've got to get this situation under control A.S.A.P. before their clients find out."

Gary jotted some notes on his tablet as a reminder of the key points Alton shared with him. Then, he called Steve.

## The Research

Gary knew the route to the furniture store from his office. Although he and his girlfriend had been there a few times over the years, this visit to the store was different. First, his girlfriend was not with him and, second, he was there to conduct a different kind of business. He was there as a potential service provider and not as a potential customer.

A chime rang as soon as Gary walked into the store. When he was greeted by a well-dressed design consultant, he couldn't help wonder if this was the person who unknowingly had brought the virus into the store.

"Welcome! Can I help you with something today, sir," the consultant asked in an upbeat voice.

"Yes," Gary replied. "I'm here to see Steve Reuben."

"Shall I tell him who's asking for him?"

"Tell him Gary Cornsilk is here."

The design consultant walked away and badged into a locked door behind the customer service area, near the store's entrance. A few minutes later, Steve walked out.

"Gary?"

"Yes, it's me, the one and only."

"I'm glad to see you. Why don't we go into my office?" Steve shook Gary's extended hand and led him behind the customer service area and through a locked door. The ambience on the other side of the door was just as posh and inviting as the showroom side. All of the office furniture shined brilliantly and there was a nice flowery fragrance just light enough to not be overwhelming. The classical music playing through the speakers evoked a sense of calm and tranquility. *By the looks of this place and the people who work here, you'd never imagine anything was wrong,* Gary thought, as he followed Steve into his office.

Steve's office looked as though one of their design consultants decorated it. It was beautiful. He had various motivational messages framed and resting on a bookshelf along with framed pictures of what Gary assumed were his wife and children. There were also pictures of Steve with some of their celebrity clients.

"So…," Steve sighed, "where do I begin? First, thank you for coming over on short notice. I'm not sure how much Alton shared with you. Maybe that's a good place to start. What do you know about our situation so far?"

Gary looked at him as empathetically as possible and repeated what Alton previously told him. He was careful not to repeat the parts about the family drama. Steve nodded his head.

"Yeah, that sounds about right. I can fill in the gaps for you. We realized our network had been attacked when one of our design consultants said she could not access any of her client's files. She said they were all 'empty.' When she opened a file, a pop up window appeared with a message indicating that the file was corrupt. At first, she thought it was a fluke, until she tried to access other client files. Same thing. All content wiped out. All corrupted. I reached out to Alton right away and asked him to come over and investigate. It was an emergency and our I.T. manager was still out for the Thanksgiving holiday."

*Hmm*, Gary thought. *That was a detail that Alton forgot to mention. The I.T. manager was on vacation when the incident occurred.* Getting the full story from Steve was already proving to be beneficial.

Steve continued, "Alton located the virus, removed it and figured out its source. But things got worse, actually catastrophic, before they got better. We lost all data for the year 2014, including customer orders and estimates. Seeing that was bizarre, to say the least, because it only affected that year. Alton explained that it was because the virus erased any file with a 2014 created or modified date, including files attached to customer and vendor profiles in our databases.

"Our saving grace was the fact that we still have some 'old school' employees around here who prefer paper files over electronic files. Some of them had paper files on the more recent orders as well as a handful of completed order files. And some of our production management team also had copies of printed orders from the customer database. With that knowledge, we went on defense. We began piecing together these orders like it was a giant jigsaw puzzle. It was tedious and time-consuming work. All hands were on deck. For a few weeks, I think many of us survived on nothing more than sugary donuts and coffee. We had to do what we had to do.

"The most important thing was keeping news of the attack away from my dad and our customers. My dad and his wife were out on a Caribbean cruise and we had hoped we could have the problem solved before he returned. So we made a collective, conscious decision to keep up the façade. We have a reputation for producing fine and quality custom furniture. If our virus attack leaked to the general public, it could cause irreparable damage. As of last week, we recovered about 65% of the 2014 customer order information. My hat goes off to the design consultants. They found all kinds of clever ways to tell our clients they needed more time to check on the status of their orders.

"The façade was working until too many of them started requesting chargebacks. I understood it, but I certainly didn't like it. In hindsight, I should have proactively communicated with all of our clients to let them know that our network had been compromised, not hacked, and that we were actively taking measures to mitigate the issue. Many of our customers are on a strict timeline and absolutely need their orders filled by the estimated date we provide them. You have to keep in mind that our clientele consists of celebrities, movie and film set designers and other affluent people throughout the metro Atlanta area. Our furniture has been featured on many TV shows and magazines whenever our celebrity clients invite camera crews into their homes. I hope I'm not rambling."

"No, not all," Gary assured Steve.

"Okay, good. So I told you about the customer order side. Then there were our financial records. My cousin, Jonathan, reported that we also lost all those 2014 records. He and his team also had several late-night marathons trying to reconcile receipts, invoices…they had to contact the bank to get copies of all 2014 statements. They even had to call some of our vendors to request copies of bills they knew we owed but had not yet paid. The last thing we needed was to get hit with collections notices."

"When our I.T. manager got back from vacation, Alton asked him the most obvious questions: 'Why don't we have a VPN?' and 'Why is there not a remote data backup system?' When Alton told us our data could have been recovered if we had a data backup system, the Princess and I both became livid."

"The Princess?" Gary asked.

"Sorry, I mean, my sister, Sarah."

"Is she a daddy's girl? Is that why you call her that?" Gary asked inquisitively, yet not wanting to pry.

"That's an understatement! But my dad calls her that because *Sarah* means *princess* in Hebrew. I guess in a way it's a double entendre."

"Indeed."

"Back to the I.T. manager," Steve said in an attempt not to deviate too far from the original conversation. "We assumed the I.T. manager had an airtight system in place to manage our data. He had been with us for eight years. We had no reason to question him. He looked and talked like he knew what he was doing. He had his own little fiefdom here. Needless to say, he felt insulted by what he called 'an attack on his character and his professionalism.' He resigned two days after he returned from his vacation. I remember us being in my dad's office when his resignation showed up in my dad's inbox. My dad read it aloud to me and Sarah. Sarah said, 'good riddance!' I think it's one of the few times we've ever agreed on anything.

"By the way, Sarah and my dad also want to meet you. Sorry for dominating the conversation, but we'll catch up again before you leave."

"No need to apologize," Gary reassured Steve.

****

Steve poked his head into his father's office and saw he was not there. "I'll take you to the back to meet Sarah," he told Gary. They walked out of the office area, past customer service and through the vast showroom. The one-story showroom featured several simulated living and working environments to help clients envision the optimal type of furniture they wanted designed. Toward the back of the showroom was a spacious lounge area with large tables and plush leather chairs. The lounge served as a place where clients could comfortably peruse catalogues while eating assorted delicatessen items provided by the store. The two gentlemen continued walking until they came to an inconspicuous door painted in the same color, black, as its adjacent walls.

Steve scanned his badge against the electronic reader on the wall to the right of the door. When the door unlocked, Gary assumed it was made of steel based on what appeared to be Steve's initial struggle to open it. Gary followed him down a narrow hallway that, eventually, opened into one massive room. One could not imagine the scale of this area based on the outside of the store; it was just as inconspicuous as the door they walked through to enter it.

Inside, there were at least 40 to 50 people distributed throughout this area, each working attentively on their designated tasks. They turned right and walked toward the far end of the area near what appeared to be a loading dock. There, Gary saw an office with a closed door and a rectangular window next to it, covered in open blinds. This, Steve told him, was Sarah's office.

Steve peeked through the window. Sarah happened to be on the phone with an angry client attempting to explain why his furniture was not ready. She looked up, saw Steve and Gary at her window, held up two fingers and mouthed, "Give me two minutes." Gary took advantage of the brief wait outside Sarah's office to respond to a text message. When she hung up the phone, she motioned for Steve to open her door. Gary followed Steve into her office and heard faint sounds of native flute and drum music.

Sarah stood up behind her desk as the two men entered her office. Instantly, she and Gary were struck by each other's appearance, not in a romantic way, but in a most peculiar way. Gary expected to see someone dressed to the nines, much like her brother. Instead, he saw a woman only one inch shorter than Steve and at least two inches taller than himself, with dark, thick brunette hair pulled back messily into a bun. She wore glasses, steel-toed shoes with khaki pants and a red plaid buttoned-up shirt. *A far cry from a princess*, he thought. *But in fairness, she does work in a warehouse.*

Conversely, Sarah expected to see a man wearing a tee shirt and blue jeans, almost slouchy in appearance. She should have known better because that was not how Alton dressed. Alton usually came to their store dressed in jeans with a buttoned-up shirt and a sports coat. But Gary was dressed in a suit and tie with shoes that seemed to shine as bright as the sun. Aside from his manner of dress, she had never seen anyone quite like him. He had high cheekbones and shoulder-length, jet-black hair pulled back neatly into a ponytail. His complexion was akin to terracotta, like the red clay found throughout Georgia and Alabama.

Steve introduced Gary and told Sarah that he explained to Gary a good bit of their virus woes. Before leaving her office, Steve asked that Sarah call him when she and Gary finished talking so that he could let their father know.

*I could just call dad directly. That would be the most efficient thing to do. But, I digress.* Sarah kept that thought to herself; she wanted to be on her best behavior in front of their guest. Soon, Steve left her office, closing the door behind him.

"Please excuse me for a second," Sarah told Gary as she sat down in the chair behind her desk. She picked up her walkie-talkie to let the warehouse manager know that she would be in a meeting. Gary looked around at the walls in her office. They were filled with motivational quotes and various charts and graphs. Sarah put down her walkie-talkie and made eye contact with Gary.

"I hear you come highly recommended by Alton. He just saved us from digital anarchy!" Sarah managed to crack a smile, but Gary knew their situation was dire and far from a laughing matter. "Steve said he told you everything. Do you have any questions for me?"

"As a matter of fact, I do. What do you do here as COO? The reason I ask is so that I can have a better understanding of the types of data your team generates and manages."

Sarah answered bluntly, "I'm the brains behind this operation. I'm responsible for overseeing client orders from production all the way to delivery. I…" Just as Sarah was getting ready to delve into the details of her role as COO, she stopped herself.

"I have an idea. I hope you have time and don't mind getting a little dirty. Why don't we walk the floor? That way, you can see what we do back here and gain a better understanding of the types of associated records. You might want to leave your jacket and attaché case here in my office." Gary agreed and placed his case on the chair next to the one he sat in. As he followed Sarah out of her office, he removed his suit jacket and hung it on a hook installed on the back of her office door.

\*\*\*\*

They walked along the perimeter of the warehouse, so as not to get in the way of the people working, through a massive sliding double door and all the way to the other side of the area. Sarah pointed out that this was the beginning of their assembly line and that each main section was marked by a bright red rectangle painted on the floor. Gary noticed the words, *Process Order*, painted in all caps and in the same bright red color every three feet along the rectangular boundary.

Sarah told him, "As soon as the design consultants enter a client's paid order into our database, our master carpenter receives that information and checks whether we have the materials in stock. We usually don't, since we build to order. But there are times when we may have enough in scrap materials, like wood, from previous jobs. He lets the design consultant know the materials' status, along with its estimated time of arrival (ETA). As a rule of thumb, our design consultants are trained to tell clients that their order will take a minimum of six weeks to build. However, that time can increase based on the material's ETA and the extent of the wood-carving required.

"The design consultants then update the order in the database. The master carpenter receives an automated email from the database. This is his cue to place the order for materials. Everything we do in the database is date and time stamped. That's why the virus was able to cleverly erase anything dated 2014."

They followed an arrow painted in neon yellow on the floor from the Process Order to the *Build Order* section of the warehouse. Sarah raised her voice so that Gary could hear her over the machinery; otherwise, her voice would be muffled by the sounds of hammers, drills and electric saws. She continued, "Once the master carpenter places the order for all materials, that information is also updated in the database. You will notice that directly across from this Build Order section is a receiving dock. We have separate receiving and loading docks. We added the receiving dock about a year after we realized the amount of wasted motion in using one dock to receive and load merchandise. People used to walk almost 50 yards [~46 meters] from the loading dock near my office to this section.

"Anyway, this is where the actual furniture making happens. The number of people working on an order depends on the type of furniture, its size and the required materials. The master carpenter updates the status of each order weekly according to its stage of production. This allows anyone with access to the database to be able to tell a client the status of his or her order.

They continued following the painted arrows on the floor until they walked through the sliding glass doors again and landed at the *Inspect Order* section. In this area were several different types of furniture that had a tag on each, indicating its inspection status. "This is my domain!" Sarah exclaimed. "We have a quality manager, but I insist on inspecting every piece of furniture before it is placed temporarily onto a storage shelf *and* when it is removed from the shelf prior to being shrink-wrapped and placed on a delivery truck. I want to make sure that each piece of furniture that leaves our warehouse meets my approval. I test it for fit, function, craftsmanship, etc."

Eventually, Sarah and Gary were back where they had started originally, the loading dock area which contained her office. "As you can see, our operation in this warehouse is basically one big assembly line and the order database is updated at every checkpoint along the way, including once the furniture is actually delivered."

"This is some operation, Sarah! Reminds me of Ford's infamous Model T assembly line," Gary told her as they walked back into her office.

"Thank you! It took a lot of hard work to get here. I know you meant that as a compliment, but I don't give Henry Ford credit with applying the assembly line concept to manufacturing. There were plenty of people who did it long before he did. Besides, he was a big time anti-Semite."

"Oh, Sarah, I'm so sorry. I didn't mean to offend you." Gary needed to quickly change the subject. "Alton mentioned you having a manufacturing background. Is that correct?"

"Yes, it is," Sarah answered. "I attribute much of my success to a plant I worked at in Ohio as an industrial engineer. We made laundry detergent there, in powder and liquid form. I was assigned several process improvement projects to improve production time. I studied the importance of timing and doing things in the optimal order to meet production targets. I've been around our store my whole life, but when I came to work here permanently, we hit a rough patch, sales-wise. I saw how the market for custom closets was taking off and asked my dad and uncle if we could start making custom furniture.

"This warehouse is triple the size it used to be. For years we only had the dock outside of my office and the storage section. That was it. We already had awesome design consultants, but even they were beginning to get bored with our limited product offering. They jumped at the chance to add variety.

"We started with wooden dressers, nightstands and chest of drawers first. We hired carpenters and other people with years of furniture making experience. It was important for me to make sure we mastered making wooden furniture before we expanded into sofas and everything else considered furniture. I got certified in Project Management, as well as Lean[12] and Six Sigma,[13] and I tapped into my engineering background to develop an estimation model.

"I even worked with a software designer to build a custom order management database for us. He put it on the network so that everyone could have access to it. However, it really needs to communicate with our CRM [Customer Relationship Management] system as well as tie into the accounting system Jonathan uses. Just as I was starting to research that, the virus attack happened.

"I'm so mad at myself. I can't believe I never thought to verify if our information was backed up or not. But, I remind myself that while I'm here in the back literally getting my hands dirty and inhaling woodchips, the 'Politician' is out front and center kissing babies and shaking hands."

Sarah instantly regretted what she said when she saw Gary's puzzled look, for she knew her comment was unprofessional and she would have to explain herself. "Sorry, I'm venting now. I call my brother *The Politician*. If we're gonna work together, you may as well find that out sooner than later."

*Oh, so they both have sarcastic names for each other,* Gary thought to himself. *Interesting.*

"Steve likes to schmooze, socialize with his pretentious friends in these fancy clubs and kill precious time on the golf course. And to think, he truly believes Dad should pass the torch on to him. The I.T. manager was right under his nose and he failed to see what was going on. But see, that's the problem around here — too many chiefs and not enough Indians!"

"I'm Cherokee."

The blood nearly drained from Sarah's face. "Oh my gosh, I am so sorry! That, that was a very racist thing for me to say and I apologize."

"Apology accepted. I guess we're even now." Gary smiled as he referenced their previous exchange about Henry Ford. Truthfully, Gary was glad he could use his ethnicity to stop Sarah's rant. "I was going to mention that when I heard the native flute and drum music you had playing in your office."

Sarah was still in shock. *So that explains his look.*

"Before I speak with your dad, can you give me a quick demo of the different systems you and Steve mentioned?"

"Sure!" Sarah told him, still embarrassed by her tirade. She turned one of her two large computer monitors to face him and gave him a demo of their ordering system, their CRM database and their accounting software. Afterwards, she called Steve. "I think we've finished up here. I gave Gary a walkthrough of the warehouse as well as the three major systems we use."

****

Sarah walked with Gary to the front of the store to her father's office and gave him one of her business cards. Steve and Sarah both bore a striking resemblance to their father, especially Steve. The only discernable difference between Steve and his father was his father's white, wavy hair. "Come on in and have a seat, Gary," Mr. Reuben said in a slight New York accent."

His office was larger than Steve's and beautifully framed artwork adorned the walls. Gary was surprised he did not see a computer in Mr. Reuben's office, only a tablet resting on the credenza across from his desk. Also on the credenza was a crystal box containing Cuban cigars.

"You've met with Steve and Sarah, so I'm sure you've heard an ear full. I probably can't add more details regarding that virus attack we had a couple of months ago, so I thought I'd share with you a little more about our history. Being that you're a risk management guy, I'm sure you can appreciate full disclosure. You'll basically get the same speech I gave to Alton."

"Yes sir, please feel free to tell me. Anything else you can share that you think is helpful is much appreciated," Gary told him.

"Very well then," Mr. Reuben told him. "Not sure if you know this, but we will celebrate 35 years in business in May. My brother and I started the company from very humble beginnings. My first wife, Steve's mother, didn't like the idea of me starting a business and leaving our plush life behind. She especially hated the idea of moving down South. Don't get me wrong, we enjoyed a very comfortable life. I was working on Wall Street as an investment banker and she worked part-time as a curator at the Metropolitan Museum of Art.

"But it was too late. I had been bitten by the entrepreneurial bug. It didn't help that my brother spoke of Atlanta as though it was a wellspring of milk and honey. I remember those phone calls from him like it was yesterday, 'Opportunities abound...and there's land, lots and lots of raw, undeveloped land! Stop all the bean counting and get your ass down here!'

"I requested a job transfer to Atlanta and my then-wife begrudgingly relocated with me and Steve. Steve was a little kid at that time. It wasn't too long afterward that my brother and I started networking, attending different events and meeting new people. Two years later we secured financing and...voilà! The wheels were in motion to open our first store. By then, Steve's mother had filed for a divorce and returned to New York with him. I met Sarah's mother, my current wife, a year later. We married a few months before we opened the first store.

"You see, Steve and Sarah grew up very differently. Sarah thinks Steve resents the fact that she grew up with me in the house and he didn't. I had joint custody of him and he usually spent the summers with us and certain holidays. That's really the genesis of this whole Princess vs. Politician thing. They've called each other derogatory names as long as I can remember. Steve is nine years older than Sarah. What's crazy is that they both work really hard and want what's best for our company. Sadly, they don't see how much they need each other. I tell them all the time that they're two sides of the Reuben coin — they're both outstanding visionaries. Steve is one hell of a business strategist and marketer. And Sarah is like a little pit bull: once she sinks her teeth into solving a problem she doesn't let up until it's solved.

"Sarah complains that Steve is like ornamentation; she says his primary purpose is to look good. She doesn't have an appreciation for the networking that he does and how it helps him keep his finger on the pulse of what's going on in the city. It was through Steve's connections that we made inroads into the burgeoning film industry in Georgia.

"Then you have Steve who complains that Sarah is like a mad scientist who buries herself in her laboratory, a.k.a. the warehouse, and never comes out to see what's really going on. But I have to tell you, if it weren't for Sarah our operations would have gone caput a long time ago. When she really started paying attention to quality, we were able to increase our prices by a flat 15% across the board. This made each order that much more profitable. She even invented a furniture protective coating formula we apply to each piece of furniture. It's funny...I often tell them their descriptions of each other as the 'Princess' and the 'Politician' are like the reverse of Bagehot's description of the Queen and the Prime Minister.[14]

"And my poor nephew Jonathan. My kids nicknamed him 'Switzerland.' He's my brother's boy. He's between the ages of Sarah and Steve, which doesn't help in conflict resolution. Whenever a new battle ensues between the Princess and the Politician, he maintains his neutral position. He's constantly trapped in the middle. He's a great kid too. I just wish he would stand up for himself more, but even I must admit that's hard to do when you're dealing with such strong personalities. It's a goddamn mess if you wanna know the truth."

Mr. Reuben leaned back in his chair and propped his feet onto his beautiful cherry wooden desk. "Let me give it to ya straight. I'm ready to start the next chapter of my life. No ifs, ands or buts about it. My brother cashed out five years ago and, ever since, I've become envious of his leisurely lifestyle. I bought a condo down in Palm Beach. My wife and I can't wait to live there permanently. Problem is, I can't retire until I know these two won't kill each other...and destroy the business in the process.

"With the steady increase in business, I worry we'll start losing our most valuable employees. Our employees have repeatedly expressed frustration over the internal family drama. They can be told literally to do two different things by Sarah and Steve. It was starting to cause mix-ups in customer orders and that was unacceptable. Some customers were starting to post bad reviews online. I bet they didn't mention that to you. That's when Sarah decided to move her office to the back, as far away from Steve as possible.

"There's something else they probably haven't mentioned: none of the systems talk to each other. I think it's a function of them operating in silos and, because they each have their own little fiefdom, we now have separate personnel, financial, CRM and warehousing systems that do not communicate with each other. Nothing is documented either. And some info is entered twice or maybe even three times. I think Sarah may have some of the processes documented for the warehouse, but you should definitely ask her. The long and short of it is this: our I.T. manager leaving and the virus are really the result of other deep-rooted issues. Even if you put a Disaster Recovery plan in place, it will only be as effective as the leadership who collectively enforces it.

"They think the stress of the business after my brother left is what caused my heart attack. Truth be told, it's *them* and their constant bickering that have me in this predicament. Sarah probably has no idea that I know about her self-medicating pot smoking and Steve's been coughing around here so much I thought he would cough up his own lung!

"Now that I've bared my soul to you, what's your judgment, St. Peter?"

Gary reached in his pants pocket to retrieve his phone. He had been at the store for nearly two hours and felt drained. "I can definitely appreciate why you shared this with me, especially the part about being told what to do by two different people. That can be an issue. Considering the severity, I'll try to get a proposal out A.S.A.P."

Gary returned to his car and drove to the Taqueria next door. He walked up to the bar and pleaded to the bartender, "Give me the strongest drink you've got!"

## The Hypothesis

During his commute to his office the next morning, Gary reflected on the previous day at the Reuben's furniture store. He was amazed at how a business that looked so amazing on the outside could be in such turmoil on the inside. *Their acting is just as good as their celebrity clients!* He sent Alton a text message to give him an update, *Met w/ the Reubens yesterday. Now I know why you gave me that background info. I can help them. Talk later.*

It was Friday. A day he usually only worked for a few hours so that he could enjoy an extended weekend. But he would likely work a full day today. Considering the criticality of the Reubens' situation, he knew he had little time to spare in preparing a proposal; he needed to get something to them before the end of the day. He would keep the information concise, yet impactful, knowing this project would require more of his mediation skills than his technical skills. He knew the end game for them after his first conversation with Alton — a Disaster Recovery and Business Continuity plan.

Such a plan would not only ensure full and timely recovery of data following an emergency, but it would also minimize business downtime. The process of achieving this would require a high touch execution for a high tech problem, sprinkled with some tough love. Getting Sarah and Steve intimately involved in this effort would be key to ensuring his success and theirs.

It didn't take Gary as long as he thought it would to prepare the proposal. As planned, he was able to narrow the content to one page. Although he completed it by 10:30 am, he intentionally waited until noon to email the proposal to the Reubens. He assumed they took their lunch breaks at this time, making it ideal for capturing their attention. However, just to be sure they would open his email, he typed the subject as *The Drama Finally Caught Up with You* and marked it as urgent. He knew it was a risk. He might offend them but, he reasoned, that was what they *needed* to hear, even if they did not *want* to hear it.

\*\*\*\*

It worked. As the grandfather clock in the hallway tolled at noon, Steve's cell phone beeped to alert him that a new email had arrived in his inbox. He saw Gary's email and opened it right away. The body of the email was brief, no more than three sentences. The gist of the email was this: Gary enjoyed meeting with all of them yesterday, he had attached a proposal and that he would like to schedule time to discuss the proposal in-person. Without hesitation, or consultation with Sarah and their father, he called Gary.

"Hello, this is Gary," he answered.

"Gary, it's Steve Reuben. Can you come over tomorrow around 8 am to discuss your proposal?"

"Yes, no problem." *Wow, that was fast!* Gary thought. It was 12:03 pm. *He couldn't have read the proposal.*

Gary's assumption was correct. Steve had not read the proposal. His intuition and instinct told him that he needed to seize the moment and get Gary back to their store as quickly as possible. He trusted Alton's recommendation. Steve then went into his office to open the proposal from his laptop. It read:

> Storing information electronically promotes paper reduction while also freeing up physical space. There is a catch, though. Without careful organization, these records can go into a sort of "black hole." All of a sudden, what should take a matter of seconds to find can turn into minutes, sometimes hours. Without adequate security and backup, there's always the risk of losing the electronic records altogether due to theft, fire, flood and viruses. Sadly, you all know this experience first-hand. I propose developing and implementing the Electronic Records Management (ERM) element of the Kasennu methodology for business infrastructure.

> The ERM specifically links together the processes, software technologies, and people needed to consolidate, organize, backup, and archive digital information in an easy-to-follow, structured manner. The ERM makes it clear how to secure confidential and sensitive information so your company's network and hard drives are easy to navigate, backup, and recover should you ever lose access.

> By documenting your company's policies and procedures for creating, naming, storing, purging, archiving, and backing up electronic records

you can:

- Protect and safeguard electronic data,
- Develop a platform for a Disaster Recovery and Business Continuity plan,
- Minimize downtime with intelligent electronic data storage and security measures,
- Organize electronic records in a system that makes sense to everyone,
- Reduce the amount of time it takes to locate electronic records,
- Create a platform for efficient virtual information sharing, and
- Increase the response rate to customers, vendors and colleagues.

The types of electronic (or digital) records is vast and includes software and database files, pictures, scanned information, videos, books, designer catalogues, presentations, and order forms.

We can complete this work in three sessions. It will require the full involvement and participation of all management as well as the design consultants.

****

Sarah read the email later in the afternoon. She had spent most of the morning trying to resolve a customer order issue. She had no reaction to the proposal, but did have some questions. Before she could open a document to type out those questions, she noticed an email from Steve also marked urgent. Apparently, he scheduled a mandatory meeting with Gary that she and their dad needed to attend.

*He could have asked me before he made that decision. He knows tomorrow is the Sabbath,* she said aloud to herself.

But her inner voice replied, *Back down, Sarah. You know how serious this is. He's as concerned as you are. You probably would have done the same thing had you seen the email first.*

****

The next day was Saturday, the last day before the third week officially began in January. As agreed, Gary arrived to the store by 8:00 am. As he approached the double doors, he tried to open each side, but both were locked. The store would not open to the public for another hour. In attempting to open each side, he made a noise that got the attention of the same design consultant, Adam, who greeted him when he first came to visit Steve.

Adam unlocked the door to let Gary inside. "Good morning! You're here to see Steve, right?"

Gary nodded his head and followed the design consultant to Steve's office.

"Good morning everyone!" Gary said enthusiastically. He really was happy to see all of the Reubens there, including cousin Jonathan. They were equally as happy to see him. "Have you all read the proposal? Do you have any questions or concerns?"

Sarah spoke first. With her technical background it was only fitting that she wanted to know the specific details of *how* Gary would execute the ERM.

"Great question Sarah! I'm glad you asked that. Here's where we are. A problem has presented itself in the form of a virus attack. Alton installed a VPN as a stop-the-bleeding solution, but it still does not address why the problem happened in the first place. When I visited this past Thursday and listened to what you, Steve and Mr. Reuben all had to say, the root cause of the problem became apparent, which is the gross lack of communication among the management team." Gary was careful not to point out the most obvious root cause — the ongoing war between Sarah and Steve.

"Operating in silos exposed a gaping hole in how data currently flows throughout this company. Knowledge of this exposure will help me to develop a plan to prevent electronic-related disasters in the future or, at the very least, minimize the impact of a disaster, whether it is natural or man-made, as in your case.

"Sarah, to specifically answer your question, the first thing I need is a copy of the company organizational chart as well as any job descriptions you have. We know the silos exist, but do they have a name? Hopefully, the chart will answer that question. These silos, a.k.a. departments, will serve as the foundation for how we will organize all electronic records to store on the network.

"Second, we'll leverage the information from the job descriptions to identify who should have access to certain records. Third, we'll take time to analyze which records belong on the network and develop a creation, naming and storage protocol and actually rearrange the files and folders on the network. And last, we'll use all of the above information to develop a Disaster Recovery and Business Continuity plan. We'll also reset security and data backup measures as deemed necessary to ensure optimal protection."

"The job descriptions and org chart… aren't those the outputs of the Business Parts Analysis and the Business Design Blueprint elements of the Kasennu methodology?" Steve asked. Much to Sarah's surprise, Steve had taken the initiative to read more about the methodology after reading Gary's proposal.

"Yes," Gary replied. "Considering the urgency of the situation here, we'll use the 'outputs' you already have and, if necessary, go back and update them after we finish the ERM."

"What time can we start tomorrow?" Steve asked eagerly. Though they expressed outward shock, Sarah and Jonathan were both wondering the same thing.

"Well, tomorrow is Sunday. What time do you open?"

"Noon."

"We can start at 8 am."

"Great! I'll let everyone who needs to be here know."

In less than 30 minutes, Gary had a signed proposal. Now the hard part was about to begin.

## The Experiment

Getting up early was never easy for Gary and this day was no different. *This ought to be a crime*, he jokingly thought to himself. *Normal people are never up this early in the morning.* As a technologist, he is used to working late at night.

Meanwhile, Sarah woke up for the first time in weeks without a crook in her neck. *This must be a good sign of what will happen today*, she told her herself. She took a hot shower and made herself a protein smoothie. Although Steve mentioned he would have breakfast available once everyone arrived at the store, she didn't want to chance there being food she doesn't eat. She was on a journey to becoming a vegan and wanted to avoid any temptations.

Steve also awakened feeling refreshed. After showering and shaving, he put on some clothes his wife had set out for him the night before. He didn't know what he would do without her. She was his oasis of calm in the center of the chaos. On his way to the store, Steve called the caterer to confirm he would meet him at the store by 7:00 am. This, he reasoned, should give the caterer's team plenty of time to set up before everyone arrived at 7:30 am. He told everyone to arrive at 7:30 am instead of 8:00 am so that they would have time to eat breakfast before Gary started the session.

****

When Steve pulled into the parking lot of the store, he was surprised to see his dad's red convertible Mercedes already parked. There was another car there, too. *Hmm, I wonder who drives that black SUV?* He unlocked the door to the store and was surprised to see Gary and his father sitting on a sofa in the showroom laughing and talking to each other. He now knew who the black SUV belonged to.

"Gary! I'm surprised to see you here so soon, buddy. How's it going? Looks like you and my dad are hitting it off pretty well."

Gary replied, "I'm almost never this chipper whenever I'm up this early. Your dad missed his calling in life, he should have become a comedian!"

Steve turned at the sound of another vehicle pulling into the parking lot. It was the caterer. He asked his dad to prop open the door to the office area so that the caterers could easily walk in and out to set up the food. As the caterer and his crew walked into the store, Steve noticed Sarah parking her car. She also drove a red convertible Mercedes, except her car had tan leather interior instead of black like their dad's.

*Copycat.* No sooner than Steve thought that, he regretted it.

He thought about what his wife told him before he left home. "Stay positive. Sarah wants what's best too. She's not going to do anything to hurt you or the store." Ironically, his wife and Sarah got along like sisters, which made his strained relationship with Sarah all the more complex.

By 7:30 am, all 13 people identified to participate in this first session of the ERM were there and eating breakfast, including Sarah. She never could resist a good bagel or croissant with homemade cream cheese. Gary quickly ate some food and went into the conference room where he would explain the instructions for the day.

Thirty minutes later, everyone sat at the table in the spacious conference room. Steve introduced Gary to everyone and reiterated why he was there and how he would help them.

Gary then stood up, "We have roughly four hours before the store opens at noon. I'll try to make today as painless as possible. I have 20 unopened packs of index cards. I'm going to give each of you a pack and I want you to go to your computer or laptop and write out the types of company-related files you have stored on the network, not the hard drive.

"Specifically, I want you to write the file *type* and not the name of each file. For example, Jonathan, instead of writing onto separate index cards, *Bank Statement December 2014* or *Bank Statement January 2015*, you should write on one index card, *Bank Statements*. The same goes for the design consultants. Write *Client Pictures* onto one index card and not *Order Number 4589. Jones. Picture 003*. This exercise does not apply to personal files. In fact, I've already asked Steve to create a folder on the network entitled *Personal Files*. That folder contains sub-folders with each of your names. Please move any of your personal files to the sub-folder with your name on it.

"You'll have two hours to complete this exercise. Let me know if you need more index cards or more time. Does anyone have any questions?" No one raised their hand. "Good, let's get started. As you walk out of this room, I'll give you a pack of index cards and a black marker."

One by one, each person filed out of the room, accepting a pack of cards and marker. The design consultants worked in the client lounge area since they did not have dedicated office space. Everyone else went into his or her respective office.

\*\*\*\*

The two hours seemed to fly by. At 10:00 am, all participants were back in the conference room, each carrying a stack of marked index cards. It was standing room only. Gary removed the chairs from the table and lined them against the back wall. In front of them were larger index cards spread across the table. Each card contained the name of a department Gary retrieved from the company's organizational chart: *Business Development, Design, Production, Delivery, Human Resources, Payroll & Finance, Information Technology* and *Legal.*

"Does this look familiar to you?" he asked the audience of employees.

"Yes," replied Diane, the H.R. manager, "these are the names of our departments.

"Precisely," Gary confirmed. "Each of you will come up to the table with your index cards and place each one under the department that file is most closely associated with. I'll use the same examples as before. The Bank Statements index card would be placed underneath the larger index card that says Payroll & Finance. The Client Pictures card would be placed underneath the larger card that says Design. Who wants to go first?"

Sarah yelled out, "Me! I'll go first. I'll be the guinea pig!"

"Very well," Gary smiled. "Come on up!"

Sarah had roughly 40 cards that quickly filled the table. Steve volunteered to go next and Gary instructed him to begin laying his index cards on top of Sarah's to make sure they would all fit onto the table. Next, each of the remaining employees placed their cards in the appropriate column on the table. The exercise generated a lot of discussion among the participants. They were saying things like, "Oh, I didn't know you stored that kind of information," "What exactly is that?" and "I never knew that…that's interesting!"

Mr. Reuben sat in one of the chairs alongside the back wall, watching the whole exercise unfold. He smiled several times throughout. Sarah and Steve both wondered what he was thinking.

By 11:30 am, every square inch of the table was completely covered with index cards. The group of participants identified those cards containing duplicate information and Gary discarded them. Carefully, he picked up each column of cards and rubber-banded them together. He then told everyone that he would take these index cards and transfer them to an ERM matrix. This matrix, he explained, would contain all of the departments and the electronic file types associated with each department. Additionally, it would also contain other columns corresponding to various attributes for each file.

"I'll email this matrix to Steve and Sarah by tomorrow and they will distribute it to you all. In preparation for our second session next Sunday, I want you to think through the attributes of this matrix," Gary instructed.

"In particular, start thinking about which files should be private versus public as well as who has access rights. Steve, Sarah, I ask that you also email a copy of your organizational chart to everyone. This will help them identify who should and should not have access to certain files. I also want you to think about the best or optimal type of digital storage for each of these files. For instance, there are certain legal or compliance documents, as well as employee files, that not everyone should be able to access. In that situation, Diane may decide that the files are stored on the network, but that only a limited number of people can actually access those files."

Before they knew it, the antique grandfather clock in the hallway chimed at noon. Steve asked one of the design consultants to go to the front of the store to unlock the door. All of the employees left the room except Gary, Steve, Sarah and Mr. Reuben.

"What'd you think about all of that?" Gary inquired.

"It was enlightening!" Sarah exclaimed.

"First of all," Steve chimed in, "I never knew you could glean so much information from an organizational chart and, second, I didn't realize we had so many different types of files! To say we're a small business, this is a lot, don't you think?"

"Yes, it's a lot. But this is a 35-year-old company! As part of the management team, it gives you a level of transparency that currently is non-existent." Gary turned to face Steve and Sarah's father. "Mr. Reuben, do you have any questions or feedback for me?"

"No, not at this time," Mr. Reuben replied.

****

The next day, Gary was at his office preparing the ERM matrix. He asked Lawrence, one of the junior technicians, to assist in transferring the information from the index cards into the matrix using their business infrastructure software. Gary reviewed the work and then emailed a copy to Steve and Sarah late Monday afternoon.

****

By the following Sunday, the main road leading to the furniture store had several patches of black ice on it. As he drove slowly along the road, Steve hoped the sun would shine long enough to melt it. Historically, Atlantans are warned to stay indoors in these types of weather conditions, especially if they must traverse steep hills and bridges to get to or from their destination. But he knew that, if customers stayed home, they would have a slow day with probably no new sales. *As crazy as it sounds, that might actually work in our favor today*, he thought. Gary scheduled an all-day session with them today so the more time they had to focus, the better.

The second session was different compared to the first. Participation would take place in groups staggered throughout the day as opposed to everyone participating at one time. Per Gary's recommendation, Sarah asked that the warehouse manager, quality manager and master carpenter arrive at 7:00 am. The plan was to work with them as a group for two hours. Afterwards, they could use the remaining two to three hours before the store opened to catch up on customer orders.

Similarly, Steve asked that the four design consultants and the showroom manager arrive as a group at 10:00 am. They too would have two hours to provide additional information about their electronic records before the store opened at noon. The remaining two managers would be the last group to meet with Steve, Sarah and Mr. Reuben to participate at 1:00 pm, after a lunch break.

When Sarah's management team arrived, they saw Gary had the index cards pertaining to the Production and Delivery Departments spread across the table. He explained, "Today's session is all about the data storage and access attributes associated with each of these files. What you see before you on the table are the index cards you gave me last Sunday. I have some stickers with me."

Gary held up four different sheets of stickers in front of the group. "This sticker has two computer monitors with a line connecting them. It represents a network." He put the network sticker sheet down and held up another one. "This sticker is a cloud. It represents those files you will need access to outside of the store. These files should not contain highly confidential information.

"This next sticker is a padlock. It represents private files. And this last sticker is an open padlock representing files that are public. Public documents are those that can be viewed and opened by anyone with network access. Private documents are those that only certain people should be able to access. There are also instances where a hybrid approach may be required but, for now, we will keep it simple and have only public versus private. Today, I want you to spend the next two hours carefully thinking through each type of file identified and place one or more of the following stickers onto each index card."

Gary picked up an index card to give a demonstration. "For example, this index card says *Material Catalogues*. If you think this belongs only on the network, then place a network sticker onto the card. If you think a copy should also be placed in the cloud, then add the cloud sticker to the card."

"Um, excuse me, Gary," Steve interjected. "About the cloud, we had a good bit of healthy dialogue about this last week. We don't think it's a good idea for us to store anything in the cloud just yet."

Sarah echoed Steve's sentiment, "Yeah, the VPN addresses our previous concern regarding remote access. We want tight control over our information. Sorry, we forgot to mention this before you came over."

"No worries!" Gary told them. "That simplifies things." He deposited the sheets of cloud stickers into his attaché case. He then asked that the three managers walk up to the table and, one index card at a time, affix the appropriate sticker(s).

It took approximately two hours and fifteen minutes for Sarah and her trio of managers to complete the exercise. There was constructive debate throughout that time. Thankfully, Gary had the foresight to recommend a one-hour buffer between them and the next group. When they finished, he picked up all of the cards off the table, rubber-banded them together and deposited them also into his attaché case before the next group arrived.

At 10:00 am, the group of design consultants arrived. Gary repeated the instructions he gave to the previous group, minus the cloud discussion. They completed the exercise within the allotted two hours. He also picked up those cards, placed a rubber band around them and deposited them into his attaché case. It was important to leave the room as he found it before he left for lunch.

As expected, the antique grandfather clock chimed at noon. Gary was alone in the conterence room with Steve and Sarah and invited them both to lunch. He knew the chances that both would accept his offer were slim, but he thought it was worth asking. To his surprise, they both agreed.

"Normally, I would suggest we walk to the Taqueria next door, but we might run the risk of sliding on ice and breaking our legs!" he said to them.

Steve laughed, "Not to mention you might fall and mess up that nice suit you have on!"

They decided to take their chances anyway and walked to the Taqueria. Gary kept the conversation light and made a conscious decision to refrain from talking about the store. He learned that Steve was married with two children and enjoyed kayaking, golfing and zip lining. He also learned that

Sarah was a self-described "vegan-in-training" and "Star Wars geek." She goes to the infamous Dragon Con event (the world's largest science fiction and comics convention) annually and she's engaged to be married later in the year.

Realizing she didn't know much about Gary, Sarah pivoted the conversation. "Gary, I must say, it's refreshing having you around! My team and I were talking about that last week. You're not like most I.T. folks. You seem to actually like talking to people and not just computers!"

Gary belted a loud laugh and nearly spit out his food. "Thanks, Sarah. I like talking to people *and* computers. When I became partner at my firm, I wanted to offer something unique to the marketplace. I found out about the Kasennu methodology after a friend of mine, who had some network woes, told me about a business coach who helped develop their Disaster Recovery plan. I did more research on the methodology and realized it was not only a missing link to identifying root causes of issues with our clients, but it also gave us a competitive advantage."

"Well, good for you, Gary!" Steve said. "I remember Alton being thrilled when you became partner."

Though their time at the Taqueria provided a nice mental break from the stress of their situation, it was time for Gary, Sarah and Steve to walk back to the store. It was good for them to be out and take in some fresh air. They had another four hours ahead of them. By 1:00 pm, Sarah, Steve, Jonathan and Diane were in the conference room. The only person missing was Mr. Reuben.

"Oh, Dad sent Steve and me a text saying he wouldn't be able to join us today," Sarah told Gary. "I think he only came last Sunday to make sure Steve and I wouldn't strangle each other." Sarah looked over at Steve who managed to crack a smile.

Gary went into his attaché case and removed the index cards associated with the Human Resources Department. Carefully, he spread them across the table and repeated the same instructions as earlier, the exception being that this group would participate in the exercise for the files associated with the Human Resources, Information Technology, Legal, and Payroll & Finance Departments.

By 5:30 pm they had reviewed all of the files for the remaining departments. As they all walked out of the store, Steve turned the main showroom lights off. Because of the time of year, it was pitch black outside. The darkness, the howling of the wind and the rustling of leaves in the parking lot made each of them all too glad to return to their respective homes.

****

On Monday, Gary asked Lawrence to review the index cards that now contained storage and access information. Lawrence filled in more of the cells in the ERM matrix using their business infrastructure software. Gary reviewed his work prior to emailing a copy to Steve and Sarah by the next day.

****

The third session of the ERM exercise arrived on the first Sunday in February. Unlike the first two sessions, Gary did not walk into the conference room with an attaché case full of index cards; instead, the case contained a small, portable projector and laptop. Another difference was the fact that this session started at 10:00 am for all participants, a much more reasonable time by all accounts. Twelve participants were there — everyone from the first session minus Mr. Reuben. As Gary set up his projector and laptop, he asked how everyone was feeling about the process so far.

Jonathan, a.k.a. "Switzerland," astonished everyone when he said, "I like what this process is doing for us. For the first time we're all together and truly working as a team, bouncing ideas off of each other and making decisions by consensus. It's a shame it took a virus to get us to do this." He looked at Sarah and then Steve who were equally embarrassed for they understood the motive behind his statement. Many of the other people in the room nodded their heads in agreement.

Then Sarah said, "I think we'll all be glad once this is behind us. But to add to what Jonathan said, I hope we keep this newfound camaraderie up."

Gary then turned on the projector. Before everyone was an enlarged ERM matrix. They had seen a blank version of this matrix from a previous email where they were asked to start thinking of private versus public record access, but this version was populated. The name of each department and the cells containing the names of its associated files were color-coded according to colors pre-assigned earlier in the week by the participants. The matrix was 28 pages long and, by first glance, looked daunting. "This," Gary told them, "is what your ERM matrix looks like to-date. Some of the matrix's cells are populated with information from our previous sessions."

Jonathan whispered, "Wow! Look at that!"

Gary began to explain the matrix in more detail. "The **first row** of the matrix highlights the life cycle of an electronic record. Reading from left to right, we have, *File Type, Full Access Rights*, followed by *Name of File, Storage Location, Backup Cycle, Retention Period, Archive Location*, and *Purge Cycle*. The **column to the far left** of the matrix contains the name of each file type identified during the first session.

"Going across to the **second column**, you identified who should have Full Access Rights to certain documents when you placed the unlocked padlock sticker on certain index cards during the second session. The same goes for the **fourth column**, the Storage Location. All cells in this column are filled with *Network*, since that is the primary focus for this round of the

ERM. I'll later explain how you all will work to populate the remaining cells with the file's proper name, backup cycle, retention period, archive location and purge cycle information. I'll give a demonstration of what I mean. Jonathan…"

"Yes," Jonathan replied.

"Let's use one of your Payroll & Finance files as an example." Gary scrolled to that part of the matrix. "The first file type listed is *Tax Returns*. Why don't you tell me how to fill in the matrix, looking at the header row."

Jonathan leaned forward. "Well, okay, the name of the file should be 'Tax Return' and include the year." Gary typed *[Year] Tax Return* into the appropriate cell in the Name of File column. He typed the word "year" in brackets to visually indicate that this part of the file's name can change depending on the year.

Jonathan continued. "The only people who have full access rights are me, Steve, Sarah and my uncle." Gary typed *CEO, CFO, CMO, COO* in the Full Access Rights column. It was important to type the name of the role and not a person's actual name.

Jonathan liked what he saw so far. "We already know this is stored on the network, but I'm considering storing copies in other locations as well. The tax return files can be backed up once a day and they should be retained for at least seven years, according to the IRS [Internal Revenue Service]. But I'm not sure where we would archive old electronic tax return data."

"That brings me to a point I'd like to make," Gary interjected. "Within each department's new folder on the network, you can add an *Archive* folder that you can cut and paste expired files to. The backup cycle for the Archive folder can take place weekly instead of daily since these are inactive files. It also ensures a faster daily backup time. That's totally up to you to decide. Please continue Jonathan."

"I don't think I'd ever want to purge the tax return files," Jonathan admitted. "It's part of our historic record. We have boxes of files in the storage closet with tax returns 20 years and older, but I get why this is important. We don't want to burden our network with outdated information. This could become very costly in the future."

"That's exactly right!" Gary confirmed. He typed *N/A* in that particular cell to indicate that a purge cycle was not applicable to the tax return file type.

| PAYROLL & FINANCE | | | | | | | |
|---|---|---|---|---|---|---|---|
| File Type | Full Access Rights | Name of File | Storage Location | Backup Cycle | Retention Period | Archive Location | Purge Cycle |
| Tax Returns | CEO, CFO, CMO, COO | [Year] Tax Return | Network | Once per day | 7 years | Network | N/A |

"Thank you Jonathan! You did a great job. Does everyone understand what we just did?"

A few people said "yes" aloud while others nodded their heads. Gary then selected one person from every department to verbalize the information needed to populate a row in the matrix for that particular department. By the end, all participants understood the purpose of the matrix and how to complete it.

Gary saved and closed the matrix file. He then opened and projected a new file. "This," he told them, "is an outline of each file type per department. Each of you will receive an email with this outline attached. You are to work with the people in your particular department to organize the files on the network according to this outline. For example…"

Gary scrolled through the outline until he arrived at a particular department. "This is the filing structure for the Business Development Department. On the network, the main folder will appear as *Business Development*. One of the sub-folders will be *Ads* and within that sub-folder there may be other sub-folders depending on the type of ad. For example, *Search Engine, Magazine, Website* or *Television*. Does this make sense to everybody?" He saw a few blank stares as he looked out and across the room.

"I'll show you an example." Gary switched screens and projected the furniture store's network. On the home screen there were folders and files all over the place; 138 to be exact. Using his mouse, Gary created a new folder. "In the future, when you access the network, the first thing you will see are eight folders. That's it. I will get you all started by creating these eight folders. I will place a zero and an underscore before the name of each department to force it to appear at the top of the list of folders."

Gary created and named each folder: *0_Business Development, 0_Delivery, 0_Design, 0_H.R., 0_I.T., 0_Legal, 0_Payroll* & *Finance* and *0_Production*. Then, he looked up to face the participants. "Your job is to move, rename and/or delete the original 138 folders and files using this outline as a guide. This will take a while considering you have your regular jobs to do, so pace yourselves. Besides, you'll need this time to become accustomed to this new electronic filing structure.

"Create as many sub-folders as you deem necessary. Just make sure that the names you choose are descriptive, especially for public files. Meet among yourselves to continue discussing their proper placement until they've all been removed from this home screen of the network and only these eight new folders appear. At that point, you can remove the zero and underscore in front of each main folder's name. Let's demo an example."

Gary clicked on a file on the home screen. "Here's a file named, *Airport Billboard.* Steve, where should I place this file?"

Steve, who happened to have a copy of the filing outline from Gary, answered, "Well…first, you need to create a new sub-folder in the 0_Business Development main folder. Name the new sub-folder, *Billboards.* Then, create another sub-folder under that and name it *Airport 2013.* That reminds me, the billboard we did last year was one of the corrupted files. I need to reach out to that graphic designer and ask for another copy. There were several files that went along with it. That's why these particular types of ads are separated by year."

Gary asked the question again. "Does this make sense to everybody now? Again, it will take some time so don't feel the need to rush. Let Steve and Sarah know if you have any questions and they'll relay those to me. I will check in periodically until our next and final session. Steve, Sarah and I will also talk through the Disaster Recovery and Business Continuity plan during this time, making sure that the network's finalized filing structure has proper protection. By that point, you will have the new file structure in place and we can add finishing touches on the matrix as well as the Disaster Recovery and Business Continuity plan.

"Before I forget, make sure to delete duplicate files on the network to save space, similar to what we did with the index cards. Now is a good time to re-name pictures and scanned files from their original generic names, for example, *IMG_0981.* This is also a good time to remove any personal files you previously identified on the network from the first session."

"Gary," Adam raised his hand. "I have a question. I'm a little nervous about moving all these files around. What if something is deleted accidentally?"

Steve answered before Gary could respond. "We're ahead of you. Sarah and I will be the two points of contact if something like that should happen. We'll continue to serve in that capacity until we can find a new I.T. manager."

Adam appeared despondent.

"Don't worry, I already know what you're thinking...that Sarah and I will give you guys conflicting information. We promise you that won't happen. We'll arrange days to go over this with you all and will try to make it as non-intrusive into your work schedules as possible. We can also take ownership of moving and/or deleting files if that makes you more comfortable."

"That's a really good idea Steve," Gary said, affirming Steve and Sarah's decision. Steve then stood up to make an announcement.

"I can't thank you all enough for all of your hard work. The past few months have been rough. We would not have made it this far without you. We're almost to the finish line. I'm asking that we each commit to coming in at least one hour before the store opens on weekdays so that we can complete the matrix and rearrange the network's filing structure. If there are days when you cannot come in an hour early, then feel free to work during your lunch break. Just let Diane know so that you can be properly compensated. I'm hoping to avoid having to come in early on weekends."

"I have no objection to that!" declared the warehouse manager. Everyone laughed.

It was almost noon and everyone left the conference room except Gary, Steve, Sarah and Jonathan. Gary reminded them that he would reach out over the coming weeks as he finalized the Disaster Recovery and Business Continuity plan.

## The Result

A month passed before Gary received the news from Sarah and Steve that all files on the network were successfully rearranged into the new electronic filing structure. During that time, Gary also worked closely with Steve and Sarah to iron out the details of the Disaster Recovery and Business Continuity plan.

Gary emailed a one-page report to all of the managers who participated in the sessions. The report summarized their work together and listed recommendations and next steps for moving forward.

### SUMMARY

Following a virus attack in late November, 2014, an important discovery was made. Though a network existed, it was highly susceptible to malware. This susceptibility was the result of a poor data protection plan.

An immediate solution was to install a VPN coupled with remote data backup. However, that solution required further refining to ensure that the right data is stored on the network and backed up. Our work together involved a conscientious strategy to invest only in data protection for those files deemed critical to the business.

Recovery from the disaster has taken nearly four months and is still somewhat in progress as employees continue to work in piecing together fragments of customer orders. During that time, we worked for a month and a half to take an inventory of all electronic file types, assessed their criticality to daily operations and assigned a document management protocol in the form of attributes. This information is summarized in the attached ERM matrix. Specific steps for recovering from and operating during a potential future disaster is now formalized in a customized Disaster Recovery and Business Continuity Plan. This plan ensures recovery within a 24-hour period.

In essence, you now have a comprehensive guide for not only organizing electronic records, but also for ensuring that information is always securely saved, stored, backed up, archived, and purged according to specific guidelines.

## RECOMMENDATIONS & NEXT STEPS

1. Work with H.R. to develop a BYOD policy that includes deactivating accounts at least 24 hours prior to the moment an employee is terminated or leaves the company. Add this new policy to the Employee Manual.
2. Create a master list of all software and web-based licenses and admin account usernames.
3. Leverage your organizational chart to formalize a CEO succession plan. This includes searching for a new I.T. manager.
4. Document processes company-wide.

\*\*\*\*

Steve arranged for Gary to come to the store and discuss his recommendations on a Tuesday in the first week of March. When he walked into the conference room, Steve, Sarah, Mr. Reuben and Jonathan greeted Gary with applause. Before he sat down, Gary handed a small sheet of paper containing a quote to each of them. The quote read:

If you talk to the animals
    they will talk with you
        and you will know each other.
If you do not talk to them,

> you will not know them,
> And what you do not know
>     you will fear.
> What one fears one destroys.
>           – Chief Dan George[15]

The silence in the room was deafening. The cheering stopped and all the Reubens looked down at the table, avoiding eye contact with each other. Gary broke the silence, "I'm not trying to be a 'Debbie-Downer,' but I've shared this with you as a reminder of how far you've come along. People fear and destroy what they do not understand. In your case, Sarah and Steve, your avoidance of each other nearly destroyed this company. That avoidance led to the silos, creating an 'us' vs. 'them' culture.

"Some of your long-time employees told me they remember a time when it wasn't like this. While thinking you're each other's enemy, the real enemy was lurking in the shadows, going unnoticed and unchecked until it manifested in the form of a virus attack. You've recovered from that attack, but your dysfunctional relationship was, ultimately, the root cause. There will be more catastrophic manifestations until you repair, at the very least, your working relationship."

Sarah had tears in her eyes. She mustered the courage to look over at Steve. "Steve, this isn't easy for me, but…I'm sorry.

Steve walked over to Sarah and gave her a hug as he whispered in her ear, "I'm sorry, too." It was the first time he could remember hugging his baby sister since she was a young child. Sarah could not believe she allowed herself to be publicly vulnerable, but the release of her anger and animosity at that moment was freeing.

Jonathan looked over at Gary and mouthed, "Thank You!"

"Gary, I'm going to have this quote framed!" Sarah told him as she wiped away the tears that managed to escape down her cheeks.

Gary smiled at her. "Now, let's talk about the reason why I'm really here! Do you have any questions for me?"

Steve shook his head "no," but Sarah raised a question about the recommendation for processes. She argued that they already have their processes documented. Gary reminded her that the processes were documented on the manufacturing or "back office" side of the business and not on the customer-facing or "front office" side of the business.

"I have a proposition for you all. Would you be willing to swap roles for a week? I think you will learn even more about what you each do here. Sarah, you'll learn firsthand about the process-deficiency that currently exists."

"That's an interesting idea," Jonathan said. "I'm game for it!" Sarah and Steve also agreed to swap roles as early as the next week.

Gary told them about a process identification and documentation workshop scheduled to take place in Atlanta next month. He highly recommended they attend, but warned that they should not delay in registering, as there were a limited number of seats available. He also mentioned that there were certain things that they needed to do in preparation for the workshop, namely going through their job descriptions to add information about adhering to the new ERM system and making sure all associated job tasks have been identified (Business Parts Analysis).

Mr. Reuben spoke, "Well, Gary, I knew you could do it. Thank you for saving our company from the threat of implosion and for helping to salvage my children's relationship. I know this wasn't easy."

"Aw, you're welcomed Jack! It was my pleasure."

Sarah, Steve and Jonathan were in disbelief. They didn't realize Gary and Mr. Reuben were now on a first-name basis. Puzzled, and somewhat disturbed, Sarah asked, "Wait, do you two know each other?"

Mr. Reuben looked at Gary and then back at Sarah, "I have a confession to make. Yes, Gary and I have known each other for quite some time. We're in the same poker club. We rarely discuss business while at the club as our focus tends to be on perfecting our card-playing technique, but I knew he was in cybersecurity. When Steve described Gary to me the day he came for that initial consultation, I sent him a text asking if he was here at the store. When he confirmed and said he was standing outside of your office, I asked that he not tell anyone we already know each other. So don't get mad! I didn't put Gary up to any of this peace-making stuff. Like I said, we never discuss the details of our business when we see each other and he never knew how much you two bickered until he started coming around here."

"Wow," Steve said looking at Gary. "You must be one hell of a poker player! You kept a poker face the entire time! I'm impressed more than I am pissed."

"I'll walk Gary out to his car," Jack Reuben said.

As Sarah stood up to walk out of the conference room, she told Gary, "Thanks, again, for everything Gary! I guess we'll call you later this week to start tackling the missing pieces of the Business Parts Analysis you described."

Jonathan was next to thank Gary, telling him, "I always figured it would take someone on the outside of our family and our company to help my cousins reach a truce."

Steve also thanked Gary, shook his hand and quickly left the room, trying to catch up with Sarah. "Hey, you gotta minute?"

"Yeah, what's up?"

Steve lifted his hand to give Sarah a high-five. "We did it!"

"Yes, we did!

"What are you doing later tonight? We [Steve and his wife] were wondering if you'd like to join us for dinner?"

"Yeah, I'd like that," Sarah said. "So… where do we go from here?"

"Long-term, I'm not sure. But I know where we're going next month — that process workshop! Come on, let's go to my office so we can register for it."

****

Jack walked Gary to his car in the front parking lot of the store. Before getting into his car, Gary turned to him and asked, "Have you made your decision? Who will replace you as CEO?"

Bashfully, Jack replied, "Yes, as a matter of fact I have made a decision. But I want to see what happens after this workshop next month. Then I'll make my official announcement."

# CHAPTER 5

# THE LEVEE AND THE LEVY

**Kasennu™**
Paper Records Management

Karen and Sharen are identical twin sisters running a mental rehabilitation facility with three locations. They have survived one disaster after another and, in the process, learned from a brush with the law the importance of protecting physical records at all costs. A recent audit exposed their lack of structural cohesion and transparency across their locations. Time is running out to demonstrate compliance. Their business is only as good as the paperwork they can produce when requested. Another failed audit could result in a shutdown while opening the door to fraud accusations. Their consultant introduces them to the Paper Records Management element of the Kasennu methodology to prove to the auditors their business operates as well as it is perceived publicly.

It was 7:15 am on a breezy Monday in New Orleans, LA. There's finally low humidity in the air, a fitting weather condition following a weekend of festivities as Karen Benoit and her identical twin sister, Sharen, celebrated their 40th birthday. It's a miracle Karen is present at her Toastmasters club meeting, considering she only arrived home from partying a few hours ago.

Karen is teetering between consciousness and unconsciousness. *Why on Earth did I sign up to speak today?* She knew, from looking at the meeting's agenda, that she was slated to be the second speaker. When prompted, she found it difficult to write her feedback on the first speaker's speech. Her hands were trembling. Just then, a timer chimed — her cue that it was her turn to speak next. But first, the designated Toastmaster for the meeting introduced her.

"Karen Benoit is a native New Orleanian. She recently celebrated her 40th birthday. This morning she will share with us her personal story — something that none of us are aware of. The title of her speech is 'Weathering the Storms of Life.' She has five to seven minutes. Please join me in welcoming Karen Benoit."

The audience began clapping. Karen stood up and swallowed hard. Her heart was racing. As she approached the front of the room, she could not believe how nervous she was. She had spoken publicly many times before, but this was different. She had to give a speech out of her Toastmasters manual that required telling her personal story. Historically, she had shared tidbits of her past, but never the whole story. It was a defense mechanism. She had learned over the years how to hold back emotion, adapt to different environments and press forward no matter the circumstances.

Now she faced a room of about 35 people, maybe 15 more than their average meeting attendance. Some people were even standing since there weren't enough seats to accommodate them. Karen interpreted this as a sign that *now* really was the right time in her life to give this speech. It was important she did well as she set her eyes on a much bigger stage: the TED Talk stage in New York City. Before she uttered her first word, she noticed an old friend, Camille Soutien, whom she had not seen in a while. They first met at this very Toastmasters club.

Karen began to speak. "Exactly 30 years ago, on a breezy, beautiful day, much like today's, the trajectory of my life forever changed. Some call a breezy day the 'calm before the storm' and truer words were never spoken. Good morning, fellow Toastmasters and guests. Today, I will share with you three storms that I've weathered throughout my life.

"The first storm occurred when my parents were in a fatal car accident on their return trip home from Houston, Texas. My twin sister and I were spending the weekend with some friends. I'll never forget when our friends' mother delivered that most devastating news. The biggest question became,

'Who will care for us?' My sister and I had just turned 10 years old. We found out later that my parents went on this trip to surprise us with a new house. Unbeknownst to us, we were going to relocate and our parents went to Houston to close on the new house. Their death was one hell of a birthday present.

"We stayed with our friends and their parents for about six months until it got to the point where the financial strain of having extra mouths to feed proved to be a mission impossible. Both of my parents were only children, so we had no immediate aunts, uncles or cousins and all of our grandparents were deceased. No one seemed to want us and so we ended up in foster care. To this day, we've never bothered to look for any distant relatives. We figured, they never looked for us, so why should we look for them?

"They say twins have a bond unlike any other and Sharen and I learned quickly that all we had was each other. We got lucky though, we were welcomed into a foster home when we were twelve. Although our foster parents never adopted us officially, we were able to stay with them until we turned eighteen and both enrolled at Xavier University.

"Eventually, I became a social worker and Sharen became a psychiatrist. We both chose professions where we could specialize in helping children who either grew up in foster care or were adopted. By the time we were in our late twenties, we started our own mental rehabilitation facility to help these very children. Things were going well until the second storm happened — Hurricane Katrina.

"I don't need to tell any of you how absolutely devastating Katrina was. It caused physical, emotional and psychological pain, a pain that binds every single one of us in the city together. A few months after Katrina occurred, our facility was audited and we failed. We failed, *miserably*. Not only were most of our patient records destroyed, but so was the facility itself. The auditing agency had little sympathy and we were levied severely. Had the levee not broken, we likely would have never received that tax. At least that's what we told ourselves. But Sharen and I are resilient. The aftermath of Katrina led to a business expansion we could not have imagined. Soon, we opened a new facility on the West Bank and extended our offering to *all* children suffering from the trauma of Katrina.

"We were making such a huge impact that we opened a second location in Metairie and expanded our offering this time to children suffering from any type of trauma. As we gained more press and attention, we opened our third and latest location here in Uptown. Growth is good, but it can also be painful, I'm currently learning, as my sister and I are now weathering our third storm."

Karen intentionally did not reveal the nature of what she described as the *third storm*. Instead, she continued, "One thing I've learned is that there is the calm before the storm, the storm and, then, the aftermath and clean-up. We've all weathered different types of storms. We may not be able to prevent the storm, but we can certainly take charge of our reactions to it. Our reaction is critical to whether or not we survive those storms. One thing I know for sure is that trauma is real. Pain is real. It's okay to cry. It's okay to release anger and frustration, but channel that energy into something that can grow and be productive.

"I have lost people, material things and, at one point, I almost lost my business; yet I can stand here today before you and tell you that forgiveness is the greatest antidote. Laughter is medicine for your soul and life is for the living. I'd like to close by quoting the last stanza of one of my favorite poems. It's called *Desiderata*.[16]

"'And whether or not it is clear to you,
no doubt the universe is unfolding as it should.

Therefore be at peace with God,
whatever you conceive Him to be,
and whatever your labors and aspirations,
in the noisy confusion of life, keep peace with your soul.

With all its sham, drudgery and broken dreams,
it is still a beautiful world.
Be cheerful.
Strive to be happy.'"

Karen turned to face the Toastmaster of the meeting, "Mr. Toastmaster…" As he approached her to shake her hand, Karen walked back to her seat amid thunderous applause.

Following the end of the meeting, Karen talked to several of her club's members as well as guests. Many of them congratulated her on a job well done. Her friend Camille patiently waited her turn to speak with Karen and when she saw an opening, she greeted Karen in her thick French-Caribbean accent.

"Karen! Bonjour!" They embraced each other tightly. Although they talked on the phone about once a quarter, they had not seen each other in a little over two years.

"Camille! I'm surprised to see you! When did you arrive? I had no idea you were here!"

"Yesterday. I logged into the club's website and saw that you were scheduled to speak. I'm here on a business trip this week, but knew that I had to make time to see you. Happy Birthday! I was hoping to surprise you and Sharen, but my flight was delayed and I did not arrive until yesterday evening. I was so tired. So much for surprises. Where *is* Sharen by the way?"

"She left this morning for a short cruise to Cozumel."

"Ooh, nice!"

"Yes, her husband and kids had to practically drag her away from the office. You know how we are. We believe in putting in that work, *baby*." Karen stressed the word *baby* intentionally in a New Orleanian accent. "It's only for a few days, though. She should be back before you leave."

"Good. I'd like to spend some time with both of you. Listening to your speech, I'm curious to learn more about what's going on. You mentioned a third storm." Camille leaned in toward Karen and whispered, "Does it have something to do with your business?"

"Yes," Karen affirmed.

"I hope I'm not prying. But the reason I ask is because I wonder if it's something I can help with."

By this point, the meeting room cleared out and Karen motioned for Camille to walk with her out of the room. "Girl, look, we need all the help we can get! The sooner we can talk, the better. I can fill Sharen in when she returns. I know she won't mind, considering the severity of this."

"Do you have lunch plans tomorrow?"

"No, but I'm fasting during the day for this entire week. I know it's still early, so if you'd like we can go to a coffee shop near our new office. I work from that location whenever we have a Toastmasters meeting since it's not a far drive to the office."

Camille checked her schedule from her phone. "I will call someone at my next appointment to let them know to expect me an hour later, at around 10 am." Camille didn't quite know how best to broach the topic of the first storm Karen mentioned, so she chose the safest approach. "Karen, your speech was phenomenal!"

"Thank you!" Karen replied. They were now in the lobby of the building where the meeting took place. "How did you get here?"

"I took the streetcar."

"You can ride with me. I want to open the office first. You can take the streetcar to your next appointment. We're only a block from the line."

Karen and Camille walked to the parking garage where Karen's car was parked. The drive to her office, though short, was a bit challenging because of all the commuters making their way downtown to go to work. Looking at all of the restored and renovated old buildings and houses en route made Camille nostalgic. She truly loved New Orleans and enjoyed comparing and contrasting the city to her native Martinique and Paris, France, where she had lived most of her childhood.

"It's just the way I remembered it."

"I hope that's a good thing!" Karen replied as she turned off of a narrow, two-lane street and down a narrow driveway that ran between two houses now functioning as businesses. The driveway led to a small parking lot in the back of one of the houses.

"Bienvenue!"

"Merci! Merci beaucoup! Ah Karen, is this it? Is this the new office? It's beautiful!"

The house they parked behind was a shotgun double with a camel-back[17] that had been converted into a mental rehabilitation clinic for children. The partially two-story building was painted in lime green and had dark green shudders framing each window. There was ornate crown molding painted in white and, though there was little land in the front and back of the building, the landscaping was picturesque.

They approached the back of the building and went up a few steps that led to a solid oak door. Unlocking and opening the door released a waft of fresh magnolias. Their office manager, Justin, was already inside the building. Karen explained to Camille that he made it a point to fill a large vase with magnolia flowers once a week inside the waiting area near the front of the building.

Camille tried to take in the beauty of the building's interior. The floors were terrazzo and stained in a beautiful bronze color complemented by various shades of green walls. She noticed a variety of ivy, ficus and peace lily plants placed strategically in the hallway and offices that they walked past on their way to Karen's office.

"I'll show you around when we get back. I'm sure you must be starving!" Karen quickly walked into her office, retrieved her wallet from her large shoulder bag and placed the bag on a chair in her office before locking it.

As they walked toward the front door of the building, Camille noted the phrase, *Laissez Les Bon Temps Rouler*, painted above the door and smiled. There was no need for her to ask the meaning, she already knew it: *Let the Good Times Roll.* It was an expression she learned early on when she lived in New Orleans and visited other parts of southern Louisiana, an expression unique to Louisiana that serves as a reminder to have a light-heartedness about you no matter the situation. Camille followed Karen out of the building and onto the main street where they walked to the coffee shop.

## The Fast Growth Predicament

By the time they sat down at the coffee shop, it was getting close to 9:00 am. Camille knew she didn't have much time to learn more about that *third storm* Karen alluded to earlier in her speech. But the situation seemed dire, so she said, without hesitation, "Karen, about your speech...I am *so* sorry. I had no idea your parents died so tragically. I thought you and Sharen were adopted as babies. How foolish of me to make assumptions. I should have..."

Karen interrupted before Camille could finish her statement, "Please don't be sorry! That's exactly why Sharen and I don't like sharing that part of our story. We don't want people feeling sorry for us. If the effect of my speech was pity and sorrow, then I failed in my delivery. My intent in sharing our story was to evoke a can-do spirit and attitude. It's important I get this messaging right as I plan to start doing more public speaking."

"Oh! So you *will* be speaking more about this?"

"Yes! That's why I wanted to practice first at Toastmasters. I want to start doing more motivational speaking. Over the years, I've spoken at many of the local schools but, recently, we hired a publicist who has already booked some interviews and panel discussions for me on major national and international media outlets. I need to be ready! My message needs to be clear, concise and, most importantly, inspirational. Not woe-is-me."

"Ah, I see." Camille responded. "Again, I hope I am not prying by asking such personal things."

"No, not at all," Karen assured her. "It's so ironic that we own a mental rehabilitation facility, but have not sought therapy ourselves. I guess we poured ourselves so much into our work that we saw that as our therapy."

"Okay. May I ask, what is the third storm?"

Karen released a deep sigh, leaned toward Camille and, in a barely audible tone, said, "Girl, we were audited again earlier this month. Our paperwork management has gotten us in trouble again. Can you believe it? Another levy? I swear, it's like the curse of the levee breaking after Katrina just won't lift. The deficiency became known when an auditor asked for a sample of patient files here at our Uptown location. The problem was there were different files for the same patients across our locations. In other words, they're not consolidated. Once he visited our other two locations, he discovered just how pervasive the record fragmentation really is. The auditor concluded that we don't have a cohesive records management system in place and explained how this lack of cohesion could impede our ability to operate in an effective and compliant manner. In his final report, he made a recommendation to get a records management system in place within the next 90 days, or else he would have to report our refusal to comply to Medicaid. That makes two citations we've received with the threat of a third."

"Oh, my goodness!"

"I know, right?" Karen looked down at her watch. "What time do you have to be at your next appointment?"

"At 10.

"Where?"

"Downtown, on Gravier Street."

"Ooh, we better hurry. Maybe you can ask the barista to put the rest of your coffee in a styrofoam cup that you can take out with you."

As they walked out of the coffee shop and back toward her office, Karen looked at Camille and grabbed her hand. "Lord, have mercy. I am so rude. Girl, how have *you* been? And why exactly *are* you here?"

"Actually, I am here to introduce the company I used to work for to a methodology I learned about and have built a business around over the past year."

"Oh, that's good!" Karen replied. "How's business? I remember you starting it. How does it feel to be an entrepreneur?"

"Great, thank you!" Camille giggled. "It is rewarding and challenging, but I love it! The travel is the most difficult part so far. I can do things remotely, but I want the hands-on experience first before I go 100% virtual. I've been working mostly with different small companies between Paris and Martinique to gain the experience of applying the methodology. So far, everything has worked well and the results are sustainable."

When they walked through the front door of the facility, the office manager happened to be standing next to the receptionist. Karen introduced them, "Justin, Jasmine, this is Camille Soutien. She's originally from Martinique but spent her teenage years in Paris. She moved back to Martinique as an adult. We met 14 years ago when her company relocated her to New Orleans. She's a dear friend of ours. Camille might be able to help us with our paperwork issue."

"Thank you Jesus!" Justin said in a semi-serious tone, raising his left hand to the air, as if testifying, and extending his right hand to Camille. "It's nice to meet you Ms. Camille."

Karen then escorted Camille around the first floor. It contained many of the elements Camille found to be common in commercial spaces throughout the city: high, 12-foot ceilings, eight-inch high white baseboards, and several framed Jazz Festival posters. They walked up a flight of wooden stairs to the second floor, the *camelback* section of the building. It contained the offices of the therapists, some of whom were already in session with their patients. The hallway walls were adorned with artwork that appeared to be original pieces. Karen spoke in a hush tone, "This is the artwork of some of our patients."

As they continued walking, Camille noted that, aside from the white noise machines placed in the hallways and the occasional sandboxes, you would never guess this was a mental rehabilitation facility. Karen explained that this was intentional. "Kids are terrified of white, stoic walls. Have you ever read *1984* by George Orwell?"

"Yes, actually I have."

"Do you remember the scene toward the end when Winston was captured and placed in an all-white room and it nearly drove him mad? Science has proven that just the sight of traditional white walls and floors, which have come to be associated with hospitals and medical facilities, is actually very disconcerting to people, especially children. We also removed all of the water fountains in our locations. After Hurricane Katrina, even something as simple and soothing as a waterfall became a painful trigger to the kids who suffered the trauma of wading through toxic waters to reach safety. People think that because it's been nearly 10 years that the kids are over it. Well, they're not! In fact, none of us are! Without proper treatment, you can suffer from that kind of trauma for the rest of your life."

Karen's cell phone vibrated. She had set an alarm to let her know when she needed to cut her conversation short so that Camille could make it to her next appointment on time. "Uh oh, Camille. I've run my mouth and now you have to leave." She opened her arms to give Camille a hug. "Why don't you come over to my house later this evening?"

"Karen, I wish I could but I have to have dinner with some potential clients tonight. After my next meeting, I should be able to tell you when I can meet again so that we can resume our conversation. I wish I could stay longer to talk. Again, it's my fault for trying to surprise you and Sharen in the first place."

Karen walked with Camille back onto the front porch and gave her directions to walk to the streetcar line. As Camille walked out of the building and down the street toward the streetcar line, she couldn't help but think of everything Karen revealed today. Even though Karen asked for no sympathy, Camille's heart began to ache for everything she and Sharen have been through. *I have to figure out a way to help them in this latest storm's aftermath and break the curse of the levee and the levy once and for all!*

\*\*\*\*

Camille called Karen later that night after her client dinner. As much as they had talked on the phone over the years, they rarely discussed business. For most of their friendship, Camille wasn't a business owner and, therefore, oftentimes couldn't relate to the plight of her friends. However, she was always empathetic and had no problem providing the proverbial shoulder to cry on.

Karen told her that it would be best to meet again on Wednesday. Sharen was expected to return from her cruise the next day, mid-day. Camille confirmed that worked better with her schedule because she expected to have a full day tomorrow, too.

Karen also mentioned visiting Camille's website to learn more about her service offering, in particular, the service that seemed to apply most to her business' situation. "Camille, why don't you tell me more about this Kasennu methodology?"

"Sure. Basically, it's a methodology designed to help fast growing companies like yours scale in a repeatable and sustainable manner. In your case, the end goal would be to have processes that ensure regulatory compliance, a consistent patient experience regardless of the location visited and satisfied employees who work for the collective good of the children. Does that make sense?"

"Yes, but I guess I struggle with why processes are needed in the first place. We're not producing any tangible goods. We provide a service. Every therapist is different and has his or her own unique style."

"That is true, but there are certain guidelines that all of your therapists must adhere to from a governance standpoint. Proper recordkeeping is one of those guidelines. This is what the auditing agency has been trying to tell you. Yes, you're attracting more and more business and you have beautiful and inviting locations that your patients and constituents love but, because you receive funding from the federal government, they need to make sure that the way you operate your business is up to code. This is the real reason why you're audited. You shouldn't take it as a personal attack on you and Sharen, nor should you think of it as a curse. Instead, it could be a blessing."

"A blessing? Are you feeling well Camille? Have you lost your mind?"

"No, not at all!" Camille chuckled. "Quite the contrary. I say it is a blessing because had this citation not happened, you would be in real danger of losing credibility if, God forbid, you all open even more locations without a centralized and formalized records management system."

"Interesting. Well, one thing's for sure, 'three strikes and you're out.'"

When Camille did not respond, Karen realized she used an idiom. As hard as she tried to be mindful when communicating with her friend, Karen never realized just how full of clichés her dialect was until she communicated with Camille.

"That's a baseball reference. If a pitcher throws the ball and you swing at it with your bat and miss, it's called a strike. After three strikes, your turn is up and..."

Camille giggled softly into the phone. "I know what baseball is, Karen!"

"Well, you didn't say anything, so I thought..."

"Yes, I was uh, how do you say it? I was pulling your leg! But seriously, why has it taken so long to get your records management system under control? You and Sharen are both incredibly conscientious people and I would have thought that the infamous 'levee that brought the levy' was an experience you'd never want to repeat."

"Yeah, I hear you. I think part of it is I've always been of the opinion that the kids, our patients, are our top priority. Everything else is secondary. But I know the severity of our actions. We just kept growing. Even though we knew we needed to address the issue, it was constantly put on the back burner. There I go using clichés again.

"Our number one mission was, is, and will always be to help children suffering from trauma. We measure our success by the number of children who mature into fully functioning adults and thrive, not by how much money we make and certainly not by the piles of paper we keep. We now have three locations spread throughout the city. With the increased intensity and frequency of natural disasters, we've received even more exposure, especially when I made the cover of one of the top magazines in the country. Sharen and I have also made several TV appearances on local news channels, but now we're starting to get approached by reporters from some of the national and international media outlets.

"We're starting to receive more inquiries from people outside of New Orleans too. You have to remember that there are parts of Louisiana that no longer exist; the coastline is continuously eroding because of manmade river diversions. The people of southern Mississippi and Texas are deeply impacted too. It's the entire Gulf Coast region. Sharen and I want to expand into these areas but we're not ready just yet. I guess that's that process thing you're talking about. For example, we know we wouldn't want anyone running a facility who isn't local to that area. There were so many scam artists after Katrina happened, it was sickening. Having the blessing to operate in a disaster-stricken area by the locals of a community means everything!"

"You have 90 days to resolve this matter, yes?"

"Yes. Problem is, neither Sharen nor I have the time to focus on this. We realize we're going to have to make the time. We don't want what we've worked so hard to build for the past 12 years to be lost overnight. We're cash flow positive, have no debt and are set to have our best gross revenue ever at $3.1 million."

"Karen, think about this. Many lawsuits are lost daily all because people cannot provide proof. Your recordkeeping policy is your insurance. Just as you have insurance for your business, your home, your car and even your life, think of recordkeeping as your insurance against lawsuits. It won't prevent a lawsuit from happening, but it gives you the protection needed to defend yourself and your business practices. Like Tom Cruise's character said in *A Few Good Men*, 'It doesn't matter what I believe, it only matters what I can prove!' The *proof*, my dear, is in the pudding." Camille laughed. "See, I know some American clichés too!"

Karen smiled to herself. "I never thought about it that way, but you're absolutely right. I tell you what, I'll fill Sharen in on our conversations. We have a meeting at Tulane Wednesday morning. Usually, we walk across the street to Audubon Park afterwards to debrief. Can you join us? We can leave straight from there and go back to the office so you can ask more questions and gather any additional information you may need to help us."

**The Research**

The next day, Sharen Benoit Joseph disembarked in the Port of Orleans with her husband, daughter and two sons. Her three-day trip to Cozumel, Mexico, was a great get-away, but she was ready to get back to work. Prior to arriving at the port, as the cruise ship neared a cell tower and Sharen had cell phone service, she saw several voice mail messages from Karen, all of which were marked urgent. She listened attentively to each message and learned that Camille was in town and that she, as Karen described it, "has the antidote" to their problem.

Sharen returned her sister's call on her ride home. As a psychiatrist, she was skillful at listening without interrupting and therefore took great care to absorb every word Karen said as she gave the highlights of her conversations with Camille.

Karen asked her, "Do you have any appointments tomorrow afternoon? I told Camille she could spend the afternoon at our office to ask additional questions."

"No. I actually have tomorrow marked as a vacation day, too. You know how I try to schedule an extra day off whenever I return from vacation."

"Okay, good! I'll let Camille know that we can meet her after our meeting at Tulane."

\*\*\*\*

The next day, Wednesday, Karen and Sharen walked from the campus of Tulane University directly across the street to meet Camille in Audubon Park at 1:00 pm. Sharen gave Camille the traditional French greeting with a kiss on both of her cheeks. Camille was genuinely happy to see both of them.

The trio was now complete. They got a kick out of being seen together publicly. All three of them were 5'2" and of similar caramel complexion, except Camille had shoulder-length curly black hair and the twin sisters had wavy, light brown hair. It seemed like yesterday that Karen introduced Camille to Sharen after meeting her in Toastmasters.

They began walking the 1.8 mile paved path around the golf-course that rested in the center of the park. The majestic oak trees formed a maternal-like canopy over parts of the path as if protecting the runners, joggers and walkers. The gentle breeze through the trees made the weather all the more appealing. As they walked, they began to catch up on personal matters before moving on to business.

Camille learned that the sisters were both ready to travel more, but with three locations they had been busier than ever. Someone suggested they apply for membership at Tulane University's Family Business Center. It has since proven to be instrumental in helping them understand the value of succession planning and processes. As they continue to expand, they told Camille it was important that they keep the business ownership within their family.

Sharen told her, "We didn't grow up with cousins, aunts and uncles, so family is everything to us. And Karen and I know we can't do it all. Attending regular meetings at the center has helped us realize that our business is really like a house of cards built on a sand foundation — it's fragile. This latest audit was a real wake up call. Frankly, as a physician, I'm embarrassed. I know fully well the importance of maintaining patient records."

When they completed a revolution around the park's paved path, the three of them walked to St. Charles Avenue to catch the streetcar and got off at the stop closest to Karen and Sharen's building.

****

When they walked into the waiting area of the facility, they could hear the sounds of local, but famous jazz greats like Wynton Marsalis and Kermit Ruffin playing softly in the background. There was a lot more activity in the waiting area today compared to the first time Camille visited. There were a few teenagers, each donning large headphones, listening to their own music, and a few younger children, some of whom were reading books and others who were playing together in a large sandbox on the floor.

Karen walked into her office to begin returning phone calls while Sharen asked Camille to follow her to Justin's office. As the office manager, it was imperative that Justin speak with Camille. The door to his office was ajar so Sharen gently knocked.

"Come in!" Justin responded to the knock. "It's good to see you again, Ms. Camille."

"Justin, Karen said you're aware of Camille's visit. You got it from here, right?"

"I sure do. Come on in Ms. Camille and have a seat. I don't bite. I promise." Camille liked Justin's personality. It was infectious and seemed the right complement to balance Karen and Sharen's personalities. Although she knew little about him, she could already tell why they hired him. From what she heard so far, Justin was friendly and worked equally well with the children and the staff.

It wasn't quite cold enough to wear longer sleeves, so Justin had on a short-sleeved, buttoned up shirt revealing his tattooed forearms, a complete diversion from the twins' dress codes. They were always dressed sharply. Camille cannot recall a time she's ever seen them in blue jeans, as a matter of fact. Camille found herself staring at Justin, partly because of a flower of life tattoo he had on one of his arms and because she realized he was probably younger than she originally suspected.

"So, I hear you're going to help us become compliant," Justin said. "Where would you like to start?"

"Can we start with you? How long have you worked here?"

"I've been here almost two years, ever since this location opened. I saw Karen and Sharen on the local news one day and knew that I wanted to work with them. I didn't know how at the time, only that I wanted to help in whatever way I could. I had worked my way up to be the office manager at my old job, but no longer had a passion for the work I was doing. It was so bland. I felt like I wasn't making a difference, you know? Music was the only thing keeping me alive at that time. I'm basically an office manager by day and a drummer by night. But being here made me realize that I could use my voice as an instrument when interacting with our patients.

"Anyway, I went to their location in Metairie, completely unannounced, and asked to speak to either or both of them. There was still a considerable amount of renovation going on at the time to convert the house into what you see today. To make a long story short, I made a plea to them and by the next week, I was hired as the office manager of this Uptown location. I was instrumental in getting this location opened ahead of schedule.

"In fact, full disclosure, I became so engrossed in helping to open this new location, that I neglected the effort I previously started in trying to consolidate our records and develop a centralized and comprehensive records management system. It was tough trying to coordinate things with the office managers at the other two locations. They were envious of me because I was so new to the company and they felt that the role I was playing was higher up than theirs.

"Now I know how they felt. At first, I was a little offended that Karen and Sharen wanted to hire you because I feel this is my job to do but, then again, part of leadership is recognizing when you need help and that's something that I've learned from these ladies. In my effort to try to do it all, I spread myself too thin and the audit caught up with us. I can only beg for their forgiveness. Before I go off on a tangent, I should show you where we keep most of the archived records here. Follow me."

Justin stood up and walked out of his office. Camille quickly removed her tablet and stylus from her shoulder bag so that she could take photographs and record notes.

He led her to the room where they kept the archived records. It was a small room, which used to be a utility room when it was a house, but neat in appearance with several black, five-drawer steel lateral filing cabinets purported to be fireproof and waterproof. "I keep telling them that this won't help them survive another storm. I know they're supposed to be waterproof and fireproof, but when Mother Nature decides to have her way, none of this matters," Justin said with a tinge of frustration in his voice.

Camille used her tablet to snap photos and jot down notes, taking into account the office location and the number of files. She asked that Justin unlock and open each drawer so that she could assess just how many files were contained in each. Each drawer, with the exception of two, was stuffed with files. The other two drawers were empty and were in the file cabinet closest to the door.

"My goodness!" Camille exclaimed, "You're already running out of space in this location!"

"Yep! Wait until you see the other locations. In fact, we should leave now before the afternoon rush hour begins. We'll go to the location on the West Bank first, since it requires crossing the Mississippi River and you never know when you may get stuck on the bridge. Then we'll come back into the city and go to the Metairie location."

Listening to the areas where the other offices were located reminded Camille that Karen and Sharen's original location in the Gentilly area no longer existed. The building containing the suite they rented was destroyed during Hurricane Katrina nine years earlier.

While en route to the West Bank location, Camille assured Justin, "You shouldn't be so hard on yourself. Karen and Sharen feel equal, if not more, responsibility. The good thing is that you've helped me identify a major root cause in why they continue to be haunted by these audits."

"Thank you Ms. Camille, I appreciate that. I've signed up for some compliance classes offered through Medicaid and I hope to go to D.C. soon to attend them. The auditing guidelines are very specific and I want to be as proactive as possible in making sure we break the curse of the levee once and for all. The last thing we need is a scandal, especially since we receive a bulk of our reimbursements from Medicaid. For example, Sharen wants to partner with the District Attorney's Office on Child Advocacy. If they find out the trouble we're currently in, they'll run! We've done a very good job of keeping up the illusion that all is well. But if we don't pass again in 90 days, that's our asses!"

\*\*\*\*

At each location, Camille met most of the staff, snapped photographs and continued taking notes. When they returned to the Uptown location, she thanked Justin for driving her around. She then went into Karen's office. Sharen had left earlier to go home and finish unpacking and recuperating from her cruise. It was Camille's first time actually sitting in Karen's office. On her desk were a beautiful collection of crystals and stones, a reminder to Karen of their healing power. She also noticed a large poster of the poem, *Desiderata,* framed and hanging on the wall across from Karen's desk.

"What do you think?" Karen asked. "Is there hope for us?"

"Absolutely! I'll need some time to prepare a proposal for you, considering the other work I have to do while I'm in New Orleans, but please expect to receive something from me by the beginning of next week."

"Okay, that's fine. Can you do me a favor? Promise me we can go out for old time's sake before you leave. You're in the Big Easy. It'd be a shame to be here and not get a chance to party."

"Oui, Madame. I promise." Camille assured her in a semi-serious tone.

**The Hypothesis**

It was Saturday and Camille was back in the tropical paradise of Martinique. She was proud of herself. In one week she gained two potential new clients: her old job that has an office located in New Orleans and the Benoit sisters. Her eight-hour flight to Martinique afforded her time to review carefully all of the information Justin and the other two office managers shared with her.

She also reviewed the auditing agency's guidelines. Camille learned, from her online research of the agency, that they exist to ensure quality care in providing health and human services. They are an independent resource and analyze certain tools to assess the quality of care. Those tools include documented processes, job descriptions, an organizational chart and records management systems. They even look for a documented service delivery process as part of their audit — literally every element of the Kasennu methodology that Camille learned over a year ago!

Once Camille settled in at home, she spent the majority of Sunday preparing proposals, first for her former employer and then one for Karen and Sharen. She emailed her proposal to the twins early Monday morning, a few days before Halloween.

**** 

Karen was at her weekly Toastmasters meeting, but Sharen had been in her office since 6:30 am on Monday. She had a day packed with appointments and she was still trying to catch up after taking a short vacation last week. She happened to be on her computer when the email from Camille arrived. Sharen opened the proposal, printed it and began to read it.

### Introduction

Your mental rehabilitation business has the opportunity to expand statewide and across the Gulf Coast region. However, there is the looming and perpetual threat of a shutdown due to a failed audit. Until this threat is eliminated, further expansion cannot take place in a sustainable way.

### How the Problem Started

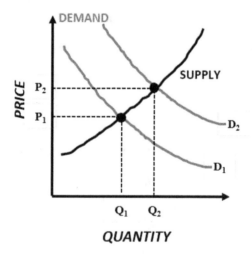

When you first started, the business focused on children in foster care. This is represented as $D_1$ in the diagram above. When Hurricane Katrina happened, the demand for your services not only increased (as more children became parentless), but your business also experienced a simultaneous shift in demand, as shown by $Q_2$ and $D_2$, respectively, in the diagram above. Over time, that shift occurred from working exclusively with children in foster care to also working with children suffering through traumatic experiences. The combined shift and increase in business forced you to raise your prices to ensure you could adequately supply that demand with a competent and capable staff, as shown by $P_2$.

That price increase meant more invoicing to Medicaid for reimbursement. More invoicing to Medicaid caused you to get onto the auditing radar again, triggering your second audit. What you see as the curse of the levee breaking is really Medicaid's attempt to ensure that the quality of services you all provide is not compromised in any way. Sure enough, the auditors determined, based on pre-established guidelines, that there were problems primarily in recordkeeping and so you were levied because of it. The latest audit exposed the fact that the archived patient records were still being stored and managed in a fragmented way.

Justin spent a good bit of his first year on the job trying to get the third location up and running. There was so much work to do that, sadly, the left hand did not know what the right hand was doing and so the curse of the levee continued. The business of running a mental rehabilitation facility has suffered, not because of the lack of quality care, but because of the lack of business infrastructure to promote cohesion and synchronization across all locations.

### Paper Records Management as the Solution

Although Green Technology is becoming the business norm for social and environmental responsibility, the truth of the matter is there are still certain records that must be maintained as an original hard copy. Medical records oftentimes fall into this category. Depending on the nature of the document, you could legally be required to retain certain paper records indefinitely.

Physical or paper records are a vital proof of original documentation. It is important that staff know where to find information when they need it in order to perform their jobs well. Unlike electronic records, paper records are tangible and therefore more susceptible to compromise. Thus, they must be handled with utmost care; without a scanned counterpart, disaster recovery is impossible, as you have learned the hard way. A Paper Records Management (PRM) system is one that links together the processes, technology and people needed to create, name, categorize, store and purge physical data in an organized, consistent and transparent manner.

PRM is one of the elements of the Kasennu methodology. The primary purpose is to create a structured system that is based on the company's business infrastructure. The secondary purpose is to reduce the amount of time spent in locating/retrieving documents so that more time can be allocated to serving your patients. The final purpose is to provide a designated employee with a documented records management system that is easy to maintain and teach to other employees.

### Value of a Paper Records Management System

By documenting your company's policies and procedures for creating, naming, storing, purging, archiving and protecting paper records you can:

- Pass industry audits the first time,
- Remain in compliance with laws and regulations,
- Create transparency in recordkeeping,
- Formalize sharing of records,
- Provide proof of certain transactions, and
- Respond quickly to subpoenas for records.

**The Scope**

The scope of your PRM system will focus on creating a centralized archival repository that takes into account that the business and its existing locations all operate in a flood-prone region that is seven feet below sea level. We will leverage your existing organizational chart as the foundation for organizing records to archive across all locations. These records include patient, legal, accounting and personnel files. We will assess the optimal storage solution and document the process for converting a record from active to inactive. Specifically, we will:

1. Take an inventory of all paper record types.
2. Group those types into main categories based on departments.
3. Create file labels and color-code accordingly.
4. Record the access, creation, naming, storage location, retention, purging, archiving and destruction cycles for each category of information.

**Proposed Time**

There were a total of 75 file drawers filled with archived records and a total of 30 file drawers filled with active records across all three locations. This work will be divided into four remote sessions before the 90-day window from your audit review expires. These four sessions can be spread over the next two months to allow you time to work around your busy schedules as well as the upcoming holidays.

****

When Karen arrived to her office, she found that Sharen was already there waiting. Sharen told her sister about Camille's proposal before forwarding it to Justin. Although she had a hunch of what Karen's answer would be, Sharen asked her anyway, "What do you think?"

"Didn't I tell you she had the antidote?!"

"Fa sho!" Sharen responded in an intentional creole pronunciation of "for sure." "In all seriousness, we need to act on this right away and get the other office managers involved. This needs to be a team effort. Let's call her right now!"

Sharen dialed Camille's number using the phone on Karen's desk and turned on the speaker. As the phone rang, Karen summoned Justin to her office.

"Bonjour!" a familiar voice greeted in French.

"Bonjour, Camille, it's me, Sharen. Karen and Justin are also in the room. We saw your proposal. When can we start?"

"Does next Monday work?"

"Next Monday it is!" Justin blurted out.

## The Experiment

The day of the first remote PRM session arrived. Per their request, Camille chose a time late in the afternoon after most appointments were over for the day. Karen, Sharen and Justin logged into the desktop sharing app from their respective offices.

Camille was already logged in. "Good morning, everyone! Thank you so much for joining! Are you all ready?"

"Yes!" Karen and Justin said at the same time.

Before them appeared a screen with a grid on it. Once Camille confirmed that they could, in fact, see her screen, she began to explain what they saw. "Before you is a grid of rectangular blocks. The top row of blocks contains the names of your departments: *Management, Clinical, Accounting, Administration, Public Relations, Human Resources* and *Quality Assurance.* I extracted that information from a copy of the organizational chart that Justin gave me. Does this look correct?"

"Yeees," Karen said slowly. Even though the proposal mentioned leveraging their organizational chart, she still wondered what this had to do with their paperwork issues.

"Stay with me Karen! I promise it will soon make sense," Camille replied. "Back to the grid. The remaining blocks of the grid are empty. The first thing we will do is assign a color to each of these departments. After that, I will explain how you will populate the remaining blocks with information about your physical files. The reason we want to assign color is because it aids in memory retention and, in the future, will decrease the amount of time spent in locating files. Once you know the meanings of colors, you can choose a color that best represents each department or grouping of paper files."

Camille then clicked on a button on the top menu of the business infrastructure software containing the grid. The button revealed a pop up window containing a color chart. As her mouse hovered over the primary colors first, the meaning or significance of each color appeared on the screen.

"As you can see, the color red represents action, energy and foundation. The color blue represents communication and loyalty, and the color yellow represents joy, confidence and attention. In choosing the right color association, a rule of thumb that us Kasennu practitioners use is to…"

"Ooh, wait! I have an idea!" Karen interrupted. "Can we start with the colors of the main chakras? That should save us a lot of time since there are dozens of colors to choose from this color chart."

"Oh boy," Sharen chimed in. "Karen, what are you talking about? Is this another one of your kooky ideas?" Though they are identical twins, they couldn't be further apart on certain spectrums. Sharen was more religious and Karen was more spiritual, and Sharen practiced traditional medicine while Karen leaned more toward homeopathy.

"Actually, I really like that idea," Justin said.

"Yes, I do too," Camille said reassuringly. "Coincidentally, the Kasennu logo actually uses the same colors of the main seven chakras. So Karen, your idea is not kooky at all!"

"We're barely 30 minutes into this conversation and already I'm outvoted!" Sharen joked.

"I'm sorry for interrupting you, Camille. That was rude of me," Karen apologized.

"No worries, Karen! Again, I like your chakra color idea. I was going to suggest that you use the color most closely associated with your business as the color for your core department. In your case, the core department is the Clinical Department. Since your company's logo is green, I would choose that color to represent the Clinical Department. Camille hovered over the color green. "Green is associated with health, balance, prosperity and safety."

"See, I keep telling ya'll, I'm not crazy!" Karen said aloud. "That's why I worked with that graphic designer years ago to create a green logo. That's also why I insisted all of our locations be painted in various shades of green. We want the children to know that, when they walk into this space, it is safe and that our mission is to restore balance and health in *all* areas of their lives."

Camille continued to hover over the remaining colors of the main chakras. Sharen and Justin learned that orange represents relationship, dark blue represents wisdom and purple represents ascension. "Now that you know the symbolic meanings of these colors, you can assign one to each of the remaining departments."

Karen, Sharen and Justin began to talk among themselves and instructed Camille on which color to assign to each department. Camille changed the color of the rectangular blocks containing the name of each department as follows: Management (blue), Clinical (green), Accounting (black), Administration (purple), Public Relations (orange), Human Resources (yellow), and Quality Assurance (red). Their reasoning for choosing black instead of green (a more traditional choice representing U.S. dollars) for the Accounting Department was because they want to stay *in the black*. They chose red as the color for the Quality Assurance Department to indicate its "red hot" importance; compliance can make or break their business.

Camille saved a copy of the grid and converted it into a document compatible with a word processing program. She emailed the copy that included additional instructions to all three session participants. "The next step is to fill in the blank, white rectangles on the grid with the names of the different types of files." She opened the page containing the instructions and read each aloud.

"Number one. Choose a starting point in your workspace and move about in a clockwise direction, taking an assessment of the various types of paperwork. For example, Justin, you might start with the files in your desk's drawers and then move on to the books you have on your bookcase across from your desk. Have the grid open and type in the name of each type of file you see.

"It's also a good time to go through your files and immediately discard or shred dated information that is no longer of use. That way, you won't log irrelevant information into the grid. It's important to record the *type* of file and not the actual file name. So, Sharen, you would not record each patient's file name in your grid. Rather, you'll type 'active patient file' in a rectangular block on the grid, in the column marked 'Clinical.' Does that make sense?"

| MANAGE-MENT | CLINICAL | ACCOUNT-ING | ADMINI-STRATION | PUBLIC RELATIONS | HUMAN RESOURCES | QUALITY ASSURANCE |
|---|---|---|---|---|---|---|
|  | Active Patient File |  |  |  |  |  |
|  |  |  |  |  |  |  |

They all replied, "yes."

"To be clear, Camille, should we record the types of books, too?" Justin asked.

"Yes, that's correct. It's a physical type of record. Any paper file, book, manual, periodical, etc., should be included. However, do not include things that are personal and therefore do not pertain to the operations of the business."

"This could take a long time," Sharen said.

"Yes and no. It really depends on how many types of files you have and the amount. The therapists may complete this inventory in one to two hours since most of their files will be patient records. But Karen's inventory may take longer considering she probably has file types associated with each department. I think you need to give yourselves about two weeks to get this done.

"Let's move on. Number two. Save a copy of your completed grid. Justin, can you make sure to distribute copies of the blank grid and instructions to everyone at the Uptown location? You'll also need to send copies to the office managers at the other two locations and ask them to distribute accordingly."

"Sure, no problem! But I'd like to go through the exercise first before I start distributing copies. I can probably knock mine out by tomorrow."

"That's great! But, please, pace yourself. And don't forget about the room with the archived files that you showed me. Karen, Sharen, do either of you have any objections to this approach?"

They both answered, "No."

"Number three. Work in four-hour increments. Depending on the amount of paper in a person's office, this exercise can be daunting to take on in one day. Besides, you won't have the time if you do this during a workday."

Justin responded, "We've actually talked about this among ourselves. We will probably have people come in the office on Saturday mornings and over the Thanksgiving break when our office is usually closed. The various offices should not take long."

"Good. Justin, can I count on you to compile all of the completed grids and email them to me in two weeks? That should put us at the end of November. I also want to recommend that you start looking for a vendor that can provide secure offsite storage."

"Sure thing! I'm two steps ahead of you! I've started the vetting process and narrowed the list down to three vendors. We want to store the records further upstate. It'll be more expensive but, at this point, we can't afford not to do it. We're looking at companies in Bossier City and Shreveport. Baton Rouge is the logical choice but even that is too risky since it's also in the direct line of a hurricane's wrath."

"Good. Any questions before we end this session?"

They all answered, "No."

"Okay, well, feel free to direct message me or email me. I'll also check in on you over the next two weeks. Thanks so much for your time today."

"No, thank *you*, Camille!" Sharen said.

"We love you baby! Talk to 'ya later." Karen told her.

Justin and Sharen both walked over to Karen's office to review their plan of action one more time. First, Justin would upload the blank grid to a cloud-based shared drive to avoid having to merge different files. Each of them would start the physical record inventory exercise as instructed by Camille. Justin would ensure their grids were separated in the file on the shared drive and, by the end of the week, he would forward the instructions to the office managers at the other two locations as well as the other employees at his location.

He spent the next two Saturdays specifically looking at the room containing all of the archived files. This particular inventory was much shorter than he had anticipated since most of the files represented one file type — archived patient records.

As planned, the week before Thanksgiving, Justin forwarded instructions along with a link to the shared drive containing the grid to the office managers at the other two locations, as well as to the other employees at his location. He also arranged a conference call to answer any questions people might have and told them that they had two weeks to complete their respective inventories.

Learning that they might have to work during the week of Thanksgiving was a strong motivator. Everyone in all three locations worked hard to get all physical records inventoried and logged into the grids in just one week. Justin downloaded and emailed a consolidated file consisting of 23 grids to Camille in preparation for their second remote session.

****

Camille received the file with 23 grids from Justin that encompassed all offices and spaces containing physical records across all three locations. She uploaded the file into her business infrastructure software in preparation for the second remote session. Doing so revealed 85 unique file types, each categorized and color-coded by department.

This remote session was different from the first in that the other two office managers joined, making a total of six people participating in the session. Camille shared her screen with everyone and revealed a matrix based on information extracted from the grids previously submitted.

"Before you is a matrix that contains attributes in the first row for each type of physical record identified. These physical records are organized by department. The attributes represent the life cycle of a physical record from creation to retirement or destruction. Reading the attributes from left to right, we have, *Full Access Rights,* followed by *File Name, Active Location, Retention Period, Archive Location, Purge Cycle* and *Destruction Type.* The column to the far left of the matrix contains the name of each physical file type.

"I'm going to spend some time describing how to fill in each column for a file type. Then, you will each work with the people in your respective locations to complete the matrix. Any questions so far?"

There was silence on the phone.

"Okay, I'll take that as a 'no.' I'll start with *Full Access Rights*. This means you will write the name of every role, not people's names, that should have access to this particular file. If anyone has questions about the names of certain roles then, as the office managers, you can share copies of the company's organizational chart to clear any confusion.

"Next, we have *File Name*. You should type in the generic way to name a file. active location represents the physical location where the document is currently stored. This should include the name of the location as well as the specific office within that location. *Retention Period* represents the length of time to keep the file in the *Active Location*. Not all of your files are governed by regulations. In those instances, you can come up with a timeline that you all agree on. Next, we have *Archive Location*. This is the location where a file will be stored once it has surpassed its *Retention Period*, which brings me to a question: Justin, have you all chosen an offsite document management vendor?"

Justin answered, "We're getting close, Ms. Camille. In fact, me, Sharen and Karen drove up to Shreveport the day after Thanksgiving and visited the three vendors we narrowed our list to."

Sharen spoke next, "Yes, we anticipate making a final decision and signing a contract with the new vendor before the end of this week. Our decision is dependent on the outcome of this session."

"That's great!" Camille exclaimed. "Back to the attributes. The next attribute is *Purge Cycle*. This represents the amount of time that a record must surpass, once archived, to qualify for destruction. You can reference the various regulatory guidelines for personnel, patient, legal and accounting records to help fill in this column for each record type. Lastly, we have *Destruction Type*. This describes how the record, once it is ready for purging, should be destroyed. Options can include shredding, recycling, scanning and simply discarding.

"As Sharen alluded to, having this kind of detailed information not only enables you to have a more intelligent conversation with the potential offsite storage vendor, but it also formalizes and centralizes a physical records management system for the entire company. I'd like to fill in an example. Let's use the most obvious record type — Patient Records."

Camille began typing into the cells on the matrix so that everyone could see how to apply the information she just shared. She asked for assistance as she typed the following information for the *Patient Record* file type:

| CLINICAL DEPARTMENT | | | | | | | |
|---|---|---|---|---|---|---|---|
| File Type | Full Access Rights | File Name | Active Location | Retention Period | Archive Location | Purge Cycle | Destruction Type |
| Patient Record | ○ Therapists<br>○ Office Managers | Patient's Last Name, First Name_Date of Birth_Last Four Digits of Social Security Number_Date of Admittance | ○ Therapist Offices<br>○ Metairie<br>○ Uptown<br>○ West Bank | Until patient file becomes inactive (file closed). | Offsite Storage Facility | N/A (store indefinitely) | Shred (scan after 3 years of archival; retain digital copy; shred paper copy) |

After Camille finished populating the matrix with the attribute information for the *Patient Record* file type, she downloaded the matrix into a spreadsheet file. She emailed a copy to Justin and asked that he upload the spreadsheet to a cloud-based shared drive so everyone could update the same spreadsheet in real time. This would prevent hours of merging data from their 23 employees.

This remote session lasted an hour and a half and ended with a recap of next steps.

****

Before uploading the matrix to the cloud for real time collaboration, Justin went about the work of carefully reviewing the auditing agency's guidelines for patient record retention. He, Sharen and Karen decided that, to be on the safe side, they would archive all inactive patient records indefinitely. Legacy patient records they were able to salvage pre- and immediately post-Katrina would be scanned. The same would be true for closed patient files after a three-year period.

To free up physical space in their three locations, they would also archive any personnel, legal and accounting records that surpassed their respective retention periods. Rather than box and store remotely, they would have the offsite storage vendor use their proprietary technology to scan and catalogue all other files that surpassed their retention period.

Armed with this information, Justin, Karen and Sharen selected the vendor they felt could best serve their needs. Justin then ordered several banker's boxes from an office supply store and had them delivered to each location. These boxes would store the files that would be scanned and/or archived initially at the vendor's offsite facility.

****

The third remote session with Camille began the first week of December. Prior to starting this session, Justin emailed her a copy of the completed matrix in the form of a spreadsheet. In the body of the email, he mentioned that he developed instructions to follow in identifying and boxing records to scan and/or archive in preparation for the vendor to pick up. Although Camille had a few days to ponder the information in the matrix, she developed some immediate recommendations to give them.

Like the first session, only Justin, Karen and Sharen joined Camille. This session lasted less than an hour as Camille's primary objective was to give some recommendations before they arranged for the offsite storage vendor to pick up the boxes of archived records.

"It occurred to me that you all do not have a designated 'headquarters.' I've given this a considerable amount of thought and I can't help but wonder if this is why the back office operations became so fragmented and siloed."

"Headquarters?" Sharen asked.

"Yes," Camille responded. "By identifying one of your locations as the official headquarters, you can centralize much of the management activity into one hub. That hub can disseminate all information that each location must adhere to. I think your Uptown office should be the new headquarters location. Think about it. Your H.R. manager is physically located there and so is the senior accountant. They service all three locations and play an integral part in establishing management protocol.

"Also, Karen and Sharen, although you have offices at all three locations, you seem to spend the majority of your time at the Uptown location. I also foresee Justin becoming an internal compliance officer. I say this based on the initiative he's taken in implementing this project, as well as the work he's done in the past to consolidate and standardize the efforts of all office managers. Since all of you play a proactive role in management, one can only conclude that the Uptown office become the headquarters. What do you think?"

Karen replied first. "That actually makes a lot of sense."

Justin said, "Karen and Sharen, you already know I'm on board. I've been saying for a while that we needed to pick a location where we could set up a conference room for times when we need to corral managers from other locations into one place."

Sharen thought carefully before she spoke. "Yes, Justin, that's true. I actually like that idea. It makes us seem more deliberate and intentional in our efforts to prove that we know and understand the *business* of owning a mental rehabilitation facility. I'm sure that would go a long way with the auditing agency."

"Then it's settled!" Camille said. "But first, we need to discuss a critical part of your PRM — getting the records ready for archival. Justin, you mentioned you created some instructions for this. I'm going to give you control of the screen-sharing app so that you can share your screen with us."

Justin gained control of the screen-sharing app and read the document aloud. Camille, Karen and Sharen were able to see a list of instructions on his screen as follows:

1. All records in every location are considered private. Therefore, each filing cabinet must remain locked at all times. You should also lock the door to your office prior to leaving for the day. Your office manager will have a master copy of all keys should you lose any.

2. Carefully sort through each piece of paper in your office and determine whether it needs to be archived based on the completed PRM matrix. If so, then place the file into a banker's box and affix a sticky note on the outside of the box indicating the type(s) of paper records inside and its associated department(s).

3. If you have a record that you want scanned and then shredded, place that into a separate banker's box and also affix a sticky note on the box indicating the type of record, its associated department and write "TO SCAN." Our offsite storage vendor will use the record type and department information as "tags" to attach to the scanned file for ease in future retrieval.

4. All active files will now be color-coded using a new labeling system. Your office manager will work with you to re-label all of your paper files.

5. If possible, place all of your boxes with archived files in a corner in your office. Your office manager will review the contents of each box with you and affix a permanent label to each box based on the information on the sticky notes you previously filled out.

All locations will be closed the last two weeks of the year for the Christmas break. This gives us more than enough time to sweep through our respective files and set aside information to archive. As a reminder, the auditing agency will be here again in January 2015 to check on our progress.

I will perform a final quality check of the contents of all boxes marked for archival at the Uptown office. Karen will do the same at the Metairie office and Sharen will oversee the West Bank office. The offsite storage vendor is scheduled to pick up all boxes marked for archival on Dec. 29, 2014. Thank you for your full cooperation in helping us to keep our facilities coordinated and compliant.

This third session ended with Camille reminding everyone to reach out to her if they had any questions along the way. She was proud of the progress they were making. In fact, they were ahead of schedule.

**The Result**

Since they were ahead of schedule, Camille used the time originally slated for the fourth remote session to present her final report with recommendations.

It was Monday, December 21, just a few days shy of Christmas. Karen, Sharen, Justin and the other two office managers all logged into the fourth remote session with Camille. Camille shared her screen and everyone saw what appeared to be a cover page of a report. This, Camille told them, was their official PRM system. It was a 31-page document that included their completed matrix, along with specific procedural steps for creating a new physical file using the new color-coded labeling system.

Other procedural steps included the protocol for: 1) working with the offsite storage vendor to pick up new archival records, 2) scanning documents and 3) testing and updating the new PRM system. "Justin, how many boxes will the offsite storage vendor pick up next week?"

"Right now, 41," Justin replied. "We also have 10 boxes of information to scan. Everything is labeled as the vendor requested. We've taken pictures of everything, too, and we plan on taking that five-hour drive and following them to Shreveport. This is our first time ever doing something like this and we're, uh, cautiously optimistic."

"Yeah Camille, this is a little scary for us," Karen added. "But I keep reminding myself that, moving forward, our system is not only going to look good, it *will* be good! It only took us 12 years to get it right. But, better late than never!"

Sharen shared Karen's enthusiasm, "Thank you so much, Camille! This new system is comprehensive and it ties together the efforts of all of our locations. It also provides a foundation that we can use as we open additional locations."

"That's so wonderful to hear! I'm glad you understand the intent and the value now and in the future. You should share this new PRM system with everyone. Let them know the expectations for adhering to the maintenance of your company's physical records. As you continue using this system, evaluate whether or not you should invest in developing your own official document management solution that includes scanning, indexing and classifying more of your records in an electronic format. You can use the information from this matrix as the *tags* to locate information in the document management solution. This is a more expensive option, since the solution would be customized to your company's specific needs, but it will significantly reduce your liability in storing active physical records onsite."

Camille closed the document describing the new system and thanked everyone for all of their hard work and the opportunity to work with them. She emailed a copy of the PRM system to all of the session's participants and hinted that she wanted to have a separate conversation with Karen and Sharen.

****

Later that night, Sharen called Camille and Karen on three-way to discuss the final recommendations Camille hinted at earlier. There were specific things Camille wanted to talk to them about as they moved forward.

Camille began by giving a recap of her first recommendation, a document management solution. Sharen asked for further clarification. Camille explained that, basically, the document management solution would be like a customized search engine for their own records — sort of like an internal *Google*, for lack of a better term. Implementing a document management solution would also mean developing a new Electronic Records Management system.

"Once the audit check-in happens next month, my next recommendation is that you go through the Business Parts Analysis and Business Design Blueprint elements of the Kasennu methodology. Yes, you have job descriptions and an organizational chart already, but both should be updated, one, to include the specific job tasks related to the upkeep of your new Paper Records Management system, and, two, to reflect the colors selected for each department.

"Three, and most important, to add at least two new roles to your business: a compliance officer and a community liaison. Again, I foresee Justin advancing into the role of the compliance officer. This role would enforce and manage the activities of the Quality Assurance Department for all locations. Right now, you have no one specifically working in that department, which is probably another reason why compliance was low in certain areas, despite best efforts. If Justin is promoted into that role, then the current receptionist can be trained and promoted to replace him as office manager of the new headquarters location. I suspect it'll be much easier to hire a new receptionist than it would be a new office manager.

"The community liaison is a new role that would help field questions from the general public and media. If the publicist you've hired does a good job, then Karen's time will be spent mostly in business development and making media appearances, not in fielding questions. It's time for Karen to function as a true CAO [Chief Administrative Officer] while Sharen remains the CEO and medical director. Sharen, as the business continues to expand, you may also be faced with choosing between being CEO and serving the role as medical director. Just something to think about."

"Camille, I'm all in favor for your recommendations! What do you think, Sharen?"

"Yes, yes, it all sounds good. In fact, Justin has expressed a strong interest in learning more about the Kasennu methodology and applying more of its elements to our business so that we can keep duplicating what we do best."

"I'm really glad to hear that!" Camille said excitedly. "Here's what I think we should do as next steps. First, pass the audit check-in next month! Then, I can start working with Justin to teach him the methodology. We'll start with the Business Parts Analysis and the Business Design Blueprint elements. That will take about a month. Next, we can look at developing the Electronic Records Management system. The conversion of more paper documents into digital files might free up enough space to create a new conference room where strategic planning meetings can take place.

"I foresee the headquarter location being used only for staff who service all locations with existing therapists at the Uptown location eventually relocating to new or other locations. The Work Space Logistics plan would encompass this body of work. Lastly, we need to identify and document your processes! Documented processes will show auditors and employees alike your commitment to Medicaid's mission to 'combat fraud, waste and abuse to ensure proper use of funds to protect Medicaid recipients.'

"By the time you look at those first few elements of the methodology, the timing should work well to attend a process identification and documentation workshop. It will take place in Atlanta in April of next year. It's imperative that you attend, especially as you start adding more locations."

Sharen did not need convincing to attend the workshop. "If this exercise has taught us anything, it's that processes help bind and stitch our operations together. It gives everybody the same compass to direct our work flow. Plus, it ties into the succession planning work that we've been learning about at Tulane. Karen, are you ready to go to the A-T-L?"

"Girl, you know I don't like those dirty birds,[19] but maybe they can benefit from our *saintly* presence!" They all laughed loudly. "But seriously, Camille, thank you again *for everything*. We have a lot of referrals for you!"

****

The following January, Karen made her first international news appearance their new publicist had scheduled a few days after they received confirmation that they had passed their audit. All that practicing at Toastmasters paid off. Telling more of her personal story was helping to bring more attention not only to the plight of children growing up in the foster care system, but also to children suffering through trauma.

Karen's phone rang constantly, but there was a phone call one day that took her by complete surprise.

"Hello, this is Karen Benoit."

"Hi...Karen?" a cracked voice asked, as if in disbelief. "My name is Lisa Benoit Aucoin. I recently read an article about you in the Times Picayune newspaper. I'm...I'm your cousin. Our grandfathers were brothers."

Karen's heart raced, much as it did when she last spoke at her Toastmasters club. She was speechless. She vaguely remembered Lisa.

"Hello? Karen?"

"Yes, I'm here."

"Can we talk?"

# CHAPTER 6

# RED PILL OR BLUE PILL?

**Kasennu™**
Service Delivery Blueprint™

Brian Miller, his wife, Vandana, and her best friend, Imana, are co-founders of a fast-growing mortgage company in Brooklyn, New York. In just three years, they managed to secure a recurring role on a new reality TV show featuring first time homebuyers in the Big Apple. This show is responsible for their most recent wave of growth. But with that growth has come the inability to meet the loan processing time predicted by their proprietary mathematical algorithm. Each co-founder is now at an impasse, especially Vandana, as they decide whether to follow their original dreams or continue down their current path. The stakes are high. All eyes are on them and they must make the right decision. Their consultant introduces them to the Service Delivery Blueprint element of the Kasennu methodology as a means to help them make the right choice.

"And…cut!" An energetic director yelled into his megaphone as the second assistant camera clapped the top layer of the clapperboard to the bottom, making a loud, clicking noise. This was the sixth, and final, take of a particular scene on a new real estate reality TV show where a young and very impressionable couple were interacting with a savvy mortgage broker to negotiate the terms of their first home loan.

That mortgage broker happened to be Vandana Thiagarajan. She was exhausted from having been on the set since 6:00 am. It was now getting close to noon and her stomach was practically tied into knots from hunger pain. Although there was plenty of food around, Vandana wanted to be away from the set more than anything else. Before she stood up from the desk in an office that did not belong to her, she couldn't help but think about the pain the illusion of this "reality" TV show was causing her.

The entire set was staged, the only similarity to their actual office was the prominent use of turquoise in the set's décor. In reality, she operated out of the second floor of a narrow brownstone in Brooklyn, not this fancy Manhattan office encased in glass with a view of the Hudson River.

"All the world's a stage, and all the men and women merely players: they have their exits and their entrances…,"[20] she said in a low tone only audible to herself.

Vandana retrieved her phone from her pants pocket. Her voicemail was full, a recurring blessing and curse. A blessing because it was an indication that her company's services were in high demand. A curse because they were struggling to meet that demand. Before she could think further, Hunter Jeffries, the consultant she and her partners had been working with for close to two months, walked up to her.

"Vandana, that was awesome! You're a natural on camera!"

"Thanks, Hunter." Vandana managed to force a smile. She was getting used to masking truth. By most accounts, she *should* be happy. At 33-years-old, she was co-owner of a fast growing residential mortgage company in New York City, arguably, one of the highest valued real estate markets in the country. December 2014, the month they initially hired Hunter, also marked their third year in business. They netted $5 million.

Yet, Vandana felt trapped. As she continued reflecting on the pressures of performing both on and off camera, she found her breathing becoming more laborious. She removed her purse from the desk she sat behind on the set, fumbling through it looking for her inhaler. The last thing she needed was to have an asthma attack.

Hunter was curious about Brian and Imana's whereabouts. Brian Miller was Vandana's husband of four years, and Imana Van Dijk was her best friend of 24 years. In an attempt to divert attention from the obvious, Vandana fibbed and said they were both at the office working.

*Where is he anyway?* She thought about her husband. *This show was his idea. I didn't sign up for this. This was his dream, not mine!* She preferred to operate in the background, as most mortgage brokers would normally be in a real estate transaction; however, when the casting director saw her, she said Vandana made for "great TV." Vandana went along with being on the show, trying to be a team player, but they were now in their second season and she was uncomfortable with the idea of making money based on her appearance.

"Don't you have a train to catch?" Vandana asked Hunter.

"Yeah, I guess it is getting to be about that time, eh?" Hunter replied in his Canadian dialect. He was scheduled to take a train to Boston for another client appointment before crossing the border into Toronto.

## The Fast Growth Predicament

Hunter was at the TV show's set per Vandana's request. She and her business partners were introduced to him upon the recommendation of Brian's childhood friend, Tim McKiver. Tim anticipated helping Brian's mother, Emily, with her non-profit organization in Washington, D.C. and, therefore, would be unavailable to assist them with their fast growth woes.

Vandana asked Hunter to come to the set because she knew the timing was perfect to speak candidly with him one-on-one. She planned this day strategically because she knew Brian would be busy at the law firm where he worked full-time and that Imana would be visiting family in their native Suriname.

As they began walking toward the nearest subway station, Vandana continued to make small talk with Hunter. She started by reiterating what Hunter already knew: the TV show was becoming more popular and more people were requesting their services as a result. The business was coming in fast and furious.

Cognizant of what Vandana was doing, Hunter asked her, "Is everything okay, Vandana? It seems like you're hiding something. I realize being on a crowded train isn't the best place to have this conversation, but I can't shake the feeling that you're withholding information. What's troubling you?"

Relieved Hunter asked, Vandana replied, "Honestly, Hunter, I don't know where to begin. I...I...ugh! How can I say this delicately?"

"Don't worry about being delicate."

"We're in trouble."

"That's why you all hired me, remember? To help you get a business infrastructure in place to make sure your growth is sustainable and replicable."

"Yes, I know Hunter, but there's some stuff I don't think Brian told you."

During his initial engagement with them, Hunter interfaced primarily with Brian. He came to know Brian as a straight shooter and couldn't imagine what Vandana could be talking about. He leaned in closer toward her so that she could speak into his ear without others on the train hearing her.

"We're unable to meet the loan processing timeline we've boasted for the past year. The show is doing well and that's why we've been asked to participate in a second season, but it's shining a spotlight on our weaknesses. We're an important piece of the puzzle in closing residential real estate deals on the show. Right before we started taping this season, a local investigative news reporter interviewed several couples who participated on the show last season. They reported shoddy contractor work and had proof to back their accusations.

"Of course, this made us guilty by association, even though we have nothing to do with the contractors on the show. That's when Brian reached out to you as a proactive measure. Don't get me wrong, I'm grateful for what you've helped us with so far, but now our clients outside of the TV show are starting to complain more and more about the length of time it takes to process and approve their loan applications.

"One client even accused us of 'going Hollywood' and not having time for people unless we can get air time out of it. It's true, the clients that come as a result of the show currently take top priority. If we're not careful, these angry clients can also call an investigative reporter to expose us directly. If we don't fix this soon, we'll lose endorsements, not to mention the opportunity to be on this show and others in the future. Film is forever."

Hunter straightened up in his seat. When he looked at Vandana, her eyes were welling with tears.

"Hunter, I feel like I'm caught up in the Matrix! I know how valuable the TV show is in getting us exposure, but I also know how important it is to remain loyal to our client base and referral network we had *before* the TV fame. Have you seen that movie, *The Matrix*?"

"Yes, I have." Hunter replied curiously.

"It's like I'm Neo and you're Morpheus. Through your work, you've presented me with the option to choose between taking the proverbial red pill and blue pill.[21] If I take the red pill, I'll see how deep this Hollywood rabbit hole takes me, while risking the possibility of losing myself and my vision for our company in the process. The fame will become my drug of choice and I might develop an insatiable appetite for it. And we'll continue the illusion that all is well as long as the money continues to flow in.

"On the other hand, if I take the blue pill, I can continue down the original path of operating a business in the real world, as we had originally planned. It might take longer for us to achieve some of our goals, but at least we would be able to keep our promises and not risk being accused of fraud."

Over the years, Vandana perfected the use of analogies in describing her thoughts and feelings. As a statistician with a finance background, she often found that people could not understand her when she spoke of or tried to explain what she did for a living. She found analogies to be a useful communication tool.

Hunter was dumbfounded. "I didn't realize I placed you under that kind of duress!"

"It's not your fault. Your presence and the work you've done and are continuing to do for us is a reminder of something I've hidden for a while…that it's all smoke and mirrors."

At that moment, they arrived at Penn Station. As they walked through the crowded corridor to the platform where Hunter would catch his next train, they searched for and found a less crowded place to sit. He had about 30 minutes before boarding.

"What do you mean when you say 'it's all smoke and mirrors?'"

"Like I said, this TV show has been great for business. But we're mortgage brokers, not actors! I feel like we're getting further and further away from our original vision, which was to help prevent displacement of long-time residents in areas undergoing gentrification. We envisioned partnering with urban planners and eventually branching into real estate development. Instead, Brian is off hob-knobbing and rubbing elbows with the Who's Who of New York, trying to secure a future partnership at the real estate law firm where he works. And Imana is on a high from all of the newfound fame. She's always traveling between here, Miami and Paramaribo.

"I'm tired of making compromises. First, I forfeited a research assistant position at a reputable university to start this business. Then, I settled for *not* having a traditional Hindu wedding back home and, instead, got married here in the States. And then, my mother-in-law gave me grief for not taking on their last name, Miller. I finally won her over with my decision to keep my maiden name when I told her I didn't want to suffer an identity crisis like her [see Chapter 2]. Thank God she finally backed off! Now, there's this issue with the TV show and our company. I want to get back to doing what I love and do so well, crunching numbers!

"When we started the company three years ago, we each brought something unique and valuable to the table. Brian came with the knowledge of real estate law, Imana came with the knowledge of urban and smart city planning, and I came with the financial acumen to structure deals for our clients. I even used my statistical training to develop an algorithm that allows us to predict accurately our loan processing and application process.

"Now, instead of us balancing each other out, I feel caught in the middle between my husband and my best friend. It's maddening!"

**The Research**

This intrigued Hunter. After working with them over the past two months, he thought he knew most of their story. But, he realized he spent most of his time talking to Brian and not Vandana or Imana for that matter. He knew that Brian's father was also a real estate attorney and that Brian wanted to follow in his footsteps.

"Are you referring to Brian's law practice? Is that what's troubling you?"

"That's part of the problem. Did you know that Brian wants to make partner at his firm? If he does, then where would that leave Imana and me?"

In all his conversations with Brian, that subject also never came up. He could understand why this would upset Vandana. There was no way she and Imana could keep up with the volume of business without Brian's full participation. They weren't quite at a point where they could convert all of their part-time employees into full-time employees with healthcare and stock option benefits.

"But that's why we're working together, remember? We've already established the tasks to perform and identified who will perform those tasks during the Business Parts Analysis exercise. Now, we just need to identify and document your processes so that, as you hire additional employees, they'll know exactly what to do and you can meet your targeted loan processing timeline again."

"Take a look at this." Vandana pulled her cell phone out of her pants pocket. The screen displayed a message indicating 23 missed calls and a full voice mailbox. "You see this? My phone is like this every day. It will take me a half hour just to listen to all of these messages. About 50% of them will be legitimate inquiries and the other half will be tire-kickers, you know, people wanting to be attached to us because of our perceived fame, not because they're serious about conducting business."

"We can solve that problem easily, Vandana. You can get a new, separate cell phone for personal use only and retain your existing cell phone, but change the number. Then, you can forward calls to your business cell phone to a temporary phone answering service until you can fill the receptionist role we identified last month."

"That reminds me, not only do we need to change our numbers, but we need to move into commercial office space quickly! Imana promised to start looking into this as soon as she returns from her vacation."

"Oh, so is *that* where she is?" Hunter asked. This was not what Vandana told him earlier when they were on the TV set and he asked about Imana.

Vandana could kick herself for slipping. "Yes, but it's not really a vacation. She's in Paramaribo. In Suriname. As I mentioned, we have business interests there, too. Lately, Imana has spent a lot of time in Miami working with the Surinamese Consulate and with real estate developers to broker deals that will help promote tourism.

"Speaking of Imana, this whole 'Matrix' situation has also placed a strain on our friendship. We've been friends since we were nine years old. She's more than a friend to me, she's my sister. We had dreams of leveraging our work here in Manhattan and using it to help strengthen the Surinamese economy. We often joke that it would be like déjà vu, except we wouldn't trade Manhattan for Suriname like the Dutch settlers did. We were gaining a lot of traction until Brian signed us up for this mentor protégé program. We've been paired with a phenomenal mentor who happens to be part of a prominent real estate family in New York. Our mentor suggested we audition for the show."

There was so much Hunter didn't know about his clients that he thought he did. It was now apparent to him why Vandana wanted to speak with him one on one.

"I'm going to think about this some more. The good news is that I believe it is possible to reach a mutually beneficial solution. Thank you for sharing this with me. I'd like to speak with Imana, too. When does she return?"

"Next week."

"I tell you what, now that I've seen what you do on set, I will draft a summary of the next thing we previously agreed to work on, a Service Delivery Blueprint. This will help get you all back on track. We can talk about the TV thing later but, for now, consider this. If you look at the TV show as a marketing and business development tool and not as a time-wasting distraction, you might develop a new appreciation for it. You might be able to use the Matrix to your advantage.

"For now, it's causing you pain because you're shouldering most of the responsibility. A lot of time is spent in multiple takes while on the set and it causes you anxiety because you're thinking of all the work that has to be done, the calls to return, the loan applications to process, etc. The sooner we spell out your delivery process, the sooner you'll sleep better and breathe easier."

"Breathe easier?" Vandana asked, thinking it was a reference to her asthma. "Are you a doctor now?" she teased Hunter.

"No, not at all. And my apologies for the breathing reference. But I think you know what I mean."

"I'm just giving you a hard time! We love working with you and I wouldn't have shared all of this with you if I didn't think you could help us. The bottom line is, it's more than just worrying about the volume of work required to keep up; it's salvaging and protecting our reputation and brand at all costs!"

"Red pill or blue pill, right?"

"Exactly!"

It was five minutes before boarding time. Hunter thanked Vandana again for the information and dashed onto the platform to board his train. Meanwhile, Vandana decided to walk outside of Penn Station and onto the street headed south for some fresh air despite the snow and biting wind ripping around the corners of the skyscrapers. She walked long enough to stop by a street vendor to order a veggie pita sandwich. It was her first time eating in nearly eight hours.

She hopped back onto a subway train at 28th Street and caught the Red Line down to Chambers Street where she again walked outside, this time to Battery Park. There were few people around in the park, which was ideal for her. She needed more time to think and liked being able to take in the wonderment of the Financial District. Seeing the New York Stock Exchange, the Statue of Liberty and all the streets with Dutch names always kept her grounded as she remembered why she was doing what she was doing.

Though she donned a thick wool scarf, heavy down coat and fur-lined hat and gloves, none proved sufficient to combat the raging winds blowing off the Hudson River. She had a mind to actually walk across the Brooklyn Bridge, but the wind gusts were too punishing. Instead, she caught the subway to Brooklyn and headed to the place she called home, a three-story brownstone she and Brian shared with Imana in the famous neighborhood Bedford Stuyvesant. As she walked toward home, she reflected on how much the neighborhood had changed in the 15 years she has lived in New York. There was no doubt about it, Brooklyn was being gentrified. They were fortunate to have purchased their brownstone right before the most recent price swell. Though she had no regrets living here, she still couldn't believe she and Imana traded living in a tropical paradise for a concrete jungle.

Imana lived on the top floor of their brownstone while Vandana and Brian occupied the main floor. The second floor was reserved for their office space and afforded them three rooms which they converted into a shared conference room and two separate offices. They rented out the basement and used the proceeds toward their own mortgage. Looking around, Vandana noticed there was no room for a physical office or home expansion; they were quickly running out of space.

*And to think, people wonder why we don't have kids! Where would we put them?* Vandana thought to herself as she walked up the stairs to the second floor. She went into her designated office, sat down and began listening to the voice mail messages on her phone.

****

When Brian came home later that evening, Vandana decided to tell him about her conversation with Hunter earlier that day.

"Can we talk?" Vandana asked in a serious tone.

"Yeah, babe. You okay?" Brian listened attentively as Vandana recapped her conversation with Hunter. He didn't like that she revealed certain things to Hunter, but he had to agree with Vandana that the more they shared with Hunter, the better he would be able to help them. Besides, Vandana argued, Hunter signed a mutual non-disclosure agreement that, if breached, Brian could easily defend in court.

****

Based on his conversation with Vandana, Hunter was not surprised when he received a phone call from Brian on a late Thursday night. But he was caught off guard when Brian relayed that Vandana shared the details of the conversation she and Hunter had.

"I feel bad for putting my wife under all of this stress and strain," Brian told Hunter. "I got so absorbed in my legal world that I lost sight of the impact it had on her and on Imana, too, for that matter. She told me about the red pill/blue pill analogy. Ironically, I feel the same way. I have to choose between continuing to work full time at the firm versus our company. How soon can we start the next phase of the methodology?"

"We can start as soon as all of you can be together at one time,"

Hunter told him, hoping to incite Brian into quick action.

"Good. Imana flew in earlier this afternoon. I'll ask both of them about the show's schedule and their availability. Hopefully, I'll have an answer for you by tomorrow."

"Sounds good. In the meantime, expect to receive an email from me explaining the next phase of the Kasennu methodology we'll work on, the Service Delivery Blueprint, in a little more detail, as well as the specific steps we'll take to complete it and the time required."

## The Hypothesis

By the time Brian was on the train to go to work the following Friday morning, Hunter sent the email he promised. Based on a quick scan, Brian was pleased to know that this effort would not be as tedious for them as the Business Parts Analysis. He sent a group text to Vandana and Imana, *GM! Check your email. Hunter sent info for next phase of work.*

Imana's phone beeped to alert her of a new text message. She had just finished showering, but quickly wrapped a towel around herself and grabbed her phone as she walked toward her bedroom. She opened her inbox to locate the email from Hunter. There were no attachments, as she had become accustomed to; rather, the details were spelled out in the body of the email itself as follows:

Hello Vandana, Imana and Brian,

We are all in agreement about the expediency of moving forward to the next phase of the recommended course of action in building a sustainable, repeatable and scalable business infrastructure — the Service Delivery Blueprint.

### The Service Delivery Blueprint

In this element of the Kasennu methodology, we will document the **steps** in delivering your core service, making sure to incorporate **all staff** identified in the Business Parts Analysis as well as the **tools** used to facilitate the client experience. We will also capture the **metrics** to monitor the client experience.

### What We Will Do

1. Document the sequential steps for delivering quality service every time.
2. Incorporate the use of various tools in delivering quality service.
3. Identify areas for automation so that you can safely handle more volume without sacrificing quality.

### The Value to You

By documenting and sharing how your company delivers its core services, you can:

- Promote your competitive advantage for approving loans without fear of retribution or a public outing;
- Re-establish credibility via a consistent, quality customer experience;
- Increase revenue by shortening delivery time to accommodate more volume;
- Improve communication with customers and among staff; and
- Get back to the "old days" when you were able to under-promise and over-deliver.

### Why This Matters

Customers want a predictable and quality experience with your company. Moreover, they expect to have an experience similar to that which they see on the TV show you're a part of. Likewise, your growing staff craves order and consistency in task allocation and job performance expectations. No one likes missing promised timelines! By taking the time to document your company's Service Delivery process and linking it to your company's job descriptions and organizational chart, you can ensure loyalty through a well-linked supply chain that communicates value to customers and staff.

There's no need to take the red or the blue pill. You shouldn't have to take a pill at all, as I believe there's a win-win solution for everyone. We can start as soon as time permits. Your full participation is necessary to ensure success. This work can be completed in as little as four sessions, both in-person and remotely, over a three-week period.

Please let me know if you have any questions.

Kind Regards,

Hunter Jeffries

Imana texted her response, *Saw Hunter's email. Sounds good. What does he mean by red pill and blue pill?* Vandana replied to the text saying she would explain on their way to the set. They agreed they would call Hunter when they all returned home later that day, though they weren't exactly sure what time that would be.

****

Early Saturday morning, they called Hunter via conference call. It was simply too late by the time they were all home, they explained, for them to call the night before.

Hunter asked if they had any questions about his email regarding the Service Delivery Blueprint (SDB). Brian asked for confirmation on the actual steps they would take and Hunter responded, "The primary purpose is to document the overall process of your company's core business and to demonstrate how this core business functions in relation to all previously identified resources and support departments. This interconnectivity can be essential in building team camaraderie and fulfilling your competitive advantage in quick loan processing. Remember, we identified your company's departments as follows: *General Management, Administration, Legal & Compliance, Operations* and *Marketing & Sales.*

"Out of these departments, the Operations Department represents the core of your business. So, your SDB will capture the steps in fulfilling the work of the Operations Department from A to Zed while simultaneously showing the activities of people in the other departments in that fulfillment."

"Zed?" Imana asked, confused.

"Sorry, that's the Canadian coming out of me. I mean 'Z.' Imana, welcome back! How was your trip?" Hunter asked.

"It was good, Hunter, thank you! Guess what? I actually saw an episode from the first season of the show while I was in Suriname! Vandana and I are like superstars over there! I received a reception at home fit for a queen! I can't wait for the second season to finish taping and air," Imana beamed.

Unlike Vandana, Imana actually liked performing and treasured the value that celebrity brought to their business. But even she could appreciate the toll that the show was taking on Vandana. With Imana's travel schedule and Brian's full-time job, Vandana bore the brunt of running the business while simultaneously filming.

"That's wonderful, Imana!" Hunter said, after a moment of awkward silence on the phone. "It's also a great segue into how I think you will be able to use the SDB to glean additional insights to help you all to better manage the deluge of business as a result of the show. For example, I took a closer look at your website and realized that you all only communicate how fast you can process a loan without providing details on your actual process. Do you find yourselves constantly answering the same questions as it relates to the steps of your process?"

"Yes!" Vandana answered. "It gets to be tiring to constantly say the same thing over and over."

"Precisely my point. After we document your Service Delivery process, you'll be able to summarize it and include it onto the website, along with a Frequently Asked Questions page that you can direct clients to in the future. The more information you provide your clients on the website upfront, without bogging them down in details, the better informed they will be *before* they call you. Elements of the Service Delivery process can also be used to develop a script for your new receptionist in answering questions."

"Can we start this weekend?" Brian asked enthusiastically. "It's short notice, but would you be able to make the trip here tomorrow? I'll pay for your flight."

"Thanks Brian, but that won't be necessary. We can actually do the first session remotely. That will give me time to plan a trip to New York for the second session. Sound good?"

"Sounds perfect!" Vandana said.

"We need to get you all to a place where your operations match your façade. You'll be able to back all of your loan processing claims and use more discretion in the future when it comes to partnering with others. I think this is what's really at the heart of what bothers Vandana. I'm just as committed to fixing this as you all are. I'll talk to you all tomorrow morning."

## The Experiment

On February 1, 2015, the first Sunday of the month, Vandana and Imana eagerly dialed into a conference call with Hunter. Brian, they told Hunter, wouldn't be able to participate due to an emergency meeting at his job. Hunter assured them that was okay because he would send a recording of their call to all of them.

"Before we start, I want to set expectations for today's call," Hunter said. "As a reminder, the goal for today's call is to document every step, from beginning to end, for delivering your core mortgage services to your clients. This call is recorded, so don't worry about having to stop along the way so that I can catch up with my typing. As you both talk, I may ask you questions if I believe there are details or steps missing. You know what you do like the back of your hand and it's not uncommon to inadvertently leave out some steps when describing what you do."

"I was under the impression this wouldn't be terribly detailed, like a regular process or procedure would be." Vandana said.

"You're right, Vandana. But as you and Imana describe what you do, if I find that the activities of certain roles that you identified during the Business Parts Analysis are missing, then I will ask you about that. The goal is for us to include the activities of everyone who works in your business to demonstrate your interconnectivity in providing value to your clients. I won't ask *what if* questions; rather, I will capture the Service Delivery process in a way that describes the flow of activities under the ideal scenario. Is that clearer?"

"Yes!" Vandana and Imana replied in unison.

"Awesome! Who wants to start?"

Vandana indicated she would start. "When prospective clients come our way, we must pre-qualify them for a loan before we enter their information into the loan processing algorithm. Then, we…"

"Wait, I need to stop you, Vandana," Hunter interrupted. "You didn't do or say anything wrong, but I want you and Imana to go further upstream into your Service Delivery process."

"What do you mean?" Imana asked.

"We need to start with how these prospective clients find out about your business in the first place. In other words, what sales and business development activities take place and by whom?"

"Oooh…we really will cover everything from A to Z!" Vandana said, as though she had an epiphany. "A lot of that is in Brian's domain. It's part of our strategy execution."

"Yeah Vandana, but we have a general idea of what he does," Imana countered. "I think Hunter just wants us to get as much of our knowledge out of our heads and onto paper so that we can collectively review and determine where information may be missing. Is that right, Hunter?"

"Exactly Imana!"

Now that Vandana and Imana were clearer on where to begin describing their Service Delivery process, they told Hunter that they constantly work to form new, and solidify existing, strategic alliances and partnerships with home builders, CPAs, financial planners, inspectors, appraisers, real estate agents, lenders and real estate attorneys. They have an entire ecosystem of people who can serve as referral sources or gate openers for them. This, they reminded Hunter, was how the opportunity to work on the reality television show came about.

Hunter probed more about the methods used to stay in contact with the members of their referral ecosystem, but knew that conversation should be reserved for the more detailed processes they would later capture. For now, he wanted to gather just enough information to show the flow of key activities from one person to another within their business. From his earlier work with Vandana, Imana and Brian, he knew how paper-intensive real estate transactions are.

Therefore, he took care to note any reference mentioned to a particular form, template, software or checklist as Vandana and Imana took turns in describing their Service Delivery process. With Hunter's guidance, they described the process from the moment prospective borrowers are referred to them all the way to when borrowers become approved for a loan and close on their homes. They discussed post-closing activities, too.

Two hours later, Vandana and Imana reported finishing their description of their Service Delivery process. Hunter told them he documented a total of 65 steps, but that he wanted to compare this information against the activities and roles previously cited during their Business Parts Analysis and Business Design Blueprint exercises. He wanted to make sure that all roles were accounted for in their description of the workflow.

"As soon as I complete my comparison, I will email a draft to all of you. It will likely include additional questions. Those will be marked in red font. I know it can be difficult to get all of you together at one time, but it's imperative that you all discuss it among yourselves before we meet for the second session.

"We can conduct the second session in person at your home office. I want to do a full walkthrough of the process as you've described it." Hunter ended the call by asking that Vandana let him know a day when they would not be filming and all of the partners could get together and go through this exercise. He asked that she reserve two half days as soon as possible for the second and third sessions so as to not lose any momentum.

Later that night, Vandana sent Hunter a text message indicating that all three of them would be able to meet with him on the upcoming Saturday and Sunday.

\*\*\*\*

As planned, Hunter flew into LaGuardia Airport and took a cab into the city on a late Friday afternoon. He took advantage of some points he had accrued from a hotel chain to book a room for the entire weekend, free of charge, in iconic Times Square. Though it was freezing cold, he opted to walk a few blocks instead of staying cooped inside his hotel room. He was always energized by the flashing lights and the hustle and bustle of the city known for never sleeping.

By 9:00 am Saturday, he found himself ringing the doorbell at the brownstone that Brian, Vandana and Imana called home as well as their place of business. Working on weekends was not ideal for Hunter but, considering the severity of their issue, he knew it was the only time they could work together as a team. Brian greeted Hunter at the door and, after a few minutes of small talk, led him up the intricately carved wooden staircase to the second floor.

Their conference room was a former bedroom and just as Hunter remembered from the last time he was there — a soothing blend and balance of traditional architecture with contemporary furnishings. Three of the walls had exposed brick while the fourth was a plastered wall painted in a bright turquoise that commanded attention. The walls were a nice accent against the pine hardwood floors and the high ceiling was complemented by some of the most ornate crown molding Hunter had ever seen. *This should be the location where they film!* But he knew that, between the value they placed on their privacy and the hassle in getting a zoning permit to allow filming, it would never be.

Vandana and Imana were already seated at the table in the conference room.

"Good morning!" Hunter greeted them.

"Hey, Hunter! How are you?" Imana asked cheerfully.

"Hunter! You're back! We haven't managed to scare you off yet?" Vandana joked.

"Nope. I'm still here. Are you all ready?"

"Yeah man, let's do this!" Brian said as he pulled out a chair for Hunter to sit at the table. "What do you want to do first?"

Hunter was a bit shocked, not by Brian's enthusiasm, but by his informality. Something was different.

"Were you able to answer the questions I provided in the Service Delivery process draft I emailed? Did it make sense? I know you all were very busy earlier this week but I hope you had a chance to review it."

"We most certainly did!" Vandana proclaimed. She then handed Hunter a printed copy of the document that included answers to all of his questions. Immediately, he noticed that the number of steps he originally captured had gone from 65 to 86. In answering his questions, they added 21 new steps.

"Wow! Look at this! This is awesome! Great job!" Hunter encouraged them. "What I'd like to do now is use this printed version and literally walk through every step, to the best extent possible. I want you to show me any and all tools used. I'll capture that information and verify who performs which steps in the process. Before we start, Vandana, I have a quick favor to ask. Can you email this version of the document to me?"

"Aye, aye captain! Already on top of it! It should be in your inbox now."

Hunter checked his email on his laptop. Sure enough, while he was en route to their home office, Vandana emailed the latest version of the Service Delivery process to him. Hunter opened the business infrastructure software installed on his laptop and imported Vandana's version of the document into the software.

Then he went about the business of fact checking the Service Delivery process, as documented. This involved making sure the flow of the information was correct and did not exclude any important steps. Hunter used the business infrastructure software to record the name of the role performing the step into the far left margin, as well as the name of any tool used into the far right margin. Tools included forms, templates, checklists, software, mobile apps and physical devices used to execute the steps.

As Hunter predicted, this exercise took about four hours. Some steps were added while others were either deleted or combined, allowing for the total steps to remain at 86. Hunter explained that, during their half-day session tomorrow, they would work to segment the steps into stages.

"The purpose for segmenting the steps is two-fold. One, these are the stages that can be used to communicate your service delivery process externally to your customers without revealing your proprietary information. Two, these stages will be used to populate a Service Delivery Matrix which will serve as an internal document to share with your staff. This will be especially critical since the bulk of your staff works remotely."

"Oh no! A *matrix* Hunter? You're going to create a Matrix? I told you, I'm trying to get out of the Matrix!" Vandana said in a joking way, though everyone in the room knew she was partially serious.

"My apologies, Vandana. We can call it whatever you like. Let me show you what it will look like."

They all gathered around Hunter and his laptop. On the screen was what appeared to be a blank grid with columns for each stage to be identified in the first row and four rows with which to populate information for each column.

Hunter explained, "The **first row** will showcase the **stages** we will identify tomorrow. The **second row** will display the **staff** needed to execute the steps assigned to each stage. The **third row** lists the **tools** needed to perform the steps assigned to each stage. The **fourth row** summarizes the steps involved in each stage of the overall Service Delivery Process. And finally, the **last row** is for **metrics** to monitor in each stage. You will be able to share this document with each new person you hire. You will also be able to figure out at what point you start the clock in determining how long it takes you to close a loan."

| OPERATIONS DEPARTMENT | | | |
|---|---|---|---|
| | STAGE 1 | STAGE 2 | STAGE 3 |
| **Required Resources** | | | |
| **Tools** | | | |
| **Steps** | 1.<br>2.<br>3. | 4.<br>5.<br>6. | 7.<br>8.<br>9. |
| **Metrics** | | | |

Vandana liked what she was hearing. This was exactly what she'd been waiting for since they began working with Hunter. She, Brian and Imana would finally all be on the same page regarding the order in which things needed to happen so that they could better pinpoint when and where breakdowns occurred in the process. She could see how this format for the process was different from a flowchart or a standard operating procedure. This matrix format provided a high-level, one page summary with just enough detail to ascertain their overall value chain.

Brian escorted Hunter out of the house. As Hunter walked down the steps of the stoop and onto the street, Brian asked that he stop as he walked down the steps toward Hunter.

"Hey man, you wanna grab a drink later tonight?"

Now, Hunter was convinced more than ever that something was wrong. "Sure, just text me a time and place and I'll be there."

\*\*\*\*

As Hunter walked from the subway station toward Brian, Imana and Vandana's brownstone, he reflected on the startling news Brian shared with him over drinks the night before. Brian was denied partnership at the firm. He was disappointed and relieved at the same time. This explained why he seemed more relaxed the day before. He had not yet broken the news to anyone except his father.

Brian would be able now to focus more on their business and he knew that would make Vandana happy. But he shared that he was still having trouble recovering from the sting of rejection.

Hunter knew he had to keep this secret and not let on about Brian's revelation while working with Vandana and Imana today. *Just concentrate on the subject at hand,* he told himself. Carefully, he navigated around the ice on the steps leading to their front door. Brian answered the door and, as if in some type of "guy" code, gave Hunter a look confirming that he had not yet revealed his secret to his wife.

Vandana and Imana were in the kitchen on the main floor of the house and offered Hunter a cup of coffee which he gladly accepted. Several minutes later, they all walked up to the second floor to begin the work for the day — segmenting the 86 steps of their Service Delivery process into stages.

"Hunter," Vandana said, as they all sat down in the conference room, "we talked a little more after you left yesterday about this uh, *matrix.* We decided we should just call it what it is: a blueprint, a Service Delivery Blueprint that provides direction for how to deliver value to our customers and keep our promises to ensure a consistent and positive experience."

"I like that!" Hunter affirmed. "Why don't we get started? First, are there any additional corrections to make to the process steps?"

The co-business owners confirmed there were no corrections to make. Hunter requested Vandana print four copies of the process. When each person had a copy of the process in their hands, Hunter led them through the segmentation of the 86 steps into stages. He explained that, like the segmentation of their business into departments (as they previously did in the Business Parts Analysis), they should not create more than nine stages to assist in simplicity as well as memory recall and retention.

Hunter began to talk through the steps of the Service Delivery process and noted that the first few steps had to do with networking, and building and nurturing relationships with their ecosystem of referral sources. Hunter challenged them to think about where the division occurred from when a potential borrower or client is referred by someone in their ecosystem to the point where they make initial contact with the person referred. This division, Brian told him, occurred around step nine of the process, where the potential borrower's contact information is entered into their database and an email is sent to establish a date and time to conduct a borrowing interview.

**PROSPECTING**

**PRE-QUALIFICATION**

**PRICING**

**LOAN SELECTION**

**LOAN APPROVAL & PROCESSING**

**CLOSING**

**POST-CLOSING**

Hunter asked them to describe those first nine steps as a stage. He suggested they refer to the stage as *Lead Generation* but Brian suggested they call it *Prospecting* instead. Hunter entered the first stage of their Service Delivery process as *Prospecting* in his business infrastructure software. He then specified that this stage included steps one through nine of the process. Those steps then appeared in the second to last row of the SDB.

Then Hunter resumed with step 10 of the process and, similar to how he helped the team figure out the first stage, he helped them identify the second stage as *Pre-Qualification*. They repeated this stage identification exercise until all 87 steps of the process were segmented into seven distinct stages: *Prospecting, Pre-Qualification, Pricing, Loan Selection, Loan Approval & Processing, Closing* and *Post-Closing.*

At this point, the SDB contained a completed first row of stage identification and the second to last row was filled with the steps to complete in each stage. Now they needed to fill in the remaining information, but this would take place during their next session.

Hunter asked if he could set up his portable projector so that he could share what the SDB looked like so far. The only wall with a smooth surface for projection was the plastered turquoise accent wall, but the wall was too dark to project a discernible image. Imana retrieved a white sheet from her living quarters on the third floor and she and Brian pinned it to the plastered wall.

Upon seeing the results so far, they all expressed great pleasure. Hunter told them that he would use his notes from yesterday to populate the rest of the blueprint with information about the tools and resources to assign per stage. Before he left, he pointed out the very last row of the blueprint. It contained information about the metrics to use in monitoring the performance of each stage.

This row, Hunter emphasized, was the most critical to their current issue of not meeting projected loan processing timelines. Assigning metrics would directly assist them in monitoring the performance of each stage of the overall process.

"I want you to start thinking about which stage correlates to the beginning point of your algorithm. Right now, I suspect that the point at which the loan processing timeline begins varies from borrower to borrower. Moving forward, you will have a standardized way to track the time it takes to close a loan. I also want you to think about which stages you want to share with your customers.

"Obviously, you wouldn't share all seven stages but maybe, just maybe, you might share three, four or maybe five of these stages. This is what you can begin communicating in all of your marketing collateral, including your website."

"Whoa! This is what I've been trying to tell you guys for months!" Vandana blurted out. She walked up to the wall and began pointing to the projected SDB. "We need to start the clock here at the Pre-Qualification stage and then stop it at the Closing stage. This means we communicate five out of the seven stages externally to our clients. Hunter, can you leave a copy of this with us? We need more time to talk through the metrics."

"Yes, that's exactly what I was going to suggest. I'll export this into a spreadsheet format and email it to all of you. But first, if it's okay, I'd like to populate the blueprint with the tools and required resources information. It won't take me long, I promise."

Vandana looked at him with suspicion. Hunter knew how important this was to her in particular. "I have an idea. I've been here two and a half hours now. If it's okay with you guys, I can work here until I get the rest of the blueprint populated."

"That's fine with me," Brian said.

"Yeah, me too!" Imana agreed. "The sooner we can get this info, the better!"

Vandana walked back toward the table, "You already know my answer," she said with a big grin on her face.

Hunter spent another two hours meticulously populating the SDB with the required resources and tools for each identified stage. He then projected a more complete blueprint onto the wall again.

Each column of the blueprint contained the name of the stage, followed by labeled stick figures representing the roles of people performing the steps of that stage. Further down the column was a listing of each tool needed to perform the steps of that stage preceded by a checkbox. Tools,

Hunter taught them, also included their cell phones, tablets and laptops since much of their work was done remotely in order to increase their responsiveness. The next row of the column included the steps they previously segmented per stage.

The last row was blank. It was reserved for the applicable metrics to assign to each stage. Vandana wanted to spend the remainder of the week thinking through these metrics as well as the five stages that would be used to calculate their expedient loan processing time to the general public.

| OPERATIONS DEPARTMENT | | |
|---|---|---|
| 1<br>PROSPECTING<br>STAGE | 2<br>PRE-<br>QUALIFICATION<br>STAGE | 3<br>PRICING<br>STAGE |
| **Required Resources**<br>• CEO<br>• CMO<br>• Sales Agent<br>• Sr. Mortgage Consultant | • Recruiter<br>• Admin Manager<br>• Tech Consultant | • Admin Manager<br>• Sector Manager<br>• Bookkeeper |
| **Tools**<br>☐ Customer Relationship Management System<br>☐ Email Template<br>☐ Tablet<br>☐ Smart Phone | ☐ Pre-qualification Questionnaire<br>☐ Authorization to Pull Credit Form<br>☐ FAQs<br>☐ Website<br>☐ Cloud Storage | ☐ Pricing Model<br>☐ Uniform Loan Application<br>☐ Request for Credit Report Form<br>☐ Website |
| **Steps**<br>1. Attend events.<br>2. Add Leads to CRM system.<br>3. Follow up on Leads. | 4. Perform preliminary interview with potential Borrower. | 5. Calculate Debt to Income ratio.<br>6. Select a Lender.<br>7. Pull credit report. |
| **Metrics** | | |

Before leaving their office, Hunter confirmed that Brian, Vandana and Imana each received a copy of the latest draft of the SDB in their respective inboxes. They could see that it was too much information to print onto a standard 8.5" x 11" sheet of paper, so Brian said he would walk a couple of blocks to a print shop to get the blueprint printed onto a larger sheet of paper.

****

When Brian returned, he had a laminated, posterboard-sized version of their Blueprint. He told Vandana and Imana that the three of them could write on this with dry erase markers so that they could wipe off markings easily if they needed to make corrections. They spent the next several hours poring over the contents of the SDB.

Later that Sunday evening, while waiting at LaGuardia Airport for his flight home to Toronto, Hunter received a phone call from Brian who thanked him for keeping his secret. Hunter told Brian he felt strongly that Vandana would be in full support, but Brian still asked that he keep the secret until further notice.

****

It was getting close to midnight and they all decided it was time to stop reviewing the SDB and go to bed. Vandana and Imana had to be on set early the next morning. To their surprise, Brian mentioned he would be there too. He was taking the day off.

*Hmm,* Vandana thought, *that's strange.* However she was happy to see that her husband and her best friend would both be there to help share the workload.

****

Later that week, Brian called Hunter to confirm a date and time to meet for their final session. He emailed Hunter a copy of the updates they made to the SDB, which included a completed row of information for metrics. They agreed to talk on Sunday via a remote session where Hunter could share his computer screen.

During their remote session, Vandana could hardly contain her excitement. As a statistician, talking about metrics was like music to her ears. She attempted to start explaining the row of metrics in their SDB before Hunter could share his computer's screen with everyone participating in the session.

"Give me a second, Vandana," he said, trying hard not to chuckle. It was the first time he'd heard Vandana sound this enthused in the three months he had worked with her. Once everyone confirmed that they could see Hunter's screen, Brian actually took the liberty to begin explaining the metric for the first stage. He argued that the Prospecting stage of their Service Delivery process was too subjective and people-dependent to be able to assign a hard number to consistently achieve for prospect-to-customer conversion.

However, he did say that what they could monitor and control was the number of times they communicated (touch points) with a referred prospect. They landed on a metric of three touch points, at a minimum, with each referred prospect per month. This would be tracked using their customer relationship management (CRM) software. The touch points included emails, newsletters, text messages, phone calls and direct messages via social media.

| | 1 PRO-SPECTING STAGE | 2 PRE-QUAL-IFICATION STAGE | 3 PRI-CING STAGE | 4 LOAN SELEC-TION STAGE | 5 LOAN APPROVAL & PROCESSING STAGE | 6 CLO-SING STAGE | 7 POST-CLO-SING STAGE |
|---|---|---|---|---|---|---|---|
| Metrics | 3 minimum touch points/ month | ←---------------------33 days---------------------→ | | | | | 5 star feed-back rating |

It was now time for Vandana to shine. She told Hunter that, although they have a seven-stage process for delivering their home loan services to their clients, they would only communicate a five-stage process to those clients. In other words, only stages two through six would be shared externally on their website. These are the stages where they would track the total time to pre-qualify, price, select, process and close a loan.

"We've decided to start tracking each of these five stages based on a series of attributes I've identified," Vandana explained. "This will allow us to segment the overall metric of 33 days to determine at what point we lose the inability to meet it. Right now, we just know whether we miss, meet or exceed the loan processing timeline communicated. We have no appreciation for where breakdowns occur in these stages.

"We've also determined the exact points at which we will begin tracking the timeline and have communicated that to all of our part-time employees. Once we've collected at least a month of data, I can start conducting a Six Sigma[22] analysis. Since Six Sigma is about eliminating errors, I consider anytime that we go over our 33-day processing timeline to be an *error*. Conducting this analysis will allow me to determine root causes for bottlenecks and imperfections and enable us to tweak our Service Delivery process until we reach a point where our algorithm correctly predicts a processing timeline 99.997% of the time."

"Vandana, I'm *very* impressed! You're clearly much more versed on process improvement than I am. I can tell you all put a lot of thought into this and I'm so proud!" Hunter expressed sincerely.

"That's why I married her!" Brian chimed in.

Everyone laughed. Imana then went on to explain the metric for the last stage, Post-Closing. "We're going to implement a client feedback survey. What's crazy is that this is something we used to give all the time in our first year in business. It became more sporadic by our second year and last year it was practically non-existent once we got involved with the show. We started taking our clients for granted. I strongly believe that if we had continued issuing and collecting feedback surveys, we could have gotten ahead of the recent rash of complaints. I'll be the first to take the blame for this. With my travel schedule, I became lax on some of these small, but critical details that make for an overall great client experience.

"So we've decided that, starting tomorrow, we'll begin tracking this metric. Anything less than a five-star overall rating will be considered an *error* and warrant immediate investigation. We also want to track how long it takes for us to follow up with clients once they've closed on their homes. This is something we have never tracked before, but need to; it helps close the communication loop and it helps us remain 'top of mind' for our customers who, by the way, can refer their friends and colleagues to us in the future."

"Well," Hunter let out a deep sigh. "This is a first for me. You all have left me speechless. Again, I'm impressed with all of the hard work and effort you've put into this."

"It's amazing what a little bad press can do for you, huh?" Imana asked.

"No kidding! Well guys, I look forward to speaking with you again in another month when you've collected data and tested your SDB. Until then, I want you to strongly consider signing up for a process workshop that will take place in Atlanta, Georgia, in April. At this point, I don't think I need to make a case for the importance of documenting processes."

"Not at all! We totally get it. We understand the value of processes," Brian assured Hunter. "Developing this blueprint alone has helped me gain a much better understanding of why not only Vandana and Imana, but also our customers, were so frustrated."

Hunter determined a date in March when they could meet again. By the time the remote session ended, Vandana had already signed them up for the process workshop in Atlanta.

**The Result**
A month later, in mid-March 2015, Hunter opened a conference call line with Brian, Vandana and Imana. In just 30 minutes, he learned of their many accomplishments in the past month. They finished taping episodes for the second season of their show; it was currently undergoing editing and would air in the summer. They were all equally committed to nailing down the right Service Delivery process before the show aired.

Starting with their website, Brian reported their realization that they needed to work with a web developer who had a technical background, as opposed to just graphic design. Their new web developer created a sophisticated back-end solution for their website to house all of their mortgage-related forms, templates and checklists. This web developer was currently in the process of implementing a tracking feature for their SDB where customers could login securely to determine the stage they were in, as well as where they were in the overall processing timeline.

Vandana reported an eye-opening journey in collecting data on their loan processing timeline. She had since made some changes to the algorithm. Hunter asked her if she secured any type of intellectual property protection for the algorithm. He told her that she should document the refined algorithm thoroughly and submit it for trade secret protection. A patent, he told her, would expire and allow competition to use the algorithm eventually, whereas a trade secret never expires and is valid as long as the secret is never revealed. Vandana also reported the discovery of areas where they could automate their process even more to streamline their operation and improve the overall customer experience.

Lastly, Imana announced she found an affordable commercial office suite to house all three of them as well as two additional offices and a conference room. She and Brian would sign the lease soon. She also found a new receptionist who would start working for them as soon as they settled into their new suite.

Once the phone lines were installed, every incoming call the receptionist received would be recorded to allow them to track the consistency in responses to frequently asked questions and fine-tune the scripts they provide to the receptionist.

Hunter told Imana that she might be able to use the processes they document as a result of the workshop next month as the basis for these scripts. "In fact," Hunter told her, "you all will learn how to identify and document processes and store them in an operations manual that you can use as a training tool for all of your existing and future employees."

Imana also mentioned that she would meet with their payroll company to determine the optimal and most cost-effective way to begin converting part-time employees into full-time employees.

"I love everything you all have done and are in the process of implementing!" Hunter told them. "Keep up the great work. Just remember that, as you start to digitize more of the tools, we'll need to develop an Electronic Records Management system. We can also leverage your SDB to develop a Work Space Logistics plan to maximize workflow in your new office suite. I'll develop a timeline for these elements of the Kasennu methodology after you attend the process workshop next month. But for now, let's focus on one thing at a time. Keep collecting data and fine-tuning your SDB. Do you have any questions for me at this time?"

"Yeah, I do," Vandana answered. "Red pill or blue pill?"

"Ha! I should be asking you that!"

"Well, it turns out you were right. I don't need to take either. I can choose *not* to choose and just *be*. In other words, by changing my perception I can change my reality altogether."

"Yep. I know how much you like Shakespeare. Didn't he say, 'To *be* or not to *be*, that is the question?'"[23]

Vandana belted out a loud laugh. She had not made that connection, but Hunter was right. "Yes! And that's the question I really should have been asking all along."

They ended their call with Hunter. But Vandana wasn't the only one who had a revelation. Listening to the exchange between Vandana and Hunter gave Brian no choice but to make his secret known. He asked that Vandana and Imana join him in the kitchen.

"Please sit down," Brian said nervously. "There's something I need to tell you."

# CHAPTER 7

## VENI, VIDI, VICI

**Kasennu™**
Work Space Logistics™

Clenard Smith II is the owner-operator of a wildly successful food distribution company. He attributes much of his success to the lessons he learned during his tenure in the military and to his first business, which failed. He prides himself on having a strategy for conquering whatever he sets out to achieve and has no problem following rules, especially if they benefit him in the long term. Clenard desperately wants to take his company public but feels he lacks the physical space to do so. The reality is he must address something personal, and his refusal to do so comes as a shock to both his family and his staff. One employee, seeing the self-destruction that is ensuing, arranges for a consultant to help. This consultant applies the Work Space Logistics element of the Kasennu methodology as a means to help him win his latest battle.

Driving from Chicago, Delores Tran knew she chanced traffic being horrendous. Intentionally, she chose to cross the state line from Illinois to Indiana via Interstate-94 East, but she wanted to bypass the most direct route into Gary. This, she correctly figured, would spare her of what seemed to be a never-ending construction zone. Instead, her selected route had her drive through Merrillville via US Highway-30 East. She would cut through Merrillville to reach Gary, Indiana, a city with a steadily declining population that was once touted as one of America's steel capitals. Delores could only hope she would arrive on time. She hated being late.

Her navigation phone app announced when she reached her final destination. She turned off a busy street and followed the well-marked signs for visitor parking. Delores parked her car at 10:00 am on the dot. *Whew! That was close*, she thought. Before her was a building that stretched an entire block. The second floor was noticeably smaller than the first floor. Grabbing her tablet, she walked briskly toward the building's front doors and placed her finger on the buzzer next to the right door to announce herself.

"Hello. My name is Delores Tran and I have a ten o'clock appointment with Jackie Adams." Although Delores said she was there to see Jackie, she was actually there to conduct an initial consultation with Clenard Smith II, the owner of this establishment.

All of a sudden, she heard the door unlock and she pushed her way in. Once inside, she signed in at the receptionist's desk and fastened her visitor's badge to her jacket's lapel. *Hmm, this is pretty official for a small business.*

The receptionist offered Delores a seat and a cup of water. She accepted the water just as Jackie Adams appeared. From the distressed look on her face, Delores could tell Jackie had probably had a rough morning already.

"Good morning!" Jackie managed to say cheerfully. "Hey, Delores, how are you? Clenard wants to speak with you before I show you around." *That didn't sound good*, Delores thought, but she could not wait to meet the self-made man behind this business.

They took the stairs to the second floor and did not walk far before reaching Clenard's assistant's office (which served as the entry point to Clenard's office). The door was open. There he was, Clenard Smith, all 6'2" of this 61-year-old military veteran whose reputation preceded him. At the sight of the two women, Clenard rose from the chair behind his desk, almost as if standing at attention to a commanding officer; the only thing missing was the hand salute. Before Jackie or Delores could utter a word, Clenard motioned for them to step inside his office. "You must be Delores," he said, as he extended his hand to shake Delores' hand. He noticed she wasn't wearing a watch. "You're late."

Jackie had warned Delores of Clenard's sternness, but she was still stunned. *Is this really going to be my first impression of him?* In her defense, Delores replied, "Despite my best efforts, I walked into the building five minutes late. You know how that commute can be from Chicago to Gary." She hoped this would help relieve the situation, but the tension in the air was undeniable.

Clenard could tell Delores was about 5'2" and, based on her last name and overall appearance, probably had Vietnamese heritage. He learned over the years how intimidating his taller frame and darker skin could be so he softened his voice and offered a seat to Delores. He looked at Jackie, "Give us about 30 minutes to talk. Then you can come back and give her a tour." Jackie agreed and closed the door to his office on her way out.

When Delores sat on the soft leather chair in front of Clenard's desk, she realized that, in getting over her shock of their initial encounter, she completely overlooked the sheer beauty of his office. It reminded her of a museum. There were solid cherry wood bookcases with glass enclosures lining the two sidewalls of his office. On top of each bookcase was recessed lighting that illuminated figurines and framed quotes above the lighting.

Each figurine stood on a wooden base with his or her name engraved on a gold plaque. They were carefully lined along the bookshelf as if guarding the inhabitants of the office. Delores recognized the names of some of the figurines as a collection of military strategists, scholars, philosophers and historians: Montezuma, Hannibal, Sitting Bull, Niccolò Machiavelli, Genghis Khan, Kandake Amanirenas, Confucious, Yaa Asantewa, Kamehameha I and Herodotus were just some of the figurines.

As she continued to look around, she was surprised by one of the figurines; it was a representation she was not used to seeing of this person.

"Tupac Amaru? Wasn't he a rapper?" she asked aloud.

"Ha! You're thinking about Tupac Amaru *Shakur*. I only know of him because of my sons. No, that right there is Tupac Amaru II, the last Incan ruler."

"Hmm, I guess it's true what they say — you're never too old to learn something new."

"How old are you?" Clenard inquired. "If you don't mind me asking."

"I'm 66."

"Ah, you got me by five years. I'm 61."

Delores risked getting a crook in her neck. She was still looking up and around, still trying to take in all of the artifacts in Clenard's office. She was bewildered as to why he would keep such an extensive and pricey collection here in his office as opposed to his home.

"Do you like what you see?" Clenard asked.

"I'm sorry, I couldn't help but…"

"No need to apologize," he assured her.

Realizing she was wasting valuable time, Delores returned her attention to Clenard who sat across the desk from her. As she turned in her chair to face him, she noticed the quote "Veni, Vidi, Vici" carved into the center of the front panel of his desk.

"I came, I saw, I conquered," she said aloud, giving the English translation of the Latin phrase.

"Do you know about 90% of the people who come into my office for the first time have no idea what this means? You've ruined my icebreaker!" Clenard belted a hearty laugh. Delores remembered Jackie telling her about his sense of humor.

"I hear you and Jackie met at a Chamber of Commerce meeting a few months ago."

"Yes, that's right. I was a panelist at an event centered around regulatory compliance in small businesses. Jackie introduced herself to me once the event was over. We've talked a few times on the phone since then. She told me that you have a big audit coming up a year from now."

"Um hmm," Clenard responded. "So, Delores, tell me a little more about yourself."

"Sure. I'm originally from Vietnam. I came to America with my parents and both sets of grandparents when I was a little girl. Growing up, I was teased a lot about my culture. You know how cruel children can be. I never had sleepovers like a lot of other kids. Their parents would tell them that my family was probably 'unsanitary.' I remember the first time I heard that word, *unsanitary*. I didn't know what it meant. When I looked it up in the dictionary, I cried.

"It was a defining moment in my life. By the time I was in high school, I knew I wanted a career in public health. It was my way of combating the ignorance so prevalent about my family and the Asian-American community at large. I went to college and obtained a degree in Nutrition and Dietetics. I later worked as a sanitarian (or public health inspector) for 35 years.

"I retired almost two years ago but still wanted to be active in the public health space so I decided to start my own consulting firm helping small businesses in the food and beverage industry become compliant and audit-ready. When I joined the Chamber, I met another small business owner who told me about the Kasennu methodology for business infrastructure. I saw this as a tool I could use to help my clients, especially when they start growing quickly. That's usually when their problems started. And..."

There was a knock on the door.

Delores asked, "Is it 10:30 already?"

"Yep, that's what it looks like," Clenard replied. "You'd know that if you wore a watch." He smiled sarcastically at Delores.

**The Fast Growth Predicament**
Jackie opened the door to Clenard's office. The time seemed to fly by and Clenard asked for a few more minutes to speak with Delores as he found

her story to be fascinating. Jackie knew this was a good sign since he purposely asks Jada, his assistant, to never schedule appointments longer than 30 minutes if he is meeting with someone for the first time.

Jackie smiled, left the office and walked back into Jada's office. She asked Jada to reschedule his other call at 11:00 am but she objected, informing Jackie that it took a long time to get this particular call scheduled and that Clenard should not reschedule unless absolutely necessary.

Jackie went back into Clenard's office to relay Jada's message.

"Fine. You see this Delores? I have all of these women telling me what to do!" He belted another hearty laugh. "Let me at least treat ya'll to lunch. Jackie, my next call should be over by noon. That should give you plenty of time to show Delores everything, right?" Jackie nodded in agreement. "Okay, we'll meet back in my office at noon."

Jackie escorted Delores out of Clenard's office and formally introduced her to Jada. A few minutes later, Jackie gently knocked onto the doors of other offices to make more introductions. "As you can see, we don't have cubicles around here. We have glass cages!" Jackie jokingly told Delores. Delores noticed that the wooden doors of the offices on the second floor each had a large, glass panel.

They turned a corner and went down a few steps that led to a closed glass door with the words *BREAK ROOM* etched onto the glass. It was on the mezzanine level of the building and had a long, rectangular shape.

"Welcome to The Watchtower!" Jackie explained that the employees dubbed the break room "The Watchtower" because of the wall encased with a one-way mirror that overlooked the distribution and warehouse areas below on the first floor. Delores walked up to the wall and peered out onto the first floor. *This place is massive!* She couldn't help but think of how the sight of the employees reminded her of Santa Claus' elves busily working in the toy shop as depicted in many Christmas movies.

As Delores continued looking out the glass wall in amazement, Jackie told her, "Downstairs is where the magic happens. This room is like an observation deck. I remember when Clenard bought this building six years ago. Originally, it had small windows, but Clenard worked with a contractor to have them and the wall removed and replaced with this durable, one-way mirror made of bullet-proof glass instead."

"Bullet proof glass?"

"Yep, that's right. Bullet proof, girl. I guess you can say, 'you can take the man out of the military but you can't take the military out of the man.' This is just one example of how extreme Clenard can get. It's also why, I believe, our turnover is so high. Don't get me wrong, he's a good person, he really is. He has a heart of gold but sometimes he can be SO extreme! I'm not sure if it's a symptom of PTSD or what, but his paranoia can definitely get the best of him. God bless Sandy. I don't know how she put up with it all those years."

"Who's Sandy?"

"Cassandra. His wife of 28 years. She passed away about two years ago. Cancer. It was hell on Clenard. To be honest, things haven't been the same since. Come. Let me show you the *real* reason why we need your help." Jackie motioned for Delores to follow her out of The Watchtower and back onto the second floor. They walked toward a set of solid, wooden double-doors, similar to the kind that led to Clenard's office. When Jackie unlocked the door, it creaked from not having been open in a long time or at least not regularly. There was also a slight stench, an odor indicative of a room that was not receiving proper ventilation. Jackie turned on the lights. The room was huge. It spanned across the entire width of the second floor.

Inside the room were stacks and stacks of banker's boxes spread as far and as high as the eye could see. Some of the boxes were labeled and some were not. There were also loose papers strewn about, as well as several filing cabinets, cleaning equipment and office supplies. Delores even saw a treadmill in there!

"Is this the janitorial closet or supply room?" she asked.

"No. This used to be Sandy's office. No one has come into this room since she passed away. I come in here occasionally; usually when we are preparing for an audit or need certain historical files as part of an RFP [Request for Proposal]. Other than that, nobody comes in here. Clenard and I are the only folks with keys to her office."

"What's in all of these boxes and filing cabinets?" Delores asked. She felt a sense of sorrow as she continued looking around. This room was the polar opposite of Clenard's office and ironically, was positioned on the opposite side of the building.

"There's a hodgepodge of stuff in here. A lot of it is Sandy's medical records. Books and articles related to her specialty treatments, basically anything that related to her illness is right here in this room. A few months after she died, he paid some of the warehouse guys to go over to his house, box things up and bring them here. He didn't want any reminder of her poor health inside the house. He only wanted memories of happier times. It was his way of coping. I've tried to broach the subject of cleaning out this room, but it's tough even for me. Me and Sandy were tight. We were good friends."

Carefully, Jackie walked through the aisles of boxed files. She turned back to look at Delores who stood near the room's entrance still somewhat in disbelief. "There are also archived files from when Clenard first started the business 13 years ago. Oh, and before I forget, another reason this room got so out of control is because of the paperwork from some of the boards he sits on, organizations where he is an active member, as well as other business ventures where he has a stake in the company.

"He is now in the mode of switching from owner-operator to owner-investor. As we keep growing, he keeps piling stuff in here. He thinks the solution is avoidance and that we just need to either relocate to a bigger building or get a zoning permit to add on to this building. But I often tell him that whether we relocate or not, whether we go public or not, he's got to clean this room out. He's got to deal with it one way or another. It's all getting so convoluted and disorganized. It's one hot ass mess if you ask me!"

Delores checked her phone. It was 11:55 am. "Jackie, I would ask if I could take measurements of this room, but I don't think it's safe to climb over these boxes. Do you have blueprints of the building?"

"Yeah, they're around here somewhere. As a matter of fact, I know *exactly* where they are."

"Okay, good. By the way, it's 11:55. Should we start walking toward Clenard's office?"

"Yeah, you're right." Jackie made her way to the room's entrance, turned off the lights and locked the door.

As they walked down the hallway, Delores stopped and stood near the door of Jada's office while Jackie went inside and asked that Jada email a copy of the building's blueprints to Delores.

**The Research**

Clenard took Delores and Jackie to a buffet-style restaurant that was in close proximity to the office. As much as Delores really wanted to get back on the road to Chicago, she knew she needed to take advantage of this opportunity to extract as much information as possible from Clenard about the root causes of his company's growing pains.

Once inside the restaurant, they wasted no time filling their plates at the buffet and securing a seat at a table. There was total silence for almost three minutes before Clenard put his fork down onto his plate. "Damn, we all must be hungry as hell! None of us have said two words to each other since we sat down."

Delores laughed so hard she thought her face would catch fire. She presumed now was as good a time as any to resume her research. "So, Clenard, why don't you tell me more about yourself. What motivates you?"

*Oh God*, Jackie thought, *why did she ask that?* She knew the answer would be a long one.

Clenard wiped his mouth with his napkin and placed it back across his lap. "I thought you'd never ask. In order to know what motivates me, you first need to know my background. You know from being in my office that I'm a military man, third generation navy man, as a matter of fact. My father and grandfather both served and, being that a black man didn't have many career options back in my youth, I followed in their footsteps. I can't ever remember a time in my life when I didn't work. When I was 13 or 14 years old, I started working at a local diner. I guess you could say that was my first introduction to the food industry.

"When I was about 17 years old, I started working at one of the local steel mills. Gary was a very different place back then. It could rival any other growing industrial metropolis. The work was good and I saved as much money as I could. My mama used to always tell me, 'waste not, want not.'"

Clenard paused long enough to take a sip of water. "A few years later, I joined the Navy and was called to duty during the tail end of the Vietnam War. Eventually, I was stationed all over the Pacific. I lived in the Polynesian Islands, Hawaii, Guam and the Philippines. Those were some of the best years of my life. I got to see the world! Whenever I had downtime, I traveled. It's like I almost got obsessed with the ancient world. Of all the ruins I've visited, and trust me I've seen a lot of them, there were two that stood out the most. The Angkor Wat complex in Cambodia and the Terracotta Army soldiers in China.

"I studied everything I could find about how these structures and statues were built. The fact that out of thousands of clay soldiers, no two Terracotta Army men look exactly alike blows my mind every time I think about it. They perfected the science of mass production long before the Model T came along. It left a permanent mark on me."

Delores smiled and retrieved a small notepad from her purse.

Jackie assured Delores, "Yes, girl, start taking notes! He's on a roll now!"

Clenard smirked and continued, "Anyway, before Jackie rudely interrupted me…" Jackie chuckled. Delores appreciated that they both felt comfortable enough to be themselves in her presence.

"I was honorably discharged after 12 years. I decided to move back home to Gary and pick up where I left off. But things had changed, it wasn't the same Gary that I knew as a kid. It was a shell of what it used to be. The steel mills closed and so went other businesses. People left in droves trying to find work. They needed to feed their families. I made up my mind right then and there that I was going to do my part to resurrect the city. If it was great once, it could be great again, right? So I dipped into my savings and started a restaurant. By that time, I met and married my wife, Cassandra. The restaurant failed, badly! It was one time when I came and I saw, but I did *not* conquer. And I hate losing!

"Thank God I had a wife who believed in me. I was down but not out. One day, I decided to re-read *The Art of War*, specifically the chapter on self-preservation. Sun Tzu wrote, '…one who knows the enemy and knows himself will not be endangered…One who knows neither the enemy nor himself will invariably be defeated in every engagement. Preservation is preferred over destruction.'[24] I know experts say we shouldn't read this book and apply its principles outside of military strategy, but I disagree. In many ways, business *is* war! Failure became my enemy number one! So I regrouped and got smarter and more strategic about stuff. I realized that, while I had owned and operated *one* restaurant, the suppliers I worked with had several restaurants as customers throughout the Midwest. But I could only serve customers here in Gary.

"It was at that moment I decided I wanted to be a food distributor. But there was one major problem. No bank would touch me. I was broke as a joke. My money was funny, my change was strange and my credit just wasn't gonna get it!"

Delores almost dropped the pen she was using to write in her notepad. *Clenard is hilarious!*

"So my wife talked to her parents and I talked to mine. They each loaned us a few thousand dollars and I started the food distribution company you now know. It wasn't much money, but it was better than nothing. I relied on factoring services to get me through my first few contracts. Of course, there were bumps and bruises along the way. I learned quickly not to have any one customer represent more than 20% of our revenue. That's why I decided to not just service restaurants and schools, but also major food events like the Taste of Chicago. People started taking notice and things really took off once I got the company certified as a Veteran Owned

Business. I knew that, if I could just get one federal contract, the others would soon follow.

"And sure enough that's exactly what happened. The orders came in faster than we could deliver them. I think I finally knew I had 'arrived' when I received an invitation for an American Express Black Card.

"But with the success came more prying eyes. Once we surpassed the $10 million gross revenue mark, we seemed to get onto the radar of every auditing agency you could think of. We're preparing for the latest one, which is why you're here. We're running out of space and we've already caught heat because of it."

"Clenard, thank you for giving me that background information. But you still haven't told me what motivates you." Delores was unsure how he would respond.

"I guess I ran my mouth so much that I forgot your original question," Clenard chuckled. "What motivates me? Well, part of what motivates me is the work that you do — infrastructure. When I told you about my worldly travels, I failed to mention the extreme poverty that I saw in many countries. It's unconscionable. War is ugly. Trust me. I saw too many children starve to death. I vowed that I would make a difference. Aside from war, I used to wonder why so many people went hungry even when there were decent crop seasons. I learned it was oftentimes due to poor infrastructure. Families living in rural areas do not have the infrastructure to get into city centers where food is sold in markets. So they starve.

"That's why I can appreciate your work with business infrastructure. Just like I use road infrastructure to distribute food so children don't go hungry here, you use business infrastructure to distribute systems and processes that keep businesses *in business*. Look, I have five grandchildren now. I want to leave a legacy for them. At the end of the day, wanting to leave a better world for them is what motivates me."

It was almost 2:00 pm. Clenard looked at his watch while Delores looked at her phone. She knew there was no doubt that her commute back home to Chicago would be hellish. However, if she asked for a tour of the first floor of the building, she could save herself from having to make another trip. As they walked out of the restaurant and got into Clenard's SUV, she asked if he or Jackie had time to give her a tour of the first floor.

Clenard offered. "I'll have Jada clear the rest of my schedule this afternoon. I want to make sure you get all the information you need."

****

Clenard knew Delores was concerned about her afternoon commute and assured her that the tour of the first floor would take less than a half hour. Before entering the area, he gave her a pair of thin, cloth booties, gloves and a hairnet. Then, he pushed through a swing door that led to the hustle and bustle of the first floor. Although Delores laid eyes on this scene earlier via The Watchtower, actually being on the floor was a surreal experience.

She walked alongside Clenard on the outer perimeter of the first floor. It was one gigantic open space with large overhead signs to designate the receiving, storage, packaging and loading areas. A heavy set man soon walked toward them.

"Hey! We got a visitor?" he asked Clenard.

"Yes. Alvin, this is Delores Tran. She's going to help us implement business infrastructure to get us ready for the audit next year in preparation for our IPO [Initial Public Offering]. Delores, this is my wingman, Alvin Johnson. Alvin's the general manager and oversees all the floor operations. He's been with me from the beginning. Alvin, I'm giving Delores a tour of this floor. I've already told her that this area doesn't need any logistical attention. We got that down pat."

"Oh yeah," Alvin agreed. "We have a hiccup every now and again, especially when several big orders come through at one time, but for the most part we operate like a well-oiled machine down here."

Clenard resumed his tour with Alvin joining them. Eventually, they reached a set of offices that also had glass doors. One of the offices belonged to Alvin and the other two belonged to the shift supervisors. Alvin asked Delores if she had any questions so far.

"Actually, I do," she replied. "I'm assuming that you all must have meetings. Where do you conduct them?"

Alvin looked over at Clenard. This was definitely a point of contention. "Well, right now we meet upstairs in The Watchtower."

"The Watchtower?" Delores knew this was not an ideal location. The Watchtower was clearly a break room intended for people to eat and, well, take breaks. It was *not* a place to conduct meetings, yet alone training. This explained why she saw two copiers and a steel bookcase with manuals on it when she was up there earlier with Jackie.

"We just don't have the space," Clenard chimed in as if to justify the rationale for meeting there.

Delores already knew that was false. She asked Alvin, "How often do you have meetings? How often do you train?"

"We have daily production meetings at the beginning of each shift," Alvin replied. "Those usually take place here on the floor. But we do have weekly and monthly staff meetings in The Watchtower. And we train fairly regularly too. We can never be too anal about cleanliness and safety training. Space becomes an issue when the folks on the second floor also need to have meetings. There are times when they can't fit everybody into their respective offices. We're competing for real estate and it's getting worse by the day."

The three of them continued walking around the perimeter of the first floor until they made a complete revolution. Alvin suggested that they go outside to take a look at their fleet of 18-wheelers, but Clenard and Delores both agreed it was unnecessary. Alvin bid Clenard and Delores farewell and Clenard escorted her back into the reception area of the building.

"Delores, I know you've seen and heard a lot today. I hope we didn't overwhelm you. Let me know if you have any more questions."

"Thank you Clenard. I appreciate your hospitality. You have quite the operation here. You should be very proud! As a next step, I'm going to review my notes as well as the blueprints Jada will email to me. From there, I'll prepare a proposal that will include a timeline for our work together. Again, thank you so much for your time today."

****

By the time Delores returned to her home office, she realized she missed a call from Jackie. She listened to the voicemail message Jackie left, "Hi Delores, this is Jackie Adams. I just wanted to thank you for stopping by today and giving us an initial consultation. I can tell Clenard likes you. He doesn't usually warm up to people so quickly. I'm sure you noticed that he didn't mention much about his personal life during lunch. More will be revealed as we work together. Have a great evening!"

**The Hypothesis**
Two weeks later, Delores emailed a proposal to Clenard and Jackie for their review. It arrived soon after Clenard logged into his computer at his office one morning. He began to read the proposal while sitting at his desk.

> The actual layout of a work space directly affects productivity, job satisfaction and profitability. If a picture is worth a thousand words, then your work space's aesthetics and functionality are worth a million. Because people are so visual, having the "right" setup for a productive work environment is vital to: 1) communicating your company's competency, 2) ensuring you continue attracting the right customers, vendors and employees and 3) creating an environment conducive for an initial public offering.

> By carefully planning and re-organizing the second floor offices, you can:
>
> - Create clutter-free offices and work stations that maximize floor space and encourage productivity;
> - Consolidate or create work zones based on how first floor and second floor employees interact with each other for more effective information exchange;
> - Use intelligent workspace design to match the perceptions of

your company's image to existing as well as future staff;

- Bide time in purchasing a bigger building until you're absolute-ly ready;
- Set aside work areas to accommodate future staff;
- Pass OSHA, ADA[25] and other legally required building inspec-tions and audits; and
- Create a comfortable, but finely-tuned environment through-out the second floor that complements the work style and company culture of the first floor.

The long term goal is to pass the August 2015 audit. However, the more immediate goal is to secure additional space. This aligns with the Work Space Logistics element of the Kasennu methodology for business in-frastructure. However, in order to implement this, we will need to im-plement other elements of the methodology first. This is because the optimal Work Space Logistics plan for the second floor will consider the proper placement of:

- All employees (according to your Business Parts Analysis, Business Design Blueprint and Service Delivery Blueprint),
- All furniture (according to your Paper Records Management system), and
- All equipment (according to your Electronic Records Man-agement system) to ensure seamless information/work flow.

This work can be completed as follows:

- Aug. 2014: Business Parts Analysis
- Sept. 2014: Business Design Blueprint
- Oct. 2014: Service Delivery Blueprint
- Jan. 2015: Paper and Electronic Records Management
- Feb. 2015: Work Space Logistics
- Apr. 2015: Business Process Manual

We will talk in more detail about the Business Process Manual at the conclusion of the Work Space Logistics element since it involves attend-ing a workshop. The entire methodology, with the exception of the Business Process Manual can be implemented prior to the audit sched-uled for August 2015.

After reading the proposal in its entirety, Clenard reached across his desk to pick up the phone. He dialed Jackie's extension. "Hey, have you had a chance to read Delores' proposal?"

"I started reading it, but then had to attend to a customer order," Jack-ie replied. "I'll let you know when I've read it completely."

"Okay," Clenard said. He hung up the phone and then walked into Jada's office. "I need you to call Delores Tran and ask if she can come in one day next week so we can discuss her proposal."

****

Delores arrived via train on her next trip to Gary. This not only saved her the headache of fighting through traffic but also allowed her to jot down last minute notes regarding things she wanted to talk about at her proposal review meeting with Clenard and Jackie. This time, she buzzed into the building 15 minutes early and waited in the lobby until Jackie came to meet her.

"Delores! How are you this morning?" Jackie seemed more alert and upbeat compared to the first time Delores visited.

As they walked toward Clenard's office, Delores told Jackie, "I heard the voice mail message you left for me. I'm going to bring it up as delicately as I possibly can. I was careful to not state anything too personal in the actual proposal. Thank you for the heads up."

"Oh, no problem," Jackie responded. "Clenard knows we need to do this work with you. He has some questions. I'm sure he'll try to challenge you. That's just his way of doing things. He needs to know that you stand by whatever you propose to him."

When she walked into his office, Clenard was genuinely happy to see Delores. "Well, look who decided to come back! I guess we didn't scare you off after all!"

Delores smiled, "No, not at all. You did not scare me. I can handle you! I do have one request though. Can we meet in an office with a white board that I can write on?"

"Sure! We can talk in The Watchtower," he offered. Delores hesitated, but realized this could actually be a good thing. She only spent a few minutes in The Watchtower during her first visit. Being there for an extended period of time should validate her proposed sequencing of work.

When they arrived at The Watchtower, there were already several people in there. Jada was standing at one of the two copiers, someone was sitting at one of the smaller roundtables eating a snack and Alvin, the general manager, appeared to be reviewing some paperwork with about five of the warehouse employees.

*Um hmm, just as I suspected*, Delores thought. *This Watchtower is detrimental to productivity.*

"How much longer you got, Alvin?" Clenard asked.

"Uh, can you give me about five more minutes?" Alvin responded.

Jackie offered her office as a place to meet. "I have a white board in my office. I'm not sure how comfortable we'll be in there, but it's worth a try. The Watchtower is the better option since it has a large table, but we

198 | BEHIND THE FAÇADE

shouldn't interrupt Alvin's training. Hey Clenard, why don't we go to my office?"

Clenard agreed as he didn't want Alvin to cut his meeting short for their sake. Once inside Jackie's office, she offered Delores her desk and chair so that she would have room to spread out her papers.

Clenard started the conversation. "Conceptually, I don't have a problem with your proposal, but I am concerned about the timeline as well as one of the elements of the methodology."

"Okay, which concern would you like me to address first?"

"The Service Delivery Blueprint. We don't need that particular element of the methodology. We already have that in place. Unless our first floor operation didn't impress you."

"Oh, it's certainly not that! The first floor operation does seem to, like Alvin said, 'work like a well-oiled machine.' It was very clear to me that you've put a lot of time, effort and energy into getting the core operations just right. But that's just it, you've *concentrated* all of the effort and attention here and, for lack of a better word, *diluted* the second floor, the more administrative operations. The Watchtower, for example, is causing more harm than good. It functions as a catch-all space and is very unsanitary, when you think about it."

Clenard looked straight into Delores' eyes as if to intimidate her but she did not flinch. "Each day you use that room for eating, administrative purposes, training, etc., is a day that you are one step closer to getting those worker's compensation claims you had before on the first floor. That room should serve one purpose and one purpose only — as a true break or lounge room! It's simply not big enough to accommodate the multi-purpose functionality it currently has. That may have worked when you first moved into this location, but the business is growing and, if you continue diversifying your customer portfolio, you'll get even more business which means more employees, which means they will need adequate space.

"I want you to think about this...*if your company went public next month, would you have the space and logistics on the second floor to handle it?* It's like needing a bigger pair of shoes. What happens when your feet outgrow your favorite shoes? Do you still hold onto those shoes and try to force your feet into them? No! Why? Because you know you'll cause more harm to yourself than good by trying to walk in a pair of shoes that are too small for you. It's not worth stunting your growth, so you get a bigger pair."

"Delores, I'm fully aware that we need more space," Clenard interjected. "I've been saying this for a while now."

"Yes," Delores agreed, "but your solution is to relocate altogether. You already have the space here. There's a large room at the end of the hall that could easily serve as a new conference room and possibly more. I know this is difficult to hear, but its time Mrs. Smith's old office is cleared out.

It's valuable space that is under-utilized. You've focused so much on your professional life that your personal life has suffered. Your employees are feeling the brunt of this. You need balance."

Jackie looked over at Clenard. His face was completely stoic. He showed no outward sign of emotion.

Delores kept talking, "Clenard, I'm sure you're familiar with the law of polarity. Being that you lived in the Pacific for many years, you've probably lost count of the number of times you've seen the yin-yang symbol. You've devoted most of your efforts on the first floor. It represents the company's logic. But you've placed less emphasis on the administrative support on the second floor, which represents your company's emotions. Until the logic, the yang, and the emotion, the yin, are balanced, you, as well as your employees, will feel the pain of those shoes you've outgrown. Turnover used to be an issue among the first floor employees, but it's only a matter of time before it spreads to the second floor."

Clenard broke his silence. "About this timeline, will it really take a year?"

Delores was somewhat stunned that he did not acknowledge her soliloquy. She sensed she struck a nerve and that she had better answer his question instead of forcing this issue of imbalance.

"Yes, it will take about a year. If we could focus exclusively on the work I've proposed, then the timing could be cut in half, but the reality is that you all are already very busy. That's why the timeline is based on working no more than 20 hours a week. Do you have any questions about the actual Work Space Logistics solution?"

Clenard shook his head, "No."

"I want to show you something."

Delores stood up and walked over to the white board in Jackie's office. "I'd like to sketch conceptually what I mean about the work flow being chaotic up here on the second floor." As Delores grabbed a dry erase marker, Clenard also stood up. He now had wrinkles in his starched pants and buttoned up shirt. His 6'2" frame towered over Delores.

"I've seen enough and you've said enough. No need to sketch anything. You've answered the main questions I had. Good seeing you again." Clenard abruptly walked out of Jackie's office.

Jackie closed the door, and in a low voice told Delores, "You've struck a nerve! But don't worry. He knows it's what he needs to hear, even if he doesn't like it. Trust me, he's going to sign your proposal. He just needs time to clear his head. Brace yourself, though. When we do get to the actual Work Space Logistics next year, you might see more of that behavior!"

"Oh my goodness, Jackie! I hope I didn't offend him. I, I should go talk to him."

"No, you don't want to do that! He's fuming and needs time to cool down. He's not mad at you, he's mad at himself. You've reminded him of his Achilles heel — Sandy's office. You know his mantra — *Veni Vidi Vici*. Well, dealing with Sandy's death is one thing he has not conquered yet in his life, even though he told you it was his failed restaurant. I'm glad you brought that up, though. I've tried telling him that we don't need to relocate now. It's money that we can save. Even if we did relocate, all he would do is just have some of the guys load all of that stuff in Sandy's office onto a truck and dump it into a room at the new location.

"I want to introduce you to his sons. I've already talked to most of them about you. They'll probably start coming around when we get to the portion of the work where Sandy's office will be cleaned out. But don't expect to see them around here unless they're dropping off or picking up their kids. They tend to stay as far away from this place as possible. Come, I'd better take you back to the lobby."

Delores was still speechless. Yes, Jackie assured her that everything was okay, but she felt a need to apologize to Clenard. On her train ride back into Chicago, she sent Clenard a text message, *Please accept my sincerest apologies if I offended you. It was not my intention.*

****

Later that afternoon, Clenard left work to pick up one of his grandsons and granddaughter from his oldest son's house. When they arrived at his house, he told them to sit on the sofa in the living room. He went upstairs and returned with a photo album in his hand. "Would ya'll like to see pictures of when me and Grandma got married?"

"Yeah!" his grandchildren yelled in excitement.

### The Experiment
To her surprise, Jada emailed a signed copy of the proposal to Delores the next day. Delores wanted to call Clenard but she could almost hear Jackie's voice warning her not to. Instead, she called Jada and asked if they could begin coordinating dates for the various sessions until the end of 2014. Delores also requested copies of existing job descriptions, their Employee Policy Manual and their organizational chart.

The first session of the Business Parts Analysis took place in mid-August. Delores was concerned they would not have the space needed to conduct the department identification exercise, but Jada actually sent a companywide email indicating that The Watchtower would not be available from 9:00 am to 11:00 am. Two hours was plenty of time for them to complete this portion of the Business Parts Analysis since most of the tasks were already identified in the different job descriptions. The area that required updating was the departments.

By the time the first session ended, they had identified 34 unique roles throughout the company, five more than what they currently have. They also re-structured and consolidated their departments into nine: *Billing, Business Development, Customer Service, Distribution Services, Human Resources, Information Technology, Operational Excellence, Procurement* and *Packaging & Delivery*.

The remaining sessions for both the Business Parts Analysis and the Business Design Blueprint went relatively smoothly. The only snag occurred when there was debate regarding the classification of certain roles as independent contractors versus employees. There was a fine line between the two and, apparently, they crossed it at one time. Delores learned they were penalized a couple of years ago following a Department of Labor investigation. A former, disgruntled employee successfully argued that he was treated, and expected to perform duties, as though he was an employee when, in fact, he was an independent contractor. He won his case and the company paid a hefty settlement.

Clenard's mood had lightened noticeably over these sessions. Though he never apologized to Delores for being curt during the proposal review, she accepted Jackie's former advice to not take it personally. After she presented the combined final report for the Business Parts Analysis and the Business Design Blueprint, Clenard was still apprehensive about the next phase of work, the Service Delivery Blueprint.

****

By the beginning of October 2014, Clenard's company had redefined departments along with all of the associated roles and their management structure. When Delores arrived for the first session of the Service Delivery Blueprint, Jackie told her they would meet in Alvin's office on the first floor.

"May I ask why?" she inquired.

"Because we're going to talk about the operations, right?" Jackie answered with a question.

Delores replied, "Yes, but we already know the packaging, delivery and distribution side of the operations. We need to capture what happens on the second floor to support the activities on the first floor. Remember the law of polarity that I mentioned back in August when Clenard got upset?"

"*Oh,* so that's what you meant!" Jackie finally understood but wondered if Clenard and Alvin did. When they walked into Alvin's office, Jackie repeated the objective to Alvin and Clenard.

They said, in unison, "We know!"

Alvin continued, "We just thought it would be a good idea to talk through what happens down here first and then we could go upstairs and finish there."

Jackie turned to look at Delores. "Is that okay with you?"

"Yes, I like that approach. I have a summary here that I would like us to talk through. It's based on the information I read in your training manuals."

Clenard looked at the stapled set of papers Delores handed him. "You condensed those hundreds of pages from the training manuals into eight pages?"

"Yes," Delores answered, "but keep in mind, this condensed version focuses on the actual activities that take place. The objective is for us to understand the flow of both information and work."

The four of them talked through the document with Delores taking note of corrections along the way. Eventually, they walked up to the second floor.

"Now," Delores said, "we need to start figuring out what people do on this floor, starting with activities that happen pre-distribution all the way to post-distribution."

They walked into each person's office on the second floor, asking questions based on imagining themselves first as a customer and then as a customer order. Three hours later, they all walked away with a greater appreciation for why people seemed to run around like chickens with their heads cut off on the second floor. It was clear that they all knew what they needed to do and when, but the spatial arrangement of their workspaces simply robbed them of productivity, efficiency and effectiveness.

Just one week shy of Thanksgiving, Delores, via the Service Delivery Blueprint, combined the supportive and administrative work performed on the second floor with the distribution preparation work performed on the first floor. For the first time, Clenard and his management team had a complete and holistic view of the company's operations. Delores helped him realize how he had, in fact, treated the employees on each floor in isolation of each other, despite the interconnectedness of their work.

However, this was only one part of figuring out the optimal work space layout. The other part involved clearing out Cassandra's office.

Clenard and his team previously agreed that they would take the month of December off. There was no point in trying to work around all of the different holidays. After Delores presented her final report for the Service Delivery Blueprint, he asked that she speak with Jada to coordinate the dates for the upcoming sessions for at least the first quarter of 2015.

As Delores turned to walk out of his office, Clenard stopped her. "Wait, I almost forgot. I want to invite you to a holiday party we're having at my house." He handed Delores a beautiful, and unexpected, invitation in a shiny gold envelope.

"Clenard, thank you so much!" she exclaimed.

"Yeah, come on out. And bring your husband. You'll get to meet my sons and my grandbabies, too."

\*\*\*\*

Delores had mixed emotions as she prepared for her first session of the new year with Clenard and his team. It had been a month since they worked together. Although she loved the transformative nature of decluttering and organizing, she knew it would be emotionally challenging for Clenard. As she sat in her home office, she reflected on her conversations with each of Clenard's sons at his holiday party last month.

She learned that they all wanted the best for their father, but, for a variety of reasons, each chose to keep a safe distance from his company. His oldest son seemed to harbor the most resentment. He spent the latter part of his adolescence feeling that his father cared more about his business than him. He especially loathed working weekends at his father's company during his formative years. It was time he missed chasing girls, playing sports and hanging out with his friends.

Clenard's second oldest son had similar feelings as his older brother, but he actually wanted to help his dad. In fact, he told Delores, he had worked there full-time at one point but, after his mother died, he could no longer stand by and watch his father self-destruct. The youngest son followed in his father's footsteps and joined the Navy, and the second-youngest son owned and operated a successful auto body shop.

*It's a new year. What better time to clean out his wife's office and start with a clean slate? A New Year's Resolution.* Delores thought. The good news was that all of Clenard's sons offered to help in whatever way they could. Delores reviewed a document Jackie gave her. It contained a listing of recordkeeping guidelines dictated by the agency that would conduct their audit later that year in August. They would use this as a compass for determining which paper and electronic records to retain and archive versus which ones to purge.

The combined Paper and Electronic Records Management sessions began on a bitterly cold day during the second week of January 2015. The frigid temperature and high gusts of wind reminded Delores that, like Chicago, Lake Michigan also borders Gary.

The paper and electronic records inventory work began in all of the currently occupied offices in two to four hour increments. Delores was mindful not to cause too much of a distraction as she helped survey the paper and electronic records of each employee with an office. She also recorded the work performed in each office, in addition to measuring all furniture and equipment and documenting their respective use.

****

The last four Paper and Electronic Records Management sessions took place on Saturdays and were reserved for decluttering Cassandra's office. These were eight-hour sessions and Clenard offered to pay double-time to some of the temporary warehouse workers to assist with any hauling required. They were joined by Jackie, Jada, his four sons and his only grand-daughter, Taylor, a cheerful seven year old who insisted on helping her Papa.

During one of those sessions, Clenard became enraged. He was searching through papers in one of the boxes in Cassandra's office and must have found something that upset him because he had an emotional outburst. After yelling a few expletives, his oldest son, Kevin, asked that everyone clear the room. However, Taylor refused. She wondered what was wrong with her Papa. In a fit of rage, Clenard had forgotten that he was not alone in the room. He stood up and punched a wall so hard that he cracked it. Taylor began to weep.

Hearing his granddaughter cry made Clenard snap out of his "episode." He walked over to her and hugged her. "I'm sorry, baby. I didn't mean to scare you."

She looked up at him and asked, "What's wrong Papa?" Seeing how hurt his innocent granddaughter was caused Clenard to tear up.

It was the first time Kevin had ever seen his father vulnerable. He had never seen his father cry. Never. Not even at his mother's funeral. "What happened, Dad? What's in that box?"

"Don't worry about it. I'll tell you later," Clenard answered. "I don't want to upset you boys either." A half hour passed before Kevin opened the door to the office and asked that everyone else join them.

When they walked in, Clenard apologized to everyone. "Sorry about that everybody. I saw something I didn't like. Something that brought back real bad memories. But one monkey don't stop no show! Let's get back to work."

Jackie and Delores looked at each other and then at Clenard. He winked at both of them. It was his way of acknowledging that he was still committed to the process of decluttering his wife's office.

Forty-five days later, all paperwork and digital files were organized, color-coded and accounted for. The biggest change was Cassandra's office. It was now completely empty. One day, Clenard and Delores stood in the middle of the room.

"This, Delores," he said with his arms spread out, "is chaos."

"What?" she asked, confused.

Clenard explained, "You know, ancient Greek mythology starts with the god, Chaos. He represented the void. The void, according to them, was chaotic." Clenard turned his body around the room with his arms still spread out. "It's so much bigger than what I remembered the first time we moved in this building. How are we going to fill this void?"

Delores now understood what he meant. She had a plan for filling the voided space of Cassandra's office, but Clenard was suffering from the void left by his wife's death. That was his source of chaos.

Delores thought, hopefully, that chaos would soon dissipate. She managed to help Clenard take a major step forward in restoring balance between his personal life and his company. "Clenard, I agree. This room actually looks larger than what the dimensions show on the blueprints. There's so much we can do with this space. How do you feel?"

"Like a man who just got his get-out-of-jail-free card!"[26]

On her train commute home that evening, Delores received a call from an unknown number. Listening to her instincts, she answered. It was Kevin.

"Ms. Delores, thank you!"

****

Nearly seven months after meeting Clenard, it was time to commence the Work Space Logistics (WSL) sessions, one of the last elements of the Kasennu methodology in building business infrastructure for Clenard's company, the remaining element being the Business Process Manual. It was mid-February of 2015 and a bad snowstorm threatened to delay the first of these sessions. However, Clenard insisted his team forge ahead. "We've come too far at this point to let a punk like Jack Frost get in our way!"

Delores revealed to Clenard that she had started much of the work originally forecasted to take place the first week of the WSL. She explained that, as she worked with each employee with an office on the second floor during the Paper and Electronic Records Management sessions, she also took an inventory of and measured all furniture, fixtures and equipment in each office. She told Clenard that this should reduce the amount of time by half that she needed to spend in each office this first week. She would use this saved time to conduct time and motion studies, that is, make additional observations about everyone's movement throughout the building.

Clenard told Delores to let him know if she needed his help with anything during this first week. Delores spent four hours each day verifying the measurements of each office in comparison to the blueprints. She also drafted her own sketches of each office onto graphing paper. Her stint as a public health inspector made her handy at reading blueprints and doing light drafting. Each office sketch, drawn to scale, also contained information on all furniture, fixtures, equipment, doorways, windows, electrical outlets, air vents and direction and timing of sunlight exposure.

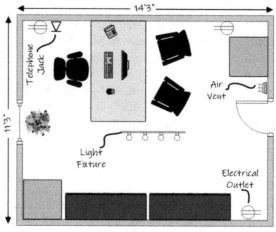

Direction of Most Sunlight
East, 8am – 2pm

Delores used the business infrastructure software on her tablet to record the purpose of each office; in particular, *who* uses it, *why* it is used and *how* work is performed in it. Her notes also included candid feedback from these employees, along with their recommendations for what would make their work environment more functional.

****

By the middle of the first week of the WSL, Delores suspected correctly that Clenard was anxious to know how things were going. He grew accustomed to playing a more active role while implementing previous parts of the methodology.

Delores knocked on the door to his office one day and asked if he would like to do a walk-through of the Service Delivery Blueprint. The goal was to test its accuracy as well as to record the average time required to cycle through the entire supply chain from order to delivery, depending on the order size.

Delores enjoyed Clenard's company. She had to reign him in from time to time. When he saw that someone was doing something he either thought they should not do or was doing incorrectly, he would stop that person. She had to remind him that the purpose was to observe and take notes. "Remember, we're like flies on a wall. Even though people see us, they are to work as though we're not standing here."

Their observations on the second floor were telling. Because the door to Clenard's office does not open directly to the hallway, he was oblivious to the constant walking back and forth that took place daily. "Damn!" he said, "so this is why Jackie says this a 'hot mess.' I always thought she was just blowing off steam, but it really is like watching a bunch of bees swarming around. It's non-stop! I'm getting dizzy."

Delores laughed. "Yes, there is quite a bit of wasted motion up here."

\*\*\*\*

Delores spent the second week of the WSL re-drawing her hand sketches into the business infrastructure software. She drew each office meticulously showing the existing configuration along with details she captured the previous week. Delores was careful to note the proximity to electrical outlets required by certain equipment. Next, she layered in stick figures to represent the people who currently occupy each office. Then, she drew an arrow to show the direction of how work flowed within each office. Referencing the Business Design Blueprint, she labeled each office with the appropriate corresponding department name and role of the occupant(s). She saved this file as *Second Floor Offices_Current State*.

She opened a new file and drew the entire second floor. It contained the layout of all offices but without the details of the first file she created. Instead, she placed the stick figures representing the person or role occupying each office at the front of each office's door. She then referenced the workflow from the Service Delivery Blueprint and drew arrows connecting one stick figure to the next. This illustrated the flow of information from one person to the next. By the time she finished connecting the stick figures with arrows, the flow pattern looked like tangled spaghetti noodles. She saved this file as *Second Floor_Current State*.

Delores took two days during the second week to digest the Second Floor_Current State drawing. It was important that she take her time to formulate an improved design to untangle those "spaghetti noodles."

After several iterations of conceptually re-arranging the stick figures on the Second Floor_Current State drawing, an ideal flow pattern emerged, one that allowed for information to flow in a straighter, more laminar pattern, as opposed to the current, more turbulent flow. She saved this version of the drawing as *Second Floor_Future State*.

Next, she set out to rearrange the layout of each individual office. Each layout needed to promote the overall second floor's re-configuration. The good thing was that many of the file cabinets in certain offices were no longer needed as most of the paperwork they contained were either archived, purged, or scanned into digital files during previous sessions. However, the most challenging part of determining the new layouts was re-arranging furniture and equipment to avoid direct sunlight.

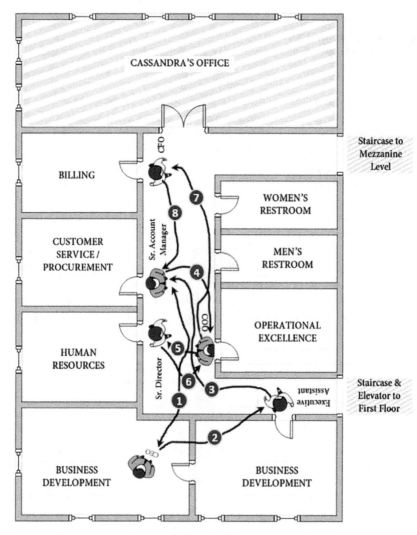

**SERVICE DELIVERY FLOW ON SECOND FLOOR (CURRENT STATE)**

1. CEO & Sr. Account Manager network to secure new account(s).
2. Executive Assistant sets appointments with potential new client(s).
3. Sr. Account Manager secures new client(s) and/or receive new order(s).
4. COO oversees order fulfillment.
5. Sr. Director secures additional staff to help fulfill order (if needed).
6. COO oversees order delivery.
7. CFO invoices client.
8. Sr. Account Manager follows up with client.

Delores spent the remainder of the second week working on the new, or future state, second floor office layouts. During that time, she consulted with an architect. Soon, the solution for the best layout of Cassandra's office became apparent. She just hoped Clenard would like and approve it.

\*\*\*\*

This onsite meeting would be unlike any Delores had previously at Clenard's company. It would take place in Cassandra's office. Per her request, Jackie and Alvin set up a fold-out table and four fold-out chairs to facilitate this particular meeting. Jackie explained, in advance, to Clenard that Delores thought it was important to meet in this room as it would help in getting them used to the idea of conducting business in this space again.

Delores arrived carrying a bag with a projector inside on her left shoulder and a blueprint tube containing enlarged copies of her "future state" drawings on her right shoulder. There were seven drawings in total, including Cassandra's office, The Watchtower break room, a future state drawing of the second floor and four of the other five offices on the second floor, excluding Clenard's. Clenard and Alvin were already in the room when Jackie escorted Delores inside.

Once Delores set up her projector and laptop, she projected the Second Floor_Current State drawing onto the wall ahead of them. "This is what the second floor currently looks like." Jackie, Clenard and Alvin saw before them a diagram that was much simpler and easier to read than a traditional blueprint. Each room was clearly labeled.

Then, Delores projected the version of the second floor overlaid with the current information flow pattern.

"Damn!" Clenard yelled.

Jackie laughed out loudly. "Uh huh, I've been telling you for years that this is a hot mess!"

"No kidding," Alvin chimed in. "I hardly ever come up here so I had no idea how bad it had gotten. But I can remember a time when the first floor probably had a similar pattern."

Delores removed the enlarged future state drawings from the blueprint tube, unrolled them and laid them flat onto the table. On top was the Second Floor_Future State drawing revealing her recommended reconfiguration. "This is what it could look like; imagine the possibilities," Delores said in a soothing voice. "I want to direct your attention first to The Watchtower room."

She removed the Second Floor_Future State drawing and taped it to the sidewall adjacent to her, revealing the drawing of a new break room in the process. "The Watchtower is officially retired. It will actually be used for its original purpose, a break room. Not a spying facility slash copy room slash training room slash whatever. Notice that the one-way mirror will be replaced with a two-way mirror. People can look out from the second floor and people can look in from the first floor."

"Wait," Clenard said, as Delores removed the new break room's drawing and taped it onto the wall next to the Second Floor_Future State drawing. "I didn't see the copiers."

"I'm glad you mentioned that. I guess now is as good a time as any to talk about the copiers. One of them will be placed in the hallway. The other will be relocated to Jada's office. If you'll recall, we eliminated two lateral filing cabinets in her office as a result of the Paper and Electronic Records Management exercises. That freed up space to make room for the other copier. And it makes sense to have it in her office. Clenard, you remember how dizzy we both got watching her constantly walk back and forth from her office to The Watchtower every time she needed to use a copier.

"I recommend fitting both copiers with badge readers. The badge readers will allow you to track how much paper is consumed and by whom. In modifying and relocating these two copiers alone, you will prevent wasted motion *and* wasted money on paper. 'Waste not, want not,' right Clenard?"

"That's right," Clenard answered, impressed that Delores remembered his mother's favorite quote.

"Are we ready to move on?" Delores asked. When they all agreed, she diverted their attention back to the table where the drawing of Cassandra's office was now on top. This time, Clenard, Jackie and Alvin all stood up to look down onto the table.

Delores asked, "Wouldn't it be great to have a dedicated, private space to conduct staff meetings, trainings and, not to mention, host auditors? This room is actually large enough to serve not only as a new conference room, but you can also install a room divider or build an actual wall to add two new offices. These new offices can accommodate some of the additional people you identified during the Business Parts Analysis exercise. This new conference room and office space will significantly reduce foot traffic throughout the break room and second floor. Combined, the recommendations proposed to repurpose and rearrange the room can reduce the overall order to delivery cycle time by 25%!"

Clenard expressed concern about the conference room being wasted space. Delores refuted that claim arguing the room would also serve as an internal library to house all training manuals and other "public" materials. Her research showed that there was at least one meeting taking place every hour somewhere in the building so the new conference room would rarely be unused. However, people would not be able to occupy the room on a whim. They would now have to either reserve the room via their email system or through Jada.

Alvin was tickled. "I can start training in this new conference room without having to be interrupted by a constant stream of people walking in and out to talk on their phones, eat, make copies of reports, spy…" He tapped Clenard on his shoulder.

"Cut me some slack, I've gotten a lot better. I don't spy that much anymore," Clenard jokingly said in his defense.

Alvin resumed, "The other good thing is that this will go over well with the auditors. What used to happen is that we'd have to ask someone to give up their office temporarily so the auditors could perform their work in private. Man, some folks around here get really pissed off, too. I won't name any names. It almost always causes them to have to work on weekends to catch up on their work, so I don't blame them for being mad."

As Jackie and Alvin marveled over the proposed layout of Cassandra's old office, Clenard noticed something that Delores did not mention. Above the sketch of the new conference room were the words, *The Cassandra M. Smith Library* & *Conference Room*. He pointed to it on the paper.

Jackie put her right hand over her mouth and gasped. Her eyes began to well with tears. "Delores, I love it, this is the perfect way to honor Sandy. Thank you so much!" Delores handed Jackie a tissue.

At that moment, Clenard excused himself from the room. Delores, Jackie and Alvin all looked at each other in silence. Roughly 10 minutes later, Clenard returned to the room. He walked over to Delores, extended his arms out to hug her and whispered, "Thank you."

"It's my pleasure," Delores whispered back. "Shall we continue?" When they all nodded yes, she revealed the remaining future state drawings of each office, one by one. As she revealed each drawing, she projected its current state equivalent onto the wall ahead of them.

Clenard asked if Delores could project the Second Floor_Current State drawing again. He also asked if she would remove the Second Floor_Future State drawing from the wall and place it back onto the table. "Can we sketch the information flow with this new design?"

"You certainly can," Delores answered. "I've actually already taken the liberty to do that, but it'll be interesting to see if your markup matches mine."

Delores handed Clenard a red marker. As he, Jackie and Alvin talked through the information flow, he began to draw a line from each stick figure positioned in front of an office to another, just as Delores previously did. When he finished, he started laughing, "Now that's as straight an arrow as you can get!"

Delores ended the session by presenting an office relocation schedule as well as a recommendation for a contractor. She also suggested that Jackie work with Jada to order furniture for the new conference room and offices.

"I have an even better idea," Jackie said, "I'm going to reach out to an interior designer I also met at the Chamber. If we're going to do this, I say we do it right. Just as we hired you as our business infrastructure expert, we need to hire an expert to help us in furnishing and sprucing up this room. Is that okay with you, boss?" She looked over at Clenard.

"Yep, boss," he replied, "sounds like a plan!"

Prior to Delores leaving that day, she emailed a copy of the future state diagrams to all of them and asked that they share it at their next company-wide staff meeting. "When will that be?" she asked.

"Not for another month," Clenard answered. "But I'll make sure we schedule one next week." He asked Alvin to work with Jada to rent more fold-out chairs. For the first time, they were going to conduct a staff meeting where everyone could sit down as opposed to standing up and around conveyor belts, as they typically do when meeting on the first floor.

Alvin reminded Clenard, "We got a big order in last week so things are going to be hectic. Can we push this meeting back by at least one more week?"

"Yeah, that's a good idea," Clenard told him.

Jackie also liked the idea of waiting another week to meet. "This will give me time to coordinate work with the interior designer and the contractor. They might need longer lead times for ordering materials, especially if it's not in stock. Can we push out the relocation schedule some more?"

Delores was not keen on the idea of delaying the relocation more than absolutely necessary. "Well, we can still relocate and rearrange The Watchtower and the other offices. Let's not wait. If the conference room furniture comes afterwards, that's fine. It may actually work better that way."

"Fair enough," Jackie said.

Delores asked one more question as she loaded her drawings and projector onto her shoulders. "Can I attend your staff meeting? I'd like to capture their feedback firsthand."

"Well, I assumed you would be here!" Clenard said as he offered to remove the items hanging from her shoulders.

****

*What better way to kick off the fourth week of the Work Space Logistics than with this staff meeting?* Delores thought as she sat near the back of the room once filled to the ceiling with boxes. All 51 current, full-time employees were spaciously seated in the future conference room eager to see the "big unveiling" announced to them the prior week. Most of them had never set foot in this room before and many of them clapped upon entry.

Clenard emceed the meeting and spent the first 15 minutes discussing the usual company updates normally presented at the monthly staff meetings. He borrowed Delores' projector to convey his updates via a slideshow. Next, Jackie, Alvin and a couple of other managers each gave a two to three-minute update on their respective departments. Clenard then opened the floor for questions up to that point. Seeing there were no questions, he asked Delores to stand so that he could introduce her.

"This is the person responsible for getting this room cleared out," he told everyone. Delores received an unexpected standing ovation. "Now, for the big unveiling." Clenard clicked to the next slide. It showed the Second Floor_Current State drawing. He explained the diagram and its associated spaghetti-like information flow, and then he showed the Second Floor_Future State drawing. There was thunderous applause when he showed the last slide — sketches of the new conference room and two offices.

Clenard opened the floor again for questions. This time, he made it clear that he also wanted their feedback. "I understand everybody might need more time to absorb this. You're probably still in shock." Some of the employees laughed.

The COO raised his hand. "Clenard, I've been reading a lot about this LEED certification. You and I have talked about going green in the past. I like having the badge access on the copiers. I think we could take it a step further and replace all trashcans in the offices with recycle bins. I've been on site visits at bigger companies and it's pretty amazing to see how cognizant people become of their paper consumption when there are recycling bins all around."

Delores raised her hand to comment, but Clenard thought he knew what she might say. And he was right. "I like the recycle bin idea, but let's add them in addition to the trash cans in each office. Over time, we can gradually remove the trash cans altogether but, if we were to do that right now, it would increase motion into the break room. We've worked too hard to try to reduce that kind of foot traffic.

"We have about five minutes left. If you have any questions or concerns about anything you saw, let your manager know or send me an email directly. Please do this by the end of this week so that we can compile all of the feedback and share it with Delores."

Delores raised her hand, "Can you mention the relocation schedule?"

"Oh, yes," Clenard said, "Thank you for reminding me. In two weeks we will begin re-arranging some offices and relocating others altogether, according to the drawings you just saw. We're gonna do this on two Saturdays. For those on the second floor, Jackie will email a copy to you. Be sure to let her know if you have any questions or concerns by the end of this week."

Clenard looked up at the wall, as if by habit, in search of a clock. He then looked at his watch and saw that the hour was almost up. "Thanks for attending everybody." Deepening his voice, he said jokingly, "Now get back to work!" As people began to file out of the office, many of them congratulated him and shook Delores' hand.

Delores spent the remainder of this fourth week and the following one collaborating with Jackie, Marco (the interior designer) and the contractor Jackie and Clenard hired. Delores shared all of her drawings with Marco who was able to make additional room layout recommendations based on Feng Shui[27] principles. Her work served as a natural complement to Marco's.

As Marco began placing orders for new furniture, Jada ordered the Audio/Visual (A/V) equipment for the new conference room. Meanwhile, Delores and Jackie reviewed the employee feedback. There were no concerns or questions, only compliments and sheer excitement over the new changes.

**\*\*\*\***

The sixth, and perhaps the most anticipated, week of the WSL was finally here. It was now March and, though the temperatures were still in the 30s (F), spring was on the horizon. Delores spent the beginning of that week working closely with Jackie to confirm all of the logistics for that Saturday. There would be a lot of moving parts on that day and it was important to make sure that their respective relocation plans were synchronized.

The plan was as follows: they agreed to relocate any applicable equipment first. This included the copiers in the newly restored break room. Jackie arranged for electricians and network specialists from the company to whom they outsource their information technology to be at the building first thing Saturday morning. This was a precautionary action to ensure minimal network downtime. Moving the equipment first would allow them to use the remainder of the day performing tests to ensure everything was working properly. Simultaneously, the contractor and his crew would erect a new wall to divide Cassandra's old office and paint it.

Next, they would focus on relocating or rearranging any furniture and fixtures identified according to the approved Second Floor_Future State drawing. As he did during the Paper and Electronic Records Management Saturday sessions, Clenard would pay a few warehouse workers double time to move the furniture as needed. The day would end with a professional cleaning crew coming over to polish all furniture as well as buff the floors on the entire second floor.

All work flowed just as Delores and Jackie planned. Everyone arrived at their designated times ready to work. The cleaning crew worked last and finished buffing the floors about 90 minutes behind schedule, since it took the paint longer to fully dry than originally projected. However, both Delores and Jackie thanked them immensely for doing such an incredible job. "Girl, I can't wait to see Clenard's face when he sees this. Knowing him, he'll probably come over here tomorrow right after church."

That's exactly what happened. Clenard drove to the building on Sunday afternoon. As soon as he badged into the building, he could smell the combined aroma of the lemon oil used in the cleaning supplies as well as fresh paint. He was almost afraid to walk onto the second floor for fear of leaving evidence of his presence. Instead, he just glanced down the hallway from his office and, later, left the building.

**** 

The following Monday marked the beginning of the seventh and final work-week of the WSL. Unlike the previous elements of the Kasennu methodology, there was no need for Delores to present a full report. Instead, she summarized in a one-page document the work they performed, along with a few additional recommendations to get them prepared for the big audit later that summer. 75% of the planned work was now complete. The remaining 25% involved getting the conference room ready.

Similar to the previous week, Delores spent the better part of this week confirming logistics with Jackie. Jackie told Delores that Marco shared good news with her yesterday: the cubicle walls and furniture for the new offices and conference room all arrived at the retailer's warehouse.

On Saturday morning, Jackie directed the contractors to the break room where they would replace the large, one-way mirror with see-through glass. Shortly afterwards, Marco told her that a delivery company called; the furniture for the conference room was on its way.

An hour later, the delivery company buzzed in at the building. They were asked to wear some of the thin cloth booties from the first floor around their shoes to prevent scuffing and scratching the second floor. They brought the largest piece of furniture in first — a large, rectangular-shaped, cherry wood table. The wood was similar to the wood in Clenard's office.

Next, they brought in the bookcases to line the two sidewalls of the new conference room. As they worked to bring the cubical walls and furniture for the new office, Delores, Jackie and Marco removed the manuals and books previously boxed from the break room and from other areas throughout the building and placed them onto the bookshelves along with various company awards and plaques.

The electricians and network specialists from the previous week arrived to set up connections to the new laptops, wireless internet and printer, as well as the new A/V equipment.

By 2:30 pm, all new furniture, fixtures and equipment were in place. "Whew!" Jackie sighed. "This was long overdue. I never thought I'd see the day! Now we just have to wait for Clenard and his family." Jackie had arranged previously for Clenard, his sons and their families to stop by the building at 3:00 pm. Delores told Jackie she needed to retrieve some things out of her car before everyone else arrived.

## The Result

When Delores went back inside the building, she had a beautifully wrapped gift tied with an exquisite golden bow. She also had copies of her one-page summary and recommendations.

"Ah, what's in the box?" Jackie inquired.

"Just a little something I have for Clenard," Delores replied.

A few minutes later, Jackie heard Clenard and his family walking down the hallway. Only Delores, Jackie and Marco were in the newly furnished conference room. "Okay, they're here!"

Taylor knocked on the door to the conference room. "Hello, anybody home?"

Jackie opened the door slowly. As Clenard's family filed into the room one by one, all Delores heard were a bunch of oohs and aahs. She was tickled at the sight of his grandchildren's uncontained excitement. Clenard walked in last. It was a while before he said anything. He walked around slowly, inspecting every square inch of the conference room and later the office with cubicles. "Ladies and Gent, you've outdone yourselves."

Delores asked that everyone take a seat at the new conference room table. She turned on the new projector that hung from the ceiling and pressed a button on the remote control. An overhead screen drew down in front of them.

Clenard's grandchildren went wild! "Ooh, Papa! Look! Did you see that? That's so cool!"

Clenard was impressed, but knew that Delores wanted to discuss important business. "Okay, okay, that's enough. Let's hear what Ms. Delores has to say."

Delores projected the one-page summary and recommendations onto the screen. The summary merely contained highlights of all the work they completed together over the past eight months. She looked at Clenard. "With your state-of-the-art corporate boardroom, you are in an even better position to showcase your company's IPO-readiness. You should pass the audit in August with flying colors. There are a few more things I would recommend to ensure the sustainability of all the work we've completed.

"First, continue working, as finances dictate, with Marco to infuse the upgraded look of this room across the entire building. Also, solicit his assistance in ensuring that other factors that affect workplace productivity are also in place. This includes lighting, noise filters and ergonomics. These factors were outside the scope of what I offered.

"Second, take advantage of the some of the site visits to larger corporations offered through the Chamber of Commerce. This will help you with ideas for extending the newfound corporate presence throughout the building. The façade of the first floor's operation and the outside perimeter of the building did their part in helping you land big customers. Now, the actual second floor's operation matches that façade and you're that much closer to having this IPO become a reality! This time, you have the business infrastructure to support the entire façade!

"Third, begin documenting the processes associated with operations here on the second floor. This is a logical next step. There will be a workshop in mid-April in Atlanta focused exclusively on the Business Process Manual element of the Kasennu methodology. It will be the last element you need to put in place to solidify the company's business infrastructure. While a good bit of the other work we've done will help you pass the audit, the business processes will be like your catalyst for going public."

Clenard stood and walked to the front of the room. "It feels good to have all of you here. It's been a long time since my sons and my daughters-in-law were last here. Jackie, thank you for having my back all these years, through thick and thin. And Delores, thank you for everything you've done!"

Jackie asked Taylor and one of Clenard's grandsons to follow her out of the room. While they were out, Delores retracted the overhead screen and packed the rest of her things. When Jackie and the two grandchildren returned, Clenard's grandson was holding a large white cake adorned with yellow flowers and Taylor was carrying the gift that Delores brought.

"Oh, ya'll went all out, huh?" Clenard helped his grandson put the cake onto the table.

Taylor walked over to him. "Here Papa, this is for you!" Clenard removed the golden bow and tore open the gift paper revealing a white box. He opened the box and removed the white gift tissue and packaging wrap. He only saw the tip of what appeared to be something in gold. Gently, he reached into the box to pull out a figurine. It was in the image of Cassandra, his late wife, wearing what appeared to be a wedding dress. The entire image was 14-karat gold plated. Like the other figurines in his office, her image stood on a cherry wood pedestal with her name engraved at the bottom.

"It's Grandma Sandy, Papa!" Taylor proudly announced.

"Yes, but how, how did you do this?" he asked.

"Ms. Delores helped us," Taylor answered. Clenard looked up and over at Delores.

Delores confirmed, "I didn't mention this to you when we first met, but one of my daughters is a sculptor. When I spoke to your family at your holiday party, I told them about something nice I wanted to have made for you to add to your collection. It was actually Taylor who suggested getting a figurine made of your wife. She said you showed her a wedding picture. I believe it was around the time when we first discussed my overall proposal to you last August. Apparently she snuck into the room where you keep photo albums at your house, used her brother's phone to snap a photo-graph of one of the wedding pictures and then texted it to me. I sent it to my daughter and the rest is history. We should go put it in your office."

"That's a good idea," Clenard said, still in awe.

When they walked out of the conference room, Jackie said, "We ain't done yet, Clenard. Turn around and look up." Above the room's door frame was a gold-plated plaque nailed into the wall that was conspicuously covered when Clenard first entered the room.

*The Cassandra M. Smith Library & Conference Room* was engraved into the plaque, along with a bird's wing on each end. There was not a dry eye in the hallway upon seeing both the plaque and Clenard's reaction.

When Clenard placed the figurine of Cassandra onto his desk, Delores told him, "Clenard, you have not lost her. Her spirit is with you and always will be. You've transformed her former office into an even more magnifi-cent area. From now on, everyone who enters that room will look up and see her name."

Everyone was now outside of Clenard's office. Some were peeking in-to the other offices, many of which had either been rearranged or relocated altogether. Jackie walked past them briskly and down the stairs to the first floor. Delores knew what she was about to do and asked Clenard if every-one could go to the improved break room.

"Whoa!" one of his grandsons said upon entering the break room. "It's spacious and spotless now!"

Delores asked Clenard to walk up to the glass and to look out onto the first floor. He did as instructed and saw Jackie on the first floor waving at him.

"Can you see me?" she yelled at the top of her lungs. Clenard turned around and walked to the large table in the break room. It still had paper, a few pens and a marker on top of it — leftovers from the last time Alvin trained in there. He wrote something in thick black letters on one of the sheets of paper, walked back to the glass and placed the paper against it so that Jackie could read it.

Jackie looked up and saw, "YOU'RE FIRED!" on a sheet of paper.

Clenard turned around with the sheet of paper to reveal what he wrote. Everyone broke out into uncontrollable laugher.

****

Later that evening, Clenard had a long, overdue conversation with all of his sons. They told him how proud they were of him. In turn, Clenard promised them that he was actively putting in motion things to free himself of the daily grind of operating his company. He even sought grief counsel-ing. The business processes represented the final leg of his journey to be-coming an owner-investor. He wanted to spend more quality time with his family. When Kevin, his oldest son, asked him, "Dad, sounds like you can proclaim another 'Veni, Vidi, Vici' milestone, huh?"

Clenard responded, "Not yet. Atlanta, here I come!"

# PART THREE
## MAINTAINING THE METHODOLOGY

"Those who cannot remember the past are
condemned to repeat it."

~ George Santayana

# CHAPTER 8

## EMERALD TABLET

**Kasennu™**
Business Process Manual

The most anticipated moment in building business infrastructure has arrived. All of the entrepreneurs converge in Atlanta, GA, in late April 2015 for a four-day workshop to learn how to identify and document their business processes. They also learn best practices for testing and monitoring their processes. Additionally, they each receive a coveted Emerald Tablet whose message, upon first receipt, seems cryptic but, by the time the workshop ends, its revelation is profound. This marks the final element of the Kasennu methodology — the Business Process Manual.

## Getting to the Workshop

As the plane touched down in Atlanta, Emily Miller (Chapter 2) looked out the window, overjoyed. For the first time in several years, she was traveling for growth and development and not simply to escape certain realities in her life. She was still on a high from the positive feedback she received from the board members of the non-profit she founded. The fact that they approved her workshop attendance was proof they forgave her for working in secret with her business infrastructure consultant because the results were too impactful to deny continuance.

Meanwhile, Albert Andoh (Chapter 3) was also celebrating. The potential investors he and his Uncle Selom had courted agreed to fund their software development business. The investors saw their participation in the Business Process Manual workshop as another step in the right direction of scaling their company. Thankfully, the workshop was scheduled to take place primarily over the weekend and Albert would miss a minimum amount of school.

Sarah Reuben and her brother, Steve (Chapter 4), did not have to travel out of town to attend the workshop as did the other participants for they already lived and worked in the Atlanta area. Things had calmed down significantly since their network virus attack. They were still in the process of not only mending their relationship but also the fragments of information missing due to the attack. Both went into the workshop hoping not only to strengthen their furniture company's business infrastructure, but also as a measure, hopefully, to make their father's decision that much easier in selecting one of them to succeed him as CEO.

Karen Benoit and her twin sister, Sharen Benoit Joseph (Chapter 5), decided to drive from New Orleans to Atlanta, stopping at historical landmarks along the way. Doing so gave them a chance to keep their finger on the pulse of the Gulf Coast region and assess the potential need for their mental rehabilitation facility's services. This workshop, they hoped, would enable them to open more locations across this region and beyond. They were both grappling with the recent discovery of a third cousin who reached out to them a couple of months ago. This road trip would allow them time to clear their minds while weighing the pros and cons of becoming reconnected to their birth family.

Excited to leave the colder weather in New York, Vandana Thiagarajan, Brian Miller and Imana Van Dijk (Chapter 6) all jumped at the chance to go to Atlanta. For the first time in a couple of years, they felt like a team again, especially after Brian revealed that he quit his job at the law firm and would be working in their business full-time. As the plane descended at Hartsfield-Jackson Airport, Vandana was captivated by the sight of the density and greenness of the trees, a far cry from the concrete and steel she had grown accustomed to in New York City. She could not help but think that Atlanta should be nicknamed Emerald City, not Seattle (as is currently). Her awe of the landscaping only intensified as they made their way from the airport up to the resort in North Atlanta where the workshop would take place.

The consummate strategist, Clenard Smith II (Chapter 7) flew into Atlanta a week before the workshop. He wanted to take advantage of the opportunity to visit a friend who offered to give him a tour of UPS' (United Parcel Service's) headquarters. Clenard was fascinated by their package delivery system and was curious to see the company from an insider's perspective. He left the tour more convinced than ever of the power of processes as a critical component in justifying and filing for his company's IPO.

****

As requested, each participant arrived with the business infrastructure software downloaded onto the laptop or tablet they would bring to the workshop. Their respective consultants gave them tutorials on using the software prior to the workshop.

## Day One – Process Identification & Prioritization

According to the itinerary, the first day of the workshop was to start at 4:00 pm and end at 9:00 pm. There would be a one-hour dinner break from 6:00 pm to 7:00 pm. Though each of the participants found this to be odd, as most business workshops are conducted during the day, none questioned it.

When the participants walked into the room where the workshop would take place, I could tell they were struck first by its size. It was a large ballroom on the resort's complex, currently separated by a partition covered in dark purple fabric. There were six long tables placed together in the shape of a U and 18 chairs, amply spaced apart. In the front of the ballroom was a small, raised platform with a large overhead screen drawn behind it. Next to the platform was a lectern serving as a command center for all audio/visual presentation needs.

D. Jude Teal, a tall man with salt-and-pepper colored hair, stood in the center of the U-shape of chairs and I sat in one of the chairs closest to the platform. Jude and I greeted each participant as they walked into the room. He asked that each person sit behind the small name tents strategically placed along the tables bearing his or her name in bold, purple-colored font.

### Introductions

"Good afternoon, everyone!" Jude said very loudly and rather enthusiastically. The collective response of "good afternoon" must not have met his expectations since he repeated himself.

"Good afternoon!"

"Good afternoon!" said the audience, in a louder, more charged response.

"Thank you and welcome to each and every one of you. My name is D. Jude Teal and it is my pleasure to kickoff this very important workshop. I know some of you traveled far distances to be here this afternoon and we appreciate that. You may be wondering why we are starting so late in the afternoon.

"The reason is because we know what it's like to be business owners and how hectic your days can be. We chose this time of day to start the workshop because we figured you're less likely to have as many distractions during this time *and* because we want to make sure that the information you receive here tonight is one of the last 'downloads' you receive before you go to bed!" Several participants laughed as Jude used his hands to make air quotes while saying the word *download*.

"I'm sure you're also wondering who the heck I am. I own this resort. I'll share with you a quick story about how that came to be. I was a witty kid growing up. I was my parents' only son and the youngest of five kids. I was cocky, too. My friends used to call me *Midas* because, they said, everything I touched turned to gold. I made everything I did look effortless. But my luck ran out one day and what I touched turned into fool's gold. I was dabbling in some illegal activities while in college and got into a lot of trouble.

"Many of my professors came to my aid when I went to stand in court before a judge. Had the judge not been convinced of my ability to become a productive member of society, this story would definitely have turned out differently.

"I didn't go to jail, but the thought of going was enough to scare me straight. I finished college with a degree in Finance. My first job was working as a junior analyst at a major hotel chain. I absorbed all the information I could and, eventually, I opened a couple of bed and breakfasts throughout Phoenix, Arizona. Things were going really well and I decided to partner with some investors to open my first hotel.

"It wasn't the transition from owning a bed and breakfast to a hotel that almost made me lose my financial shirt; it was trying to expand the hotel into other locations. That's when someone recommended me to this lady you see sitting here, Alicia Butler Pierre. She introduced me to her Kasennu methodology and I was hooked! I was so impressed by the results and her vision for her company that I became an investor.

"My company now owns a portfolio of bed and breakfasts, hotels and resorts around the world, this location being one of them. I can personally attest to the wonderment of what this methodology can do for you and your business, *if* you apply and maintain it. The Business Process Manual is the most tedious and time-consuming element of the methodology, but stick to it and I guarantee you will not be disappointed with the results.

"Enough about me. I'd like for each of you to introduce yourselves. But first..."

****

Jude pressed a button on the clicker he held in his hand to activate the large screen behind him. It revealed a slide with the following information:

**The Five Main Reasons to Document a Business Process:**
1. Succession planning
2. Selling or franchising
3. Intellectual property protection
4. Training and performance evaluation
5. Software development (automation)

Jude explained that processes can be used to help business owners looking to transition out of the lead role in their businesses as part of their succession planning strategy. Processes can also help those owners looking to sell or franchise their business by providing the detail necessary for this *business-in-a-box* approach.

Processes also provide the detail necessary to file for trade secret, copyright and patent protection of a business' intellectual property. They also provide the detail required to adequately train existing and new team members to ensure consistent product and service delivery. Metrics make it possible to monitor processes for performance and suggest areas for improvement. Last, processes aid in describing the workflow necessary to allow software developers to create and integrate automated solutions.

"Now that I've explained the five main reasons to document a process, I'd like for each of you to stand. In one minute, tell us your name, the type of business you own and the primary reason you need to document processes." Jude then looked at the person sitting closest to him and no ticed her name tent. "Emily, we'll start with you."

Emily stood, "Good afternoon everyone. My name is Emily Miller. I'm the founder and managing director of a non-profit that helps seasoned professionals in the D.C. area who are too young to retire to find their next amazing opportunity. My primary purpose for documenting processes is for succession planning. I have transitioned myself into a new role and have ideas for other ventures. I want to make sure that my replacement as the executive director has all of the tools needed for continued success."

The next participant, and by appearances clearly the youngest, stood. "Um, hello," the soft-spoken teenager said. "My name is Albert Andoh. I own a software and app development company in Dallas, Texas. My primary purpose for documenting processes is for training and performance evaluation."

Albert's uncle stood next. "Hello everyone! My name is Selom Andoh. Albert is my nephew and I also hold an ownership stake in the company. As he mentioned, we need processes for training and performance evaluation. This is imperative considering most of our development team is in another country."

A tall woman stood next. "Hi! I'm Sarah Reuben. I'm the COO of a furniture company right here in the Atlanta area. We can actually check off several reasons why we need processes but, from my perspective, the primary purpose is for intellectual property protection. My brother can explain the other purpose."

Sarah's brother then stood. "Greetings! It's a pleasure to be in your company today. My name is Steve Reuben and I'm the CMO of our furniture company. One of the other main reasons for us documenting our processes is for succession planning. Our dad is planning to retire as CEO very soon. The other reason, aside from what Sarah stated, is for training and performance evaluation. Looking ahead at that list makes me realize that documenting processes for software development is also a critical need for us since we need systems that can communicate with each other."

Steve's introduction was no doubt longer than 60 seconds and so the next set of participants, identical twins, decided to stand together. "Hi, I'm Karen Benoit," one of the sisters announced. "And I'm Sharon Benoit Joseph," the other sister said. Karen continued, "We own a mental rehabilitation facility in New Orleans. We have three locations and, until listening to your explanation, Jude, we never thought of our locations as franchises, but they are. So, we need processes for franchising purposes as we expand into other locations."

Following in the twins' footsteps, a group of three people stood next. "Good afternoon. My name is Vandana Thiagarajan and this is my husband, and Emily's son, Brian Miller. And this is my best friend, and our business partner, Imana Van Dijk." Emily beamed with pride at the sight of her son and daughter-in-law. Brian spoke, "We're co-owners of a residential mortgage company in New York." He looked over at Imana, who was on the other side of Vandana, as her cue to speak next. "Like the Reubens, we also need to document processes for multiple reasons, but if we had to choose a primary one, it would be for training and performance evaluation purposes. Our company is featured on a TV show and we have a lot of new people on our team as a result. They need to know what to do, and how, so we can continue meeting our fast loan processing time."

The final participant stood. He extended his arms wide open, "Looks like we've saved the best for last." Everyone laughed. "Hello. My name is Clenard Smith. I am the proud owner of a food distribution company in

Gary, Indiana, and an even prouder father of four and grandfather of five. I live by the mantra, *Veni, Vidi, Vici*, and I play the entrepreneurial game to win. But winners know when it's time to gracefully bow out. I want to sell my company to the public via an IPO. That's why I need processes. It's a larger part of my succession plan, which as my consultant has helped me figure out, can actually become a part of my Living Will and Trust."

Jude thanked all the participants for introducing themselves. He told them that, in stating their primary reason for documenting processes, it would serve as their compass for the workshop and beyond. Business owners, he explained, have different drivers that motivate that primary reason for documenting processes. Those drivers include retirement, audit and certification readiness, business renewal and licensing preparedness, tighter financial controls, regulatory compliance and expansion into other locations. Jude alluded to the fact that they would find out later how their primary reason for documenting processes would also affect how those processes are actually documented.

"I have a question for each of you. Think of the one person you'd like to have lunch with, living or deceased. What if you did, in fact, have lunch with that person and it did not live up to your expectations? Would you be disappointed? Would you tell others about your experience?" Jude inquired.

"Suppose you *are* disappointed. You believed in the façade or the image that person projected, whether intentional or not, and your actual experience did not live up to the hype. Do your clients have a similar reaction when they do business with you? If the answer is 'yes,' then how will you work to make sure their experience, which is an output of your operations, matches their expectations, which is the output of your marketing and branding?

"Ladies and gentlemen, I ask myself this question every day. As the owner of a portfolio of businesses in the hospitality industry, I want every guest to report a 5-star experience to match the 5-star amenities we work hard to provide. And, I worked tirelessly until that became the reality. You, too, can do the same thing!

"With that being said, it is with great pleasure that I introduce Alicia Butler Pierre. She will lead the remainder of the workshop and teach you how to develop a Business Process Manual as a critical element in your strategy to match your company's operational reality with its marketing perception. In doing so, she will present you with an Emerald Tablet." Jude could see the puzzled looks on the faces of the participants. "It won't make sense now, but it will later. Trust me. So, without further ado, here's Alicia!"

**Business Processes 101**
I recall walking to the front of the room and onto the platform. I thanked Jude for the introduction and the participants for being there at the work-

shop. I stated the primary objective of the workshop: to gain a deeper understanding of processes and how all of the work that each of them has done up to this point was in preparation for capturing their processes. A major goal was for each of them to walk away with at least one of their processes documented.

As an ice-breaker, and to set the tone for the remainder of the workshop, I shared a short story with the participants. "Clenard, I think you'll appreciate this example. I remember the first presentation on business processes I ever gave to a group of entrepreneurs. During the Q&A session, a man raised his hand and adamantly professed, 'What you said sounds nice, but it doesn't apply to my business!'

"After probing about his business, I learned that this entrepreneur, like you Clenard, owned a packaged foods distribution company. I told him that his entire distribution chain is a process. 'Just like Amazon®,' I told him, 'you have a process for accepting payments for new orders, a process for fulfilling those orders, a process for confirming order shipments and many more. It's not a matter of whether or not processes apply to your business. They do! The issue is whether your processes are documented.' Needless to say, he was speechless.

"At the time, I wasn't sure if that was a good thing or bad thing. Now I look at that experience as a defining moment. It helped me understand how prolific the myths, misconceptions and misinformation about processes are.

"For starters, the term 'process' is used loosely. The entrepreneur at that presentation could very well have been confused just by my use of the term 'process' to describe something he already has in place. It's no wonder why so many entrepreneurs and corporate executives alike resist the adoption of continuous process improvement initiatives. Usually, they have different ideas of what processes are and question the value.

"It's similar to when I hear people say that something is 'chemical-free.' As a chemical engineer, I know there's no such thing. Chemistry is a science with omnipresence, meaning it's everywhere, including in our bodies! I think what people intend to say is that a substance might be synthetic versus naturally-occurring.

"This workshop is designed to provide a simple, yet comprehensive introduction to the world of business processes and to show you how you can use them to increase the efficiency and effectiveness of your company's daily operations. It is not a complete discourse; instead, it is enough information to whet your appetite so that you can oversee implementation in your respective businesses.

"This workshop will focus exclusively on the identification, documentation, testing and storage of processes into a Business Process Manual. We will discuss process improvement, but the act of actually improving one of your processes is out of this workshop's scope. Keep this in mind: **before you can improve a process, you must first identify and document that process.**"

I activated the screen behind me and began clicking through a series of slides as I continued speaking and answering questions throughout my presentation. "There are three general classifications for processes:

1. **Natural:** processes that involve a flow or rate of change without human intervention. An example is the metamorphosis process that a caterpillar undergoes to transform into a butterfly.

2. **Manufacturing**: processes that involve the flow of tangible, raw materials to produce finished goods as a result of human intervention.

    a. *Chemical:* flow of liquids and gases (i.e., process to produce clean drinking water)

    b. *Electrical:* flow of electrical current (i.e., process to deliver electricity to operate machinery used to produce clean drinking water)

    c. *Industrial:* improved flow of pre-assembled goods (i.e., improve process to fill water into plastic bottles)

3. **Transactional**: processes that involve the flow of intangible goods (i.e., services) as a result of human intervention. These types of processes are commonly known as **business processes** since they involve the flow of work or information to produce a desired result.

"A **business process**, therefore, represents the sequential steps necessary to produce a desired result consistently. Another way of describing a business process is the consistent conversion or transformation of inputs into outputs.

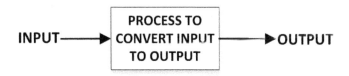

**Figure 8.1** Simplified Illustration of a Business Process

"In examining Figure 8.1, think of the process for making lemonade. The inputs are lemon juice, water and sugar. Those inputs are mixed in a container for a certain amount of time until the desired taste is achieved and later cooled. The output is cold, refreshing lemonade.

"In this way, business processes are like recipes that describe your business. Collectively, these recipes (or processes) become a cookbook (or Operations Manual). With recipes, the key is consistency and details! One missed ingredient or an inaccurate measurement is guaranteed to result in an inconsistent output.

"How would you feel if your favorite meal at your favorite restaurant is *different* (and not in a good way) than what you've grown accustomed to? You'd probably be really frustrated, maybe even angry. The same is true with how your customers experience your business. If their first experience with your product or service is bad, then they will likely never patronize your business again. However, if their first experience is good, then customers will expect that same experience in future transactions.

"Business processes are also like plays. There's a saying, 'same script, different cast.' A well-written script should provide the basis for the same play being performed simultaneously around the world with roughly similar audience feedback. The quality of the play's performance remains intact despite changes in geographical location, directors and actors.

**By documenting your firm's mission-critical operational processes, you can:**

- Ensure consistent, high quality work output,
- Leverage in-house knowledge to design a salable, replicable business that attracts top quality staff and savvy investors,
- Decrease employee training time, and
- Concentrate your efforts on revenue-generating activities.

**Business Processes are intended to be:**

- A platform for standardizing operations,
- A tool for measuring quality and performance,
- A tool for sustainable expansion, and
- A tool for creating consistent results.

**Business Processes are NOT intended to be:**

- The same as company policies,
- The same as a system,
- Used only in large, publicly-traded organizations, or
- A primary tool for reducing staff.

"One may argue that the challenge with business processes are the involvement of people because, unlike machines used in manufacturing processes, people are unpredictable and cannot easily be repaired or replaced.

"That is true, but consider this: the successful execution of a business process is not only affected by the **people** performing and/or monitoring the process, but also by the **tools** used to facilitate the process and the working **environment** in which the process is performed.

"It's now time to break for dinner. We will reconvene in an hour. Make sure you have your laptops or tablets with you when we come back because we will use the business infrastructure software to start identifying your processes."

****

The participant introductions yielded great conversations during the dinner break. Many of them discovered shared interests as well as business pursuits. They were all fascinated with Albert and his platform for bridging existing software technologies, since each of them seemed to identify an immediate need for that service.

When they walked back into the ballroom, the rectangular tables were replaced with several roundtables covered with purple linen tablecloths. The same name tents were placed onto these tables and each participant's consultant now sat at the table with their respective client(s).

I knew that each minute was precious and, once everyone was seated, I quickly resumed. "Before dinner, I shared some basic information about business processes. I've compiled a list of 29 processes that every small business, regardless of industry, should implement." I projected a slide containing a listing of those 29 processes, similar to what is shown in Appendix B.

"You may not refer to these processes, or their associated departments for that matter, by the same name, but you understand the general idea. Every one of you has to market your business, collect and pay out money, recruit and hire people to help you, guard your intellectual property via contractual agreements and select and protect the optimal technology to help your business run efficiently."

The next slide featured a solid black background with a question typed in bold, white letters, "Are You Hoarding Information?" The silence in the room broke when I said, "Information hoarding is the practice of thinking that no one can do things the way you can and so, whether intentionally or not, you keep the information to yourself, effectively preventing others from doing the work. Some people actually hoard information as a job security tactic. Either way, it is detrimental to the advancement of your company's long-term success.

"Your business," I told everyone, "must be able to operate without your daily presence." I asked the participants if being away from their business at this conference bothered them. To my surprise, no one raised his or her hand, at least, no one was brave enough to do so.

Eventually, Emily Miller raised her hand and said, "I'll admit it. If you had asked me that question a few months ago, my answer would have been 'yes.' But now I understand how, by my insistence on doing everything and not getting the proper help, I was getting in the way of our organization's success."

I showed a slide explaining what can be accomplished in a culture of transparency.

**Business Processes can help you:**

- Leverage resident intelligence to document precise company operations;
- Establish process metrics and key performance indicators (KPIs) to expose inefficiencies, measure performance, and increase staff accountability;
- Onboard new employees through well-documented training manuals;
- Set performance-based controls for staff accountability;
- Minimize sabotage through a monitored system of checks and balances;
- Create a pitch-ready presentation of your business concept to investors;
- Increase equity via intellectual property valuation that can be patented, copyrighted, or retained as a trade secret; and
- Improve cash flow and increase profitability via streamlined operations and faster delivery times.

## Leveraging the Business Parts Analysis

It was now time for the participants to identify their business processes. I asked that they each open their respective business infrastructure software on their laptops or tablets. "Retrieve your listing of job tasks from the Business Parts Analysis exercise. Follow along with me as I demonstrate how to begin identifying your processes using an example set of data."

I walked over to the lectern to begin navigating the business infrastructure software on my laptop from which the screen was projected.

"First, I'm going to select a department and its associated job tasks. I'll choose *Accounting* since all of us, whether we run for-profit or non-profit organizations, handle money." I scrolled down the listing of tasks associated with the Accounting Department in the example set of data.

"I now need to determine which of these tasks describe similar activities." I selected three tasks: *Email invoice to client, Collect payment from client,* and *Generate invoice.* By right-clicking on the mouse, the selected tasks were grouped together as one, unnamed process.

"I've grouped these tasks together because they describe a new *Accounts Receivable* process." I typed the words *Accounts Receivable* onto the new grouping of tasks, then repeated grouping like tasks until every task was assigned to a new process.

"We have about 90 minutes left. We will use that remaining time here tonight to begin identifying your processes. Your consultants are here to help you. You will have most of the day tomorrow to resume and finish this exercise. Take your time. Do not rush. By the time we meet tomorrow afternoon, you should have the first two columns of this table completed."

I projected an image of a table where the first row contained the following information: *Department, Priority, Process, KPIs, UOM (Unit of Measurement),* and *Gatekeeper(s)*. The first column, Department, had generic names like "Department 1" and "Department 2."

| Department | Priority | Process | KPIs | UOM | Gatekeeper(s) |
|---|---|---|---|---|---|
| DEPARTMENT 1 | | | | | |
| | | | | | |
| | | | | | |
| DEPARTMENT 2 | | | | | |
| | | | | | |
| | | | | | |

I explained, "As you identify processes within each department, the **Department** and **Process** columns will automatically populate with that information. Then, you will prioritize the order in which you will document processes. Fill in the number, starting with '1' for most critical, in the table's **Priority** column. Whichever process you identify as number one is the process you will document during this workshop. Are there any questions?"

No one asked a question. They were all eager to start. Each consultant worked with his or her client(s) to help identify their processes.

Ten minutes before 9:00 pm, I requested that everyone save their work and turn off their laptops and tablets. I had something to show them. I distributed a beautiful, dark green plaque with a faux marble face to each of them. Etched onto the front of the plaque in light green font were guidelines for a process-dependent business. This, I told them, was their *Emerald Tablet*. "As Jude said earlier, you may not understand what this means now, but you will by the time you leave Atlanta. I promise. Have a good night and I look forward to seeing you tomorrow."

## THE EMERALD TABLET FOR A PROCESS-DEPENDENT BUSINESS

**People before Process.**
**Process before Automation.**
~
**Document before Testing.**
**Test before Enforcing.**
**Enforce before Monitoring.**
**Monitor before Changing.**
**Change before Deviating.**

There are no shortcuts on the journey to long-lasting success. Rework is the enemy of efficiency, but internal complacency and apathy will destroy a business before any external threat. Survival rests on keen observations and the willingness to adapt accordingly.

## Day Two – Process Documentation

It was Saturday. By midday, the temperature had climbed into the early 70s (F). The sun shone brightly, the birds chirped feverishly, the trees swayed and the wind provided a welcomed breeze. It was difficult for anyone to resist the resort's amenities, but they knew better than to over-indulge. Some of the participants were able to squeeze in time before the afternoon session began to go horseback riding, swimming or play golf.

By 4:00 pm, all of the participants and their respective consultants were back in the ballroom. The roundtables were still set up. I learned that most of them identified and prioritized all of their processes by noon that day. On average, 43 processes were identified per company. Though they reported the identification exercise as "enlightening," many of them expressed concern regarding the length of time required to document the processes. That length of time, I told them, varies depending on the complexity and the number of people involved in executing a process.

I opened the business infrastructure software on my laptop and projected the intermediate results of the process table, based on the example data set from yesterday. "The format of this table should look familiar," I said. "Each department listed on the far left is color-coded according to your previous color selection. The **Process** column lists every process identified within each department and the **Priority** column showcases the order in which these processes will be documented. In this example, the Accounts Receivable process is top priority, as indicated by the number one in front of it and the thick black line that surrounds it in the table.

| Department | Priority | Process | KPIs | UOM | Gatekeeper |
|---|---|---|---|---|---|
| MARKETING | 4 | Lead Generation | | | |
| | 6 | Sales | | | |
| ACCOUNTING | 1 | Accounts Receivable | | | |
| | 2 | Collections | | | |
| TECHNOLOGY | 3 | Technology Support | | | |
| | 5 | Software Maintenance | | | |

"Now that these two columns are filled, we will focus on how to document your processes." I switched the image projected on the overhead screen from the example process table to the slide presentation.

**The two most common ways to document a business process are:**
1. Standard Operating Procedure (SOP)
2. Process Map


**The Standard Operating Procedure**
"An SOP is a step-by-step description of a process. This is a default format that I highly recommend you use first since all other formats are derived from it. Those other formats include a process map or flowchart, job aids and intellectual property applications.

"A process map is a visual illustration of a process. This format is incredibly useful in identifying problems within a process that are, otherwise, invisible when analyzing the process in any other format.

"Today, we will focus on documenting your process in the SOP format." I switched the screen from the presentation back to the business infrastructure software.

"In this example, since the Accounts Receivable process is top priority, let's look again at the three tasks that make up this process: Email invoice to client, Collect payment from client, and Generate invoice. I need to place these tasks in the order they are performed." I clicked and dragged each task until they appeared in sequential order. The following result emerged:

### Accounts Receivable Process

1. Generate invoice.
2. Email invoice to client.
3. Collect payment from client.

I scanned the room to get a feel for people's reactions before I randomly asked, "Karen, if I gave these steps to you and asked you to bill my client, would you know what to do?"

Karen Benoit looked confused. "No, I would not. Not at all."

"Why?"

"Well, for one, *how* do I generate an invoice? How is payment collected? Via credit card? Direct deposit into a banking account? Do you accept cash? What forms of payment *do* you accept? There just isn't enough detail for me to know what to do."

"Exactly! Remember what I told you all yesterday. You have to think of your processes as recipes. One missed step can skew the results of the process and you'll waste more time and money trying to correct the mistake. I'll add in more detail to answer the questions Karen asked." The following result emerged:

### Accounts Receivable Process

1. Generate invoice in the software.
2. Add the due date and a thank you message to the invoice.
3. Email the invoice to the client.
4. Collect payment from client. Payment options include direct deposit and credit card.
5. Mark the invoice as "paid" in the software.

"There's still something missing. Can anyone guess what it is?"

Sarah Reuben, who has a background in industrial engineering, knew the answer but waited to give others a chance to answer. Finally, seeing that none of the other participants were going to respond, she raised her hand, "There are no conditional statements."

"Correct! Sarah, please explain to the group what you mean by *conditional statements*."

"A conditional statement is an if/then statement indicating an action to take based on a condition. The problem with this SOP is that it's written as a perfect, or best case, scenario, as though there will never be any problems."

"Ah, I get it!" Albert Andoh said to everyone's astonishment. "This is what we use in programming. I never thought of it in this context. This is interesting."

"We're all familiar with the expression, 'The devil is in the details,' right?" Everyone nodded. "As you document your SOP, first write it considering the 'perfect' scenario as Sarah described, then go back and play 'devil's advocate.' What I mean is, you should try to figure out everything that can go wrong in the process and embed conditional statements accordingly. This alone will play a key role later when you are ready to improve or streamline your process."

I added conditional statements throughout the SOP. The following result emerged:

**Accounts Receivable Process**

1. Generate invoice in the software. *Is software working properly?*
   a. If yes, then go to step 2.
   b. If no, then go to the **Technology Support** process. Repeat step 1.

2. Add the due date and a thank you message to the invoice.

3. Email the invoice to the client. *Did client receive the email?*
   a. If yes, then go to step 4.
   b. If no, then resend the email. Repeat step 3.

4. Collect credit card payment from client. *Did the payment post?*
   a. If yes, then go to step 5.
   b. If no, then go to the **Collections** process. Repeat step 4.

5. Mark the invoice as "paid" in the software.

"Notice that, not only did I include conditional statements, I also cross-referenced other processes as part of troubleshooting this process. This is where process work can become complex. Eventually, you'll want to link your documented processes together. It's rare that a process will operate in complete isolation of other processes. The things that you cross-reference can include an actual process or checklists, templates and videos, which we collectively refer to as 'job aids.'

"There is a science to this, however. You don't want to go too deep down the rabbit hole in figuring out all process nuances."

Before I could finish my train of thought, Vandana Thiagarajan blurted, "Trust me, you do *NOT* want to go down the rabbit hole! I call it the 'matrix.' I've been there and it's not pleasant!"

"That's an interesting way of putting it Vandana. Yes, we do not want any of you getting caught in the 'process matrix.' You want enough detail to eliminate confusion but not too much to where following the process becomes unnecessarily cumbersome. As you'll learn tomorrow, testing is key to determining whether or not the amount of detail you've provided is sufficient. This is a nice segué to my next question. Karen, looking at this latest version of the SOP, do you now feel comfortable enough to bill my client on my behalf?"

Karen looked at me suspiciously, as though I asked her a trick question. After a few seconds she responded, "No. What if I don't know how to use the software."

"Precisely! This is a perfect time to show cross-referencing to a video. I won't demonstrate this but, hypothetically, I could create a job aid called, *How to Use the Software*. I would write out those steps in the form of an SOP and then leverage that SOP as a script for a video that I would create.

"All of you should make a note of this. Whenever your SOP involves use of a software technology or piece of equipment, you should consider capturing a video to demonstrate its use, as opposed to writing out the steps and capturing screenshots. The reason is because software is constantly updated. The moment you complete an SOP describing how to use software, you will likely have to change a significant portion of it depending on the nature of the update. This can be incredibly time consuming, not to mention costly.

"Some people may find that it's easier to capture a video first and then have it transcribed into an SOP. It's really a matter of preference, and transcription is becoming more cost-effective by the day. There are an abundance of screen-recording tools to create videos that capture your navigation within software on your computer. You can also use a tool as simple as your smart phone to record yourself using a piece of equipment as part of an SOP.

"Here's what the SOP looks like with cross-references to video tutorials and other processes."

### Accounts Receivable Process

1. Generate invoice in the software. *Is software working properly?*
   a. If yes, then go to step 2.
   b. If no, then go to the Technology Support process. Repeat step 1.

2. Add the due date and a thank you message to the invoice.

3. Email the invoice to the client. *Did client receive the email?*
   a. If yes, then go to step 4.
   b. If no, then resend the email. Repeat step 3.

4. Collect credit card payment from client. *Did the payment post?*
   a. If yes, then go to step 5.
   b. If no, then go to the Collections process. Repeat Step 4.

▶ 5. Mark the invoice as "paid" in the software.

"Notice that there are not only video icons in the left margin of the SOP, but there's also an information icon too. This icon visually denotes that there is a documented policy associated with this particular step. In this example, the policy referenced is an *Email Etiquette* policy."

\*\*\*\*

"This is a good time to distinguish the difference between a policy and a procedure. A policy establishes the rules and guidelines necessary to maintain company culture and goals. It has breadth in its application. In contrast, a procedure is very specific and narrow in its application. Policies are collectively stored in an Employee Manual whereas procedures are collectively stored in an Operations Manual."

## Process Map

"For purposes of this workshop, we've discussed all the key points you need to know to thoroughly document your SOP. Although the goal for today is to document your top priority process, here's a peek at what the process map equivalent for our example looks like. I'll explain all of the symbols when we begin mapping tomorrow."

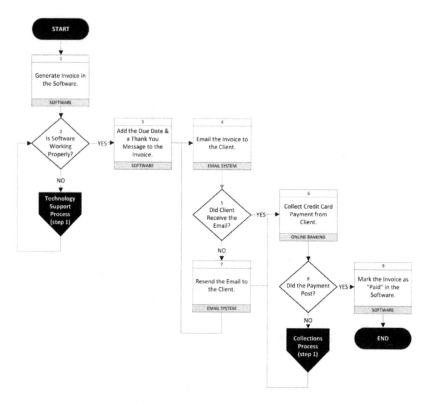

**Figure 8.2** Example Accounts Receivable Process Map

## Intellectual Property Documentation

"Many service-based small businesses often overlook the value of their intellectual property. Documentation of proprietary information in the form of a business process makes an otherwise intangible asset more tangible and easier to valuate. Suppose, there was something proprietary about this example Accounts Receivable process that warranted intellectual property protection. In keeping with the example, let's say we actually developed the software that is used to generate invoices. In order to describe its use, a utility patent application requires that we include both a written and flowchart description of how the software works. Take a look at this…"

I projected an example of what the Accounts Receivable process might look like for a utility patent application.

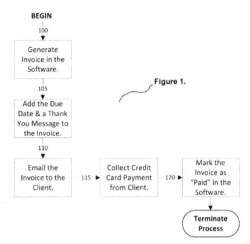

**Reference Figure 1.**
Prepare to execute the Accounts Receivable Process. At 100, generate invoice in the accounting software. If no problems are reported with the software, then at 105, add the due date and a thank you message to the invoice. The invoice is now ready to send to the client. At 110, email the invoice to the client. There are times when a client may report not receiving an email. If the client confirms email receipt, then prepare to collect credit card payment from the client, 115. Else, resend the email to the client. If the payment did not post, then initiate the defined process for Collections. If the payment does post, then mark the invoice as paid in the software, 120.

**Figure 8.3** Example Process Format for a Patent Application (Accounting Software)

"As you can see, a utility patent application leverages both the SOP and process map formats."

****

"We will use the rest of our time in tonight's session to start documenting your top priority process. The output of what you capture will be known as the **current state** of your process; it describes the way the process currently functions, *as-is*. This is not the time to capture how you want it *to-be*. You may also find that, in documenting the current state, the process is performed differently by different people. You'll want to make a note of that as well so that, ultimately, you can determine the best way to perform the process moving forward.

"By going through this exercise at least once, you will understand the time required when you begin delegating this work to others in your company.

**Remember, every process you document:**

- Must be repeatable,
- Must yield the same result, every time, and
- Must not be dependent upon one person's knowledge or skill set.

"In documenting the steps, you are like a scientist. You must carefully record the correct order of steps and any tools needed. When I worked as an engineer in chemical plants and oil refineries, a missed step could lead to a potential explosion. Think about how a missed step in your transactional business process can cost your company money. This usually shifts the perspective of a process' value from a *nice-to-have* to a *must-have*.

"Once you've worked with your consultant to capture your SOP, I also want you to think about who will be the Gatekeeper of your process. The Gatekeeper is the person responsible for maintaining and enforcing the process. If the person responsible for performing and maintaining the process versus actually enforcing the process are two different people, then you can add another column to your process table called 'Administrator,' and add the name of the assigned role to the table."

Each entrepreneur spent the remainder of the session on their respective top priority process using the instructions and lessons learned earlier. They were encouraged to show up the next day with a complete SOP.

## Day Three – Process Mapping

It was now Sunday, the third day of the workshop and, according to the itinerary, it would be a full, eight-hour session starting at 1:00 pm. Each participant showed up with a fully documented SOP for their highest priority process. Most of them admitted to staying up into the wee hours of the night trying to make sure they captured all the information. Some even had their key employees on standby to answer on-the-spot questions that arose. The good news is that they all were beginning to see the value of these exercises and were excited about the possibilities of having airtight operations.

I began the session by asking each participant to share any revelations they had in documenting their respective SOPs. Although each had different revelations, they all reported having a greater appreciation for the time commitment involved.

"Yes! It is not for the faint at heart!" I told them. "As you've experienced, process documentation is a *process* in and of itself. Though effective documentation does not happen overnight, knowing that you have a systematic way to identify and document processes that will support and facilitate future growth and sustainability plans is worth its weight in gold. It requires dedication, patience and a willingness to be exposed.

"To that extent, process documentation is like putting your business in front of a mirror. It can make some entrepreneurs anxious, not to mention resistant, especially if you learn that your perception of your company's operational health is different from reality. Though processes can range in complexity, the one thing they all have in common is *flow.*"

### Types of Process Flows

"It's always about flow," I told the captive audience of participants as I began the slide presentation for the day. "Think of water. Like electricity, it flows along the path of **least resistance**. As you map your process today, think about whether you control the flow of work or information, or does the flow control you?

"From a process perspective, flow represents movement and can happen in a variety of ways." I projected a series of slides to explain and illustrate the different types of process flows.

### 1. Series

A type of process flow where steps occur linearly or one right after the other.

**Figure 8.4** Example of a Process with Activities Flowing in Series

"In Figure 8.4, steps A, B, C and D occur sequentially before reaching the end of the process."

### 2. Parallel

A type of process flow where two or more steps can take place at the same time.

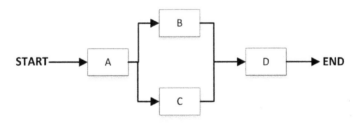

**Figure 8.5** Example of a Process with Activities Flowing in Parallel

"In Figure 8.5, the process can happen quicker (in comparison to the series flow in Figure 8.4), since two paths of steps (B and C) occur simultaneously. The paths merge at step D before reaching the end of the process."

### 3. Batch

A type of process flow that includes temporary stopping points or waiting periods.

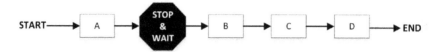

**Figure 8.6** Example of a Batch Process

"In Figure 8.6, step A does not flow directly to step B. There is a temporary stop along the way. This is known as **waiting in queue**, and is a perfect representation of what can happen in our example Accounts Receivable process — if the software is down, then the process cannot continue until it is up and running again."

### 4. Continuous

A type of process flow where movement happens without interference.

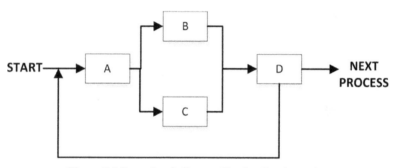

**Figure 8.7** Example of a Process Flowing Continuously

"In Figure 8.7, the process does not end with step D. Instead, it splits in two directions. Part of D's output goes to another process and another part of its output feeds into an earlier part of the process (i.e., it is recycled). Recycling is common in manufacturing processes and is not necessarily a bad thing. However, in a transactional process, this can be a sign of trouble and is known as *rework*. Think of the step in the example Accounts Receivable process where an email must be resent if the client did not receive it the first time around."

### Process Mapping

"Knowing how work or information flows in a business process can help tremendously in improving a process. You may create an initiative to eliminate batch flow in your process to save time and money. Or, you may try to automate steps in a series flow so that steps can be performed simultaneously to, again, save time and money. Speed, efficiency, accuracy and precision are tantamount to process management.

"It's no wonder that a process map is the perfect blend of science and art. The way you map can strongly influence people's decisions about how and where to best optimize a process. Mapping, if done correctly, can also expose things that may not be obvious in an SOP format."

Next, I advanced to a slide that included a table of standard process mapping symbols provided by the American National Standards Institute (see Appendix C). I pointed out that diamonds are used for decision points, squares or rectangles for steps/activities and ovals for starting and ending points, also known as terminal points. These, I explained, were the symbols used to create the example Accounts Receivable process map (Figure 8.2).

"Another point I'd like to add is that inputs to a step or activity should be drawn as arrows pointing to the left and/or top of the step. Outputs should be drawn as arrows pointing from the right and bottom of the step. This is in accordance with how chemical engineers draw manufacturing process maps to demonstrate the law of conservation."

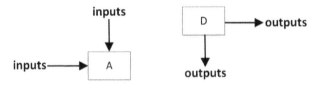

"Each of you will now spend the next four hours creating a process map version of your top priority process. I suggest printing your SOP and using it, along with the standard process mapping symbols, to create your map. You can either use a stand-alone process mapping software or your consultant will show you how to use the business infrastructure software to convert your SOP into a process map. The choice is yours. Be sure to print the map. Errors often go unnoticed in digital copies."

As instructed, the participants spent the next four hours mapping their respective top priority process. They were surprised at how quickly the time passed. Almost all of them found themselves toggling between the SOP and process map versions to make corrections until the two versions mirrored each other to the best extent possible.

## Process Testing

After a one-hour dinner break, the workshop resumed. Each participant now had a printed copy of his or her SOP and process map.

I told them that the next step was to test their processes for accuracy. I could tell that some of the participants looked puzzled. Later, I learned that some of them thought they had already exhausted the means for ensuring accuracy. Sharen Benoit Joseph said, "Testing? It seems to me we've done a considerable amount of due diligence in documenting this process. It's in two formats for God's sake!"

Before I could respond, Albert Andoh came to my defense. "Actually, Ms. Sharen, as a programmer I know the importance of testing before releasing any product."

Sarah Reuben also chimed in, "Same for us. If we don't test and inspect our furniture before delivering it to our clients, the results could be catastrophic. We've learned the hard way — bad news always travels faster than good news." Steve looked at his sister with admiration. After years of fighting, he was starting to gain an appreciation for all the effort Sarah put in over the years to establish their furniture making processes.

"Thank you Albert and Sarah," I said, relieved that there were participants in the room who validated the need for process testing. "In addition to what you both said, you all should consider that your process is currently documented from *your* perspective and you may have inadvertently left out some steps.

"The best way to test your process for accuracy is to give it to people who are completely unfamiliar with the process and ask them to follow it. If they are able to follow the process and achieve the desired result, then you'll know you have a well-documented process. If they have trouble following the process, then you'll know exactly where you'll need to update the process for clarity.

"I'd like for each of you to pair yourself with another participant. You'll spend the next two hours testing each other's processes. Of course, I realize this is not a lot of time and that some of your processes may involve the use of tools that are inaccessible. The point is for you to swap processes, talk through it and ask questions. When you return home to your respective businesses, you can perform a full testing of the process."

The participants started shuffling themselves around the roundtables present in the ballroom as if they were playing musical chairs. In a short time, they paired themselves as follows: Emily with Karen and Sharen; Sarah and Steve with Clenard; Albert and Selom with Vandana, Brian and Imana. The consultants sat together separately at a table near the entrance to the ballroom.

Two hours later, each participant revealed additional notes they wrote onto their printed SOP and process map resulting from the testing simulation exercise.

## Process Enforcement

After the testing simulation exercise, the participants were also rejoined with their respective consultant. I advanced to the next slide of the workshop presentation; it displayed a message:

## A Process is Only as Good as its Enforcement.

I explained the message by saying that enforcement is linked to quality assurance. "It does you no good to invest your time, effort and energy into documenting and testing a process, if you never enforce its performance.

"One way to enforce your processes is to assign **KPIs**. Key Performance Indicators represent metrics that let you know whether a process is performing optimally. Notice I said *process* and not *people*. Going back to our Accounts Receivable process, suppose we assign the amount of aging receivables in a month as an indicator or measure of the process' performance." I updated the process table to include aging receivables less than 30 days as a sign of acceptable process performance.

| Department | Priority | Process | KPIs | UOM | Gatekeeper |
|---|---|---|---|---|---|
| **ACCOUNTING** | 1 | Accounts Receivable | Aging Receivables < 30 days | Number; Zero per month | Bookkeeper |

"By communicating that one of the KPIs for the Accounts Receivable process is to have receivables less than 30 days old, I am letting the **Gatekeeper**, in this case, the bookkeeper, know that anytime an invoice goes unpaid past 30 days, it is a sign of trouble. If an invoice does go unpaid after 30 days of sending it, then the first course of action that the bookkeeper will take is to look at the process, make sure every step was followed and, after conducting an internal investigation, send a reminder invoice to the client.

"Notice how the default response to a missed KPI was not to automatically blame the bookkeeper. The bookkeeper did his or her part to follow the process for invoicing; however, whether the client actually pays on time is out of his or her control. Further investigation might show that part of the reason the invoice went unpaid within 30 days of notification is that there could have been software issues.

"The **UOM**, or Unit of Measurement, represents the unit and frequency with which to report the KPI. The UOM could be a whole number, a percentage or a ratio. The UOM for the Accounts Receivable process is zero aging receivables reported each month. All KPIs and their associated UOMs should be linked directly to the overall company goal to make money.

"If you'll take a look at your business infrastructure software, you'll notice there's an area in the top menu of the Business Process Manual screen called 'KPI.' Click on that to display a full listing of potential KPIs [see Appendix D] you can select for your process.

"Yes, you can select more than one KPI for a process, but you want to make sure you **measure the right things.** Choose metrics that not only directly tie to your company's ability to make money, but also choose metrics that are both customer-centric *and* employee-centric, since both represent the life force of your business. It's flat out wrong to blame people for bad or broken processes. But, if you do find that the person performing the process is, in fact, the problem, then you can take corrective action measures according to your H.R. policies."

**In addition to identifying performance metrics, you should also:**

1.  Create a forum that allows for ongoing employee feedback on the process as opposed to an annual performance evaluation;
2.  Document and test at least three processes every month for accuracy; and
3.  Develop protocol for ongoing process improvement and maintenance.

### Process Monitoring

"We're going to switch gears a little in preparation for tomorrow's session on process improvement. Before attempting to improve a process, you should monitor it first to understand where breakdowns occur. Process breakdowns are better known as *bottlenecks*. Just as the neck of a bottle slows down the flow of the substance it contains as it is poured out, so does a process bottleneck slow down the flow of information or work as it is performed.

"As a business owner, you already have more work to do than time to do it. The last thing you need are slow processes that negatively impact daily operations. I'm sure you've all heard of the importance of 'systematizing' your business, that is, having a **process-dependent business** as opposed to a **people-dependent business**. But what does that really mean?"

I displayed a different representation of the Accounts Receivable process using a pictorial flow diagram with symbols illustrating manual versus software activities and the average time to flow, or move, from one activity to the next. In the first diagram displayed, the software that the bookkeeper uses performs optimally and an invoice is sent to the customer. "If the customer pays within 30 days, the entire process would have a total cycle time of 30 days or less."

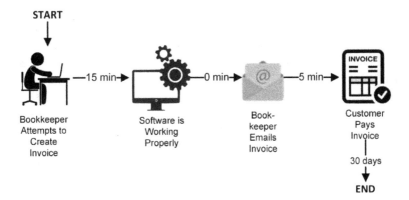

Then, I displayed a second diagram with different conditions. "Let's look at what happens when, at the moment services are rendered and you're ready to bill the client, the bookkeeper is out on a two-week vacation (10 days). The total cycle time increases from 30 days to 40 days because there is no one else who can create the invoice.

"If the software is down when the bookkeeper returns to work, it could take a full day or more to troubleshoot. The total cycle time now increases to 41 days. The net effect can be detrimental to your cash flow. The slower you are to bill your client, the later you will receive payment, even if the client pays within the requested time of 30 days.

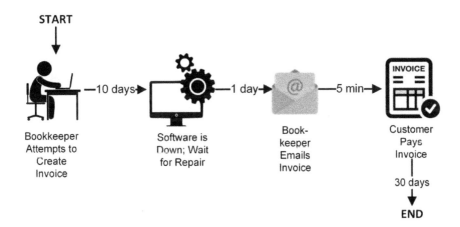

"How can you tell if your business' operations are people- or process-dependent? One way is to record the amount of time that it takes to flow from one step of your process to the next. Do some steps take an unusually long time? Would changing the flow pattern, for example from series to parallel, help reduce the overall time? Would automation of some sort help to reduce time and potential errors without sacrificing quality?

"Another way to tell is by testing the process using different scenarios to determine the impact on a process if certain people were unable to perform an activity, if certain software or equipment is malfunctioning and/or if a natural disaster occurs. Where are the bottlenecks? How much time would pass before you'd have to completely shut down operations? If the scenarios prove that the absence of certain people has a far-reaching impact, then you have a people-dependent business."

I projected a new slide. "The good news is there are ways to mitigate and safeguard your business' operations against known process bottlenecks. Some ways include:

1. **Cross-training Staff.** This allows for replacement staff when the person who normally performs a process is not physically present.

2. **Establishing an Out-of-Office Policy.** Such a policy can buy you time to find replacement staff: a simple, yet highly effective solution.

3. **Conducting a Failure Modes Effect Analysis (FMEA).** This is a Six Sigma tool for contingency planning where you brainstorm what can either go wrong or slow down your process and develop a plan of action to either mitigate or eliminate those possibilities. This could serve as an extension of your Disaster Recovery and Business Continuity plan as you identify steps to take in the event of fire, theft and flood.

4. **Trusting, but Verifying all Software Technology.** Software technology is wonderful, but it has its limitations. It's enticing to invest in the latest gadget but, before spending your hard-earned dollars, consider the following:

   • Will it improve your customers' experience?
   • How will it save you money or help you make more money?
   • Is it compatible with your existing technology?
   • Does the use of it add more steps to the existing process?
   • Is there a steep learning curve in adopting it?
   • Is there ongoing customer support for it?

"Be sure all technology you invest in passes your litmus test for operational excellence."

****

"We're at the end of today's session. You've all had to digest quite a bit of information in a relatively short period of time. Think about questions you may have and we'll discuss them tomorrow. I'll see you all in the morning."

## Day Four – Process Optimization & Team Selection

This final day of the workshop was the toughest for the participants, considering the fact that it began the morning following the eight-hour session the day before.

"We covered a lot of territory yesterday," I re-assured them. Congratulations on having your top priority process fully documented! Today, we will resume the discussion on process monitoring and improvement and end with how to select the right people to help you complete your initial Business Process Manual. I encourage building internal knowledge in your company so that you won't become overly dependent on your consultant."

I activated the slide presentation and began talking through the various points to cover.

### Process Improvement

"How many of you have heard of Six Sigma?" All hands raised except Albert's. "How many of you have heard of Lean?" Again, all hands raised except Albert's. "How many of you actually know what either of those is?" This time, only Sarah, Vandana and Clenard raised their hands.

"The short answer is that they are both continuous improvement methodologies designed to minimize waste, defects and errors. It's unfair to simplify their definitions, but in a nutshell, Lean focuses on stripping waste or non-value added activities from a process. Six Sigma focuses on preventing errors or defects resulting from a process. The process map, though fundamental, is one of the dozens of tools used in implementing both methodologies.

"Lean projects tend to be shorter than Six Sigma projects. Like Kasennu, the way a Six Sigma project is implemented is rooted in the scientific method. The Define, Measure, Analyze, Improve and Control phases (collectively known as DMAIC) of a Six Sigma project require a more rigorous examination of the root causes of a problem and consistent data collection and analysis before making improvements to a process. Process improvements made via Six Sigma are steeped in statistical analysis whereas improvements made via Lean can be based merely from observations and the measured reduction in overall cycle time. More people are beginning to combine the tools, principles and concepts of both methodologies in executing process improvement projects for maximum impact.

"Let's re-examine the pictorial flow diagram of the Accounts Receivable process we reviewed yesterday. By monitoring data over a 90-day period, you may determine the number of times the aging receivables KPI is over 30 days is unacceptable. By looking at the process map, you realize that having the bookkeeper involved in sending invoices and collecting payment is a bottleneck or non-value added activity (Lean). However, you want data to support this observation (Six Sigma). At this point, you already know the status of aging receivables, but to increase customer satisfaction, prevent erroneous information on the invoice and reduce the overall billing cycle time, you decide to re-engineer the process altogether. After conducting a series of tests, you find that the improved process works.

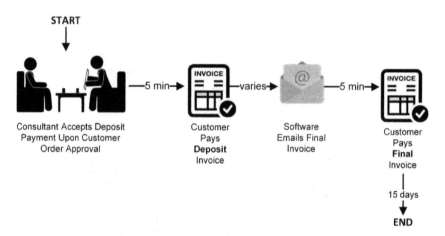

"It works because, now, instead of the billing cycle beginning once a consultant delivers a completed order, it begins the moment a consultant receives order approval from the customer. By using an automated invoicing system, the consultant can collect payment directly from the customer without having to wait on the bookkeeper to process the payment. The fact that a deposit payment is accepted also improves cash flow. Through a combination of Lean and Six Sigma tools, you could reduce the overall billing cycle time to 15 days plus the amount of time required to deliver the actual order. The improved process is no longer dependent on the bookkeeper's physical presence; it frees up time for the bookkeeper to work on other value-added activities and your customers are ecstatic because of the convenience.

"Both Lean and Six Sigma consider the *upstream* and *downstream* effects of a potential change to a process. By upstream effect, I mean the impact of changes that precede a particular step. By downstream effect, I mean the impact of changes that follow a particular step. Improvements, therefore, are not made in isolation of the overall net effect on the entire process.

"These are basic principles that lay the foundation for continuous process improvement. Here are some others." I continued advancing through the slide presentation.

## Process vs. People-Dependency

"As we discussed yesterday, people come before processes, but processes should not be people-dependent. No, this isn't meant to be a riddle. When you convert your company's processes from being people-dependent to process-dependent, the goal is **NOT to get rid of people;** rather, it is to optimize operations for maximum value to your customers and your employees. Your employees are more than just FTEs.[28] When you shift your perspective from thinking of them as liabilities and, instead, as *institutional knowledge assets*, then your relationship, and company, can change for the better.

## Employees are NOT Entrepreneurs

"Some of you have made the transition from entrepreneur to CEO. Do you remember when you were first starting out? You were probably a masterful juggler; you might still be. You had no problem rolling up your sleeves and doing whatever it took to meet customer demand and keep the doors to your business open. The unpredictability of each day fueled you and got your creative juices flowing.

"Guess what? Your employees will likely not be the same. Although they may be passionate and hard-working, they've had *specific training* to perform a *specific role* in your company and expect to do only that."

## Semantics Can Kill Efficiency

"This is a big one! Even though you and your employees speak the same language, work flow can still break down as you explain a process and communicate expectations. This happens because of the way humans listen, comprehend and interpret information. To the best extent possible, be clear instead of cryptic. When explaining something, ask your employees to repeat their interpretation of what you said so you'll know for sure if they understand your instructions."

## Employees are NOT Robots

"In transactional environments, most processes are likely performed by people. Every employee brings with him or her a unique set of experiences that affect the performance of a process. Use a balanced approach when capturing business processes. They should be flexible enough to capitalize on different employees' experiences but not rigid to the point where individuality is completely suppressed. This is key in providing excellent customer service.

"Unlike manufacturing processes, process improvement methodologies like Six Sigma can be more challenging to apply to business processes. Why? Because of people. In manufacturing environments, processes largely center around equipment and software. Employees monitor that equipment and report and troubleshoot problems as they arise.

"The same is not true for business processes, especially when they rely heavily on manual activities. As you learned on day one of the workshop, people are not predictable like machines. But they are no less valuable. Some think the solution is robotic replacement. However, they fail to consider that people are still required to collect data and monitor performance of the robot, perform maintenance on it and possibly re-program it. Invest in innovation to raise the bar but, remember, there's a delicate balance that should be maintained between the natural or analog world and the artificial intelligence or digital world. You can conduct impact studies to understand the long-term effects."

## Outsourcing the Work

"As a small business owner, you likely cannot afford a large consulting firm to do process work for you. That brings on the next challenge — who exactly can you hire? Unfortunately, there is a plethora of conflicting descriptions online regarding business process professionals.

"Here's a cardinal rule to remember:

---
### Process Specialists are NOT Created Equal.
---

"You could invest in the educational development of those of your existing staff who express a desire to learn how to do process work. However, that's a longer term goal and, if your needs are more immediate, you'll need to outsource this work. I developed a list of 10 factors for you to consider. Keep in mind that these factors depend on your company's industry and the complexity of your operations."

1. Educational Background
2. Technical & Analytical Skills
3. Troubleshooting Skills
4. References & Work Samples
5. Ability to Scope Your Project
6. Personality
7. Knowledge of Intellectual Property Laws
8. Independent Contractor or Employee
9. Ability to Work Remotely/Virtually
10. Flexibility

[See Appendix E for an explanation of each factor.]

"Whether you leverage your existing employees, hire new ones or outsource the work, one thing is for sure, you *will* need help in your process documentation and improvement initiatives. There are process engineers, lean and six sigma consultants, data scientists and technical writers, all of whom can play a role in performing process design, documentation and improvement. You may have to have a combination of these roles in your company as some of these resources may not be equipped to handle the work all the way through from identification to documentation to mapping to monitoring and improving. Revisit your Business Parts Analysis and Business Design Blueprint to add these potential activities and roles to your business infrastructure."

## Accountability

"Work with the people you identify as Gatekeepers (and Administrators, if applicable) to distribute controlled copies of your Business Process Manual to your staff. Leverage the work you completed during the Electronic Records Management and Paper Records Management elements of the Kasennu methodology to determine the best digital and/or physical location for your Business Process Manual.

"If you decide to keep a physical copy of your Business Process Manual, I recommend storing processes in separate binders according to department. Each binder would be a different color based on the color assigned during the Business Parts Analysis. It would house all processes, along with all job aids specific to that particular department.

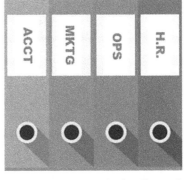

"However you decide to store your processes, make it clear that they are now 'etched in stone,' and are, therefore, part of your company's intellectual property. The contents of the Business Process Manual should not be duplicated or distributed outside your business without your permission."

****

"Does anyone have any questions before we wrap up?"

As I scanned the room, I saw a sea of eyes glazed over from information overload. "I know this was a lot of information to absorb in a short amount of time. In fairness, I did warn you!" I said, hoping to lighten the mood. "Keep in mind that you should focus on identifying and documenting your processes first. When the time comes for process improvement, you or one of your designated employees can attend one of my advanced workshops on Lean and Six Sigma."

Clenard offered to his fellow business owners, "My company's floor and field operations went through an entire Lean Six Sigma transformation a few years ago. Feel free to reach out to me anytime if you have questions. I can't guarantee I can answer your questions, but I can certainly help point you in the right direction."

"Me too," Vandana added. "I have a background in statistics and we just implemented a process improvement initiative to improve our loan processing time."

Sarah offered to help as well. I reminded everyone that they were not alone — their respective consultants would be there to offer guidance along the way.

### The Emerald Tablet

"We're now coming to a close. It's been a pleasure getting to know and work with each of you. I'm so proud of the progress you've each made thus far and I can't wait to share in your journey from this day forward.

"If you'll recall, at the close of the first day of the workshop, I handed each of you an Emerald Tablet. Can you please retrieve that?" Each participant looked through their workshop materials in search of their coveted Emerald Tablet.

"Take a few seconds to re-read this," I requested. After a brief pause, I continued. "This should make more sense now, wouldn't you agree?

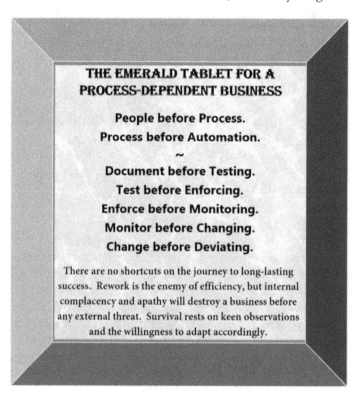

**THE EMERALD TABLET FOR A PROCESS-DEPENDENT BUSINESS**

**People before Process.**
**Process before Automation.**
~
**Document before Testing.**
**Test before Enforcing.**
**Enforce before Monitoring.**
**Monitor before Changing.**
**Change before Deviating.**

There are no shortcuts on the journey to long-lasting success. Rework is the enemy of efficiency, but internal complacency and apathy will destroy a business before any external threat. Survival rests on keen observations and the willingness to adapt accordingly.

"Your customers and your staff are the reason you are still in business. Always put them first! Of course, you must identify the processes you want to document upfront. Always document a process before attempting to improve it, and a process must be tested for accuracy before you can enforce it. Don't automate for automation's sake; you should not waste resources on fixing something that isn't broken. Change, or improvement, should occur when the data indicates there is a way to streamline the process and make it better. Always try to change a process before you make a complete deviation or departure from it altogether. And last, I think it goes without saying what complacency and apathy can do to your business. Remember, **rework is the enemy of efficiency**."

I thanked everyone and they applauded. My work was done, at least for the time being. The feeling of knowing you have made a positive difference and possibly saved a small business from ruin never gets old. At that moment, Jude entered the ballroom. He thanked everyone for staying at his resort and asked that they take time to complete a short, online survey regarding their experience at the resort as well as at the workshop.

By noon, all of the participants were on a plane back to their respective businesses.

#### **** One Year Later ****

### Emily Miller

The past year had been a whirlwind for Emily. Because of the new business infrastructure, she transitioned successfully out of her role as executive director and into managing director of the non-profit she founded. Thanks to a solid hiring strategy and processes, there were now more people in place to do the work and she was able to spend more quality time with her father before his battle with dementia ended.

She even bought a mental rehabilitation facility franchise from Karen and Sharen that specialized in providing support for caregivers of people suffering with mental illness. Emily realized that, through it all, she never really lost her identity — she just needed to reclaim it.

### Albert Andoh

By April 2016, Albert was one month away from graduating from high school. Since the workshop, he and his development team in Ghana developed an app for Vandana, Brian and Imana's mortgage company. He also led an initiative to link various systems at Sarah's and Steve's furniture store. Vandana took a particular liking to Albert and wrote him a stellar recommendation to her alma mater, Columbia University. He accepted a full scholarship to Columbia where he would pursue a degree in a financial technology (FinTech) discipline. This was on par in demonstrating to his new team of investors his desire to learn more about the *business* of software development. Albert matured from a tunnel-vision teenage coder into a well-rounded young man.

## Sarah & Steve Reuben

Sarah and Steve were stunned when their father announced that Jonathan, their first cousin and the current CFO of their furniture company, would replace him as CEO. Both felt the sting of rejection, but it turned out to be a blessing in disguise. Sarah, Steve and Clenard developed a special bond that started during the workshop. Clenard encouraged Sarah to secure trade secret protection for her signature furniture coating. Soon after, she and her husband started selling it to other furniture companies. Sarah no longer had a need to become CEO at her family's furniture store, she was now the CEO of her own company!

Meanwhile the arguing with Steve stopped and so did the name calling. In fact, Steve had an equity stake in Sarah's new company. He retained his position as CMO of their furniture company and Sarah sat on their advisory board. Steve and Brian also developed a friendship that started at the workshop when they realized their shared desire to work more in the entertainment arena. Steve was currently auditioning for a recurring role on Brian's TV show to help new homebuyers furnish their homes, and he hoped to open a branch of their furniture store back in his native New York.

## Karen Benoit & Sharen Benoit Joseph

After the workshop, Karen went into full drive with her media campaigning. She had new material to talk about, considering her and Sharen's decision to reconnect with a long-lost relative. The healing process would be a long one, for there was so much hurt and misunderstandings, but they recognized they would be better business owners if they underwent their own healing process. As Karen ramped up the publicity for their mental rehabilitation facilities, Sharen worked with all of the locations to oversee proper implementation of their newfound business infrastructure. They were far better prepared for the next potential levee breach, or any other natural disaster for that matter.

They no longer waited for external auditing to expose problem areas; rather, they developed a quarterly internal auditing system. It was paying off, too. In a year, they opened new locations in Lake Charles, Louisiana and in Houston, Texas, both without a hitch. The success of their first out-of-state location gave them the confidence to extend a franchise opportunity to Emily in Washington, D.C.

## Vandana Thiagarajan, Brian Miller and Imana Van Dijk

Vandana, Brian and Imana found themselves busier than ever, except there were no complaints this time. They were each doing what they loved which made for meaningful contributions in collectively expanding their business. Vandana no longer felt trapped in the matrix. They were now in their third season of their reality TV show. It was Imana who, a year earlier, thought it would be good to get ahead of the media to let people know that they recognized some of their internal issues and were proactively taking corrective measures.

This proved to be effective. Not only did demand for their mortgage services increase exponentially, they were getting closer to launching their new real estate development business in Suriname. Ironically, Brian's old law firm even called him, asking if he'd consider coming back to the firm and becoming a partner. His answer was a resounding "no!"

## Clenard Smith II

Clenard was actively working with his attorney to arrange for an IPO of his food distribution company. His company successfully passed its rigorous audit for IPO-readiness and he boasted of having all of their major processes documented. He was closer to conquering his vision of an IPO by the day. He was aware that going public meant a loss of control, but he valued being able to spend more quality time with his family, especially his grandchildren, more than anything.

He also accepted two board positions on non-profits, both with missions to help children. Clenard was even able to work with zoning officials to build a new facility next door to his existing location. He invited Sarah Reuben to take a look at his operational facility so that they could brainstorm the pros and cons of possible robotic process automation[29] for her new business.

# CHAPTER 9

## SANKOFA

"se wo were fi na wosan kofa a yenki"

The above quote summarizes the essence of "Sankofa." Loosely translated it means, "It is not taboo to go back and fetch what you forgot."[30] Sankofa, a philosophical construct, comes from the Akan tribe of Ghana. It embodies the idea of **learning from the past in order to move forward**.

Symbolically, Sankofa is represented sometimes as a mythical bird with its feet facing forward and its head turned backwards while carrying a precious egg in its mouth. That egg represents a life force, the seed or nucleus of an idea that should be held onto.

From a business perspective, I propose that Sankofa communicates in order to move forward, you must go backward and remind yourself of why you started your business in the first place. In that remembrance, take hold of that precious idea so that you do not lose focus as you forge ahead toward mega success.

Since this book's introduction began with a fable about a peacock and a crane, it seemed fitting to use the symbolic Sankofa bird to close this book. When you started your business, you had a vision. A dream, if you will. You are fortunate to still be in business and, at some point in your entrepreneurial journey, you made (or either will have to make) a decision to stop operating your business as the proverbial peacock and, instead, extend your company's flight distance and height by operating as the crane.

Choosing to be the crane means your business continues on a path of ascension. That ascension can be frightening. You'll have to hire more people, whom you probably don't know, and make sure they have all the tools needed to ensure a consistently positive experience for your customers. Ascension also means paying more in taxes, payroll, equipment, building maintenance and software. There's always the eminent danger of fines, lawsuits and exposés that threaten to undermine what you've worked so hard to build.

Yet, you continue on the quest to soar like a crane anyway. In that quest it can be tempting to do something counter to what makes your business so special in the first place. Some call it your "secret sauce," others, your "mojo." Whatever you call *it*, you must protect and preserve it at all costs. In other words, Sankofa!

As your small business expands rapidly, ask yourself, *Are the things that made my business so valuable to my clients in the past holding up during this period of expansion?* It's easy for your vision to become clouded and the waters to become muddied in the midst of fast growth.

Do you know what a snake does when it outgrows its skin? It sheds it! Like a snake, and in the spirit of Sankofa, you must be confident in shedding the things that no longer serve you and your business as you forge ahead.

Steve Jobs said, "You can't connect the dots looking forward; you can only connect them looking backwards. So you have to trust that the dots will somehow connect in your future." Sadly, some entrepreneurs never bother to connect the dots. They remain as the peacock, stuck on the ground and unable to fly for extended periods of time. They are caught in the minutia of the day-to-day grind of their businesses and lack the ability to see things holistically.

It makes sense. After all, the business operating as the peacock can only see things from its vantage point on the ground, whereas the business operating as the crane can fly high and see everything with an eagle's eye. The owners of these types of businesses understand that business infrastructure can help them connect the dots.

The business operating as the crane also understands that what it took to get to a certain point is not necessarily what it will take to get to the next level. They know how to integrate the past with the present to move forward into the future.

## Birds of a Feather Flock Together

Just as birds of a similar species congregate and fly together, so must we as small business owners. Think about the business owners that are currently in your inner circle. Assess their businesses for what they truly are. Can their businesses be described as peacocks or cranes? Do you truly know how successful they are? Are they successful because they've stayed true to the principle of Sankofa?

If you find it difficult to make an accurate assessment, it could be that some of the business owners in your flock operate businesses under the guise of success when they may be suffering on the inside. They've erected a façade that all is well when, in fact, it is not.

A business' façade and its back office operations, you see, can be like the case of Dr. Jekyll and Mr. Hyde.[31] On the one hand, the façade makes you feel good because it attracts business to you but, on the other hand, it causes you immense pain because of a missing or ineffective business infrastructure. The façade can be a dirty secret that no one wants exposed. If it is discussed, it is done so under oaths and NDAs — pacts that we make to protect ourselves legally from exposure. This may explain why we often do not learn of our fellow entrepreneurs' struggles until after the fact, when they have resolved the issue.

Sometimes the experience of being on the verge of losing it all forces us to take a look at our past. As a small business owner, you must align yourself with people who believe in you, support your vision and can share resources with you to help move you forward. Your flock can consist of other business owners, consultants, employees and even your clients.

Build your flock knowing there is no need to clip another bird's wings in order to sustain your own flight. The point is, don't fly alone! As Emily Miller's consultant told her in Chapter 2, even the president of a country has advisors.

# Revisiting the Three Laws

## Sankofa in the Law of Supply and Demand

In the law of supply and demand, you learned that, as a small business owner, you will constantly need to adjust your ability to supply fluctuations in demand for your product or service with the right labor while charging the right price. It's one thing to experience a change, or increase, in demand. But a *shift* in demand presents another unique challenge.

Shifts in demand, as you learned in the story of Karen Benoit (Chapter 5) and her mental rehabilitation facility, can be prompted by changes in your customers' preferences. For example, Coca-Cola® and Pepsi® were both

*Source: antiquesnavigator.com*

originally formulated and marketed as medicinal products. Over time, customer preferences for cold, caffeinated beverages caused them to shift their branding from curing ailments to curing thirst. The same is true for Kleenex®. Originally, the product was created as "a sanitary way to remove cold cream and makeup,"[32] but customer preferences to use the product in other ways, such as a disposable handkerchief, caused them to shift their marketing strategy.

Here is something to think about: what happens when your customers request something that does not represent a *change* or a *shift* in demand but an actual *deviation* from your original offering? This is where Sankofa comes into play. Changes and shifts in demand do not cause you to diverge from your original product or service in the way a deviation does. Think about the word itself: the prefix, "de-" means "to remove or take away from."

I'll share my story as an example of what can happen when customer preferences require a deviation from your original product or service. When I started my company, Equilibria, Inc., it was a professional organizing company. As I shared in Chapter 1, it evolved into the operations management firm it is today. In the beginning, there were many times when clients requested services outside of the scope of my core service offering. I usually obliged, to my detriment.

Without fail, the requested deviations caused me pain in more ways than one. I realized that, as long as I stayed true to the original purpose of my company (Sankofa), I enjoyed the projects I worked on. However, whenever I deviated, I loathed the project. Now I recognize the importance of staying true to my company's roots.

Whenever a deviation is requested, rather than change your business, consider creating a new category, product or service line or new business altogether. This is what the Benoit sisters (Chapter 5) did when they offered Emily Miller a franchise opportunity. It also led Sarah Reuben (Chapter 4) to start her own company to market her furniture product.

This recognition of creating new spaces when deviation is required or requested is what gave way to the various genres of music we enjoy today. With every deviation from the *accepted* music of that time emerged a new genre, like jazz, blues, rock and roll, and hip hop. It has also led companies like Coca-Cola to create new product lines, like Dasani® water, to meet a customer preference that represents a complete deviation from their original soda product.

**Sankofa in the Law of Conservation**
In the law of conservation, you learned that energy is neither created nor destroyed; it is merely transformed and should therefore be used wisely. Use your energy to build a stronger business and remove the people, places and things that historically have not worked for the betterment of your

business if they cannot be transformed.

An excellent example of applying Sankofa in the law of conservation is the story of Harriet Tubman. Harriet was born into enslavement in the U.S. Growing up working on a plantation against her will in Maryland, she had a singular goal, freedom! Freedom not only for herself, but for anyone else who wanted it. Using the North Star as her navigation tool, Harriet relied on her wits, quick thinking and a sophisticated network of people who shared equally in her quest for freedom, to walk over 100 miles to Pennsylvania, a *free* state.

When she arrived in Pennsylvania, she could easily have used her energy to create a new life as a free woman. Instead, in the spirit of Sankofa, she made the conscious decision to make the perilous trip back into enemy territory at least 19 more times to, literally, lead others to their freedom; the return trip that time being several hundred miles further north to Canada.

Harriet reserved her energy to work with those who wanted freedom. She carried a shotgun to dissuade escapees from changing their minds en route for, as she put it, "Dead men tell no tales." In helping over 300 people escape enslavement, she proudly touted that she never lost anyone in the journey. They were all transformed from enslaved *chattel* to free men, women and children.

Source: Unknown

Just as Harriet shed the title of "slave" as part of her transformation, so too did Emily Miller (Chapter 2) and Albert Andoh (Chapter 3) relinquish inaccurate titles, transforming themselves into more savvy businesspeople in the process.

## Sankofa in the Law of Polarity

In the law of polarity, you learned that the net effect of opposing forces, when properly balanced, can provide the perspective needed to propel your business forward. Over the years, I have found that people are less likely to appreciate the structure that the Kasennu methodology offers until their businesses experience the chaos it is designed to quell.

An example of applying Sankofa in the law of polarity is the story of McDonald's®, arguably one of the most successful franchise restaurants in history. The company was the brainchild of brothers, Richard and Maurice McDonald, and saw its first location in San Bernardino, California. Maurice was a marketing and branding guru while Richard had a laser-like focus on processes and systems. A chance encounter with the persistent milkshake mixer salesman, Ray Kroc, forever changed the trajectory of their already successful business.

Ray saw the ingenuity in the brothers' expedient system for making fresh hamburgers, as well as the mass appeal of their branding. He wanted in! Sadly, the story did not end well for the brothers. The scales became unbalanced as the brothers debated whether to expand into other locations. Ray exploited the imbalance of their operations-focused

*Source: huffingtonpost.com*

vision and, ultimately, took the company right from underneath them by laying claim to the real estate on which their very restaurant sat.

To Richard McDonald's credit, he did use Sankofa in warning his brother about partnering with Ray Kroc. They had tried, unsuccessfully, to open additional locations in the past. However, Maurice assured Richard everything would be okay.

Fortunately, for Vandana Thiagarajan (Chapter 6) and Clenard Smith II (Chapter 7), they were able to weigh the value in both sides of their respective dilemmas before it was too late to save their respective businesses.

## Emerald City (the Façade) + Emerald Tablet (the Foundation) = Manageable Growth

As we learned in *The Wonderful Wizard of Oz*, the path to building and maintaining Emerald City is not straight and narrow; it is full of deception, distractors and deterrents. Do not allow the application of the Kasennu methodology to serve as one of those deterrents. The amount of time required to implement Kasennu varies based on your availability, the number of people you have on your team to help you and the complexity of your business' situation.

Operating a business in a world of instant gratification makes it is easy to be enticed with promises of overnight solutions. You should be realistic with yourself when fixing any problem in your fast growing business. If it took you nine years to build your business, do you really think you can turn it around in 30 days? Your company did not get to where it is overnight, so fixing it will not happen overnight. It will take practice, commitment and dedication, the same ingredients it took to build it in the first place.

In applying Kasennu, you also need to give yourself and your team time to absorb the changes that result from implementing the methodology. Too much change too fast can be disastrous. As Robert Greene penned in his 45th law in the *48 Laws of Power*, "Preach the Need to Change but Never

Reform Too Much at One Time."

This is why people who win the lottery usually go broke within a short period of time. They did not work to earn the money and, therefore, do not have the same type of appreciation for it as a person who worked, invested and watched their money grow over an extended period of time. Often, I tell my clients, "A fool with a tool is still a fool." The Kasennu methodology is no exception. Its success is not in the knowledge of it; rather, the success is in its application and ongoing maintenance.

\*\*\*\*

Running a business is hard. *Real* hard. Using business infrastructure to develop your proverbial Emerald Tablet can provide the clarity, direction and foundation needed to duplicate and document the precious, golden egg that you must hold onto as your business advances. With the greatest risk comes the greatest reward; therefore, keep giving birth to new ideas.

Embrace the unknown. Take comfort in the uncomfortable. Know who you are. Use discernment. Remember your vocare, your calling, and soon your company's façade will be matched with unbridled professionalism and supported by an invincible business infrastructure. Stop keeping up with the Joneses[33] and actually *be* the Joneses! Be the model of success, inside and out, that others will want to emulate. In doing so you can:

- Reclaim your identity like Emily did in Chapter 2;
- Be humble and remain open to learning new things like Albert did in Chapter 3;
- Recognize when you may be getting in the way of progress as Sarah and Steve discovered in Chapter 4;
- Be vigilant at all times and watch out for business landmines as Karen and Sharen were forewarned in Chapter 5;
- Choose the path that aligns with your passion and not your pocketbook, for, as Vandana, Brian and Imana learned in Chapter 6, the money will come; and
- Develop a winning mentality and leave a legacy of excellence like Clenard was inspired to do in Chapter 7.

**Your Business is More Than a Beautiful Bird**
Congratulations are in order to you! Despite the astronomical failure rate for small businesses, you started and are doing whatever it takes to maintain your business. You have tapped into your natural skills, talents and abilities to create companies that provide jobs, sustain communities and make for a brighter future. Use your company's agility to your advantage and transform what may appear as a liability into your greatest asset.

You can use the Kasennu business infrastructure methodology as a stand-alone solution or as part of your operational excellence toolkit for managing fast growth. This is a journey of continuous improvement, so don't ever think that, once you've applied all elements of the methodology, that your work is complete. Keep learning, yearning and earning! Eventually, you will (hopefully) outgrow even this methodology as your company's needs become more sophisticated and advanced.

Therefore, do not shy away from the rigor required to continue on your path to mega success. Like many civilizations, your company cannot be destroyed from the outside unless it is already destroyed on the inside.

Eleanor Roosevelt said, "The future belongs to those who dare to believe in the beauty of their dreams." So keep daring. Return to your origins and claim your future! The façade works best when it covers a solid business infrastructure. Therefore, the façade does not need to be fixed per se; it just needs to be matched. Now that you know how to build and maintain business infrastructure, reflect on the possibilities it can offer in taking your company to new heights.

Reflection will lead to revelation and revelation will lead to revolution in your business. Thank you for sharing in my quest to revolutionize the way small businesses operate!

> "The Peacock, they say, did not at first have the beautiful feathers in which he now takes so much pride. These, Juno, whose favorite he was, granted to him one day when he begged her for a train of feathers to distinguish him from the other birds. Then, decked in his finery, gleaming with emerald, gold, purple, and azure, he strutted proudly among the birds. All regarded him with envy. Even the most beautiful peasant could see that his beauty was surpassed.
>
> Presently the Peacock saw an Eagle soaring high up in the blue sky and felt a desire to fly, as he had been accustomed to do. Lifting his wings he tried to rise from the ground. But the weight of his magnificent train held him down. Instead of flying up to greet the first rays of the morning sun or to bathe in the rosy light among the floating clouds at sunset, he would have to walk the ground more encumbered and oppressed than any common barnyard fowl.
>
> **Moral:** Do not sacrifice your freedom for the sake of pomp and show."[34]

### Your business is more than a beautiful bird.
### It is a beautiful bird capable of flying high!

# APPENDIX A
## SIMPLIFIED STEPS OF THE KASENNU METHODOLOGY

### Business Parts Analysis (BPA)
1. List all tasks to perform.
2. Group like tasks into nine or fewer categories.
3. Assign a department and a color to each category/grouping of tasks.
4. Identify the core department.
5. Identify all staff to perform tasks per department.
6. Create new or update existing job descriptions based on task allocation.

### Business Design Blueprint (BDB)
1. Draw all departments (see BPA) as boxes across a page horizontally.
2. Place names of upper management roles above the departments (see BPA).
3. Place names of other staff roles underneath the departments.
4. Distinguish type of staff (i.e., contractor, employee, vendor).

### Electronic Records Management (ERM)
1. Take an inventory of all electronic document types.
2. Group into main categories/folders based on departments (see BPA). If possible, color-code according to the BPA.
3. Rearrange electronic documents according to the new digital folder assignment.
4. Record the access, creating, naming, storing, purging, archiving, and back-up protocols for each document type.

### Paper Records Management (PRM)
1. Take an inventory of all paper record types, including books and periodicals.
2. Group into main categories based on departments and color-coding (see BPA).
3. Color-code (see BPA) and rearrange paper records according to new physical storage assignment.
4. Record the access, creation, naming, storage location, retention, purging and destruction protocol for each category of information.

### Service Delivery Blueprint (SDB)
1. Document all steps in delivering the core service or product (see BPA).
2. Segment those steps into stages.
3. Assign staff to each stage (see BPA).
4. List all operational tools needed per stage (see ERM, PRM, BPM).
5. Define metrics to monitor and improve each stage.

### Work Space Logistics (WSL)
1. Divide physical work space into stations based on the BPA and SDB.
2. Assign occupants to each work station.
3. Measure all furniture and equipment to determine optimal setup (see PRM and ERM).
4. Rearrange furniture and equipment accordingly.
5. Relocate work stations accordingly.

### Business Process Manual (BPM)
1. Evaluate primary need for business processes.
2. Identify processes by grouping like job tasks within each department (see BPA).
3. Assess all tools needed to execute each process.
4. Document each process in a procedural and flowchart format.
5. Measure process performance, assigning KPI(s) and a Gatekeeper (see BPA).
6. Store processes per department as physical and/or electronic manuals.
7. Improve processes to enhance the customer, staff and vendor experience.

**Continuously update, monitor and evaluate the effectiveness of the resulting business infrastructure and make improvements across all areas accordingly.**

# APPENDIX B
## 29 PROCESSES EVERY SMALL BUSINESS SHOULD IMPLEMENT

**Marketing**
1. Networking
2. Lead Generation
3. Sales
4. Relationship Management

**Operations**
5. Service Delivery
6. Records Management
7. Inventory Management
8. Customer Support
9. Facilities Management

**Accounting**
10. Accounts Receivable
11. Accounts Payable
12. Collections
13. Account Reconciliation
14. Tax Preparation & Filing

**Human Resources**
15. Recruiting, Interviewing & Hiring
16. New Hire Orientation
17. Payroll
18. Performance Evaluation
19. Termination
20. Continuous Education

**Legal**
21. Contract Development & Review
22. License/Certification Renewal
23. Internal & External Auditing
24. Insurance Selection & Maintenance
25. Intellectual Property Maintenance

**Technology**
26. Equipment Selection & Maintenance
27. Software Selection & Maintenance
28. Disaster Recovery & Business Continuity
29. Electronic Data Storage & Backup

# APPENDIX C
## Standard Process Mapping Symbols

| Common ANSI Symbols Used in Flowcharts[35] | | |
|---|---|---|
| SYMBOL | NAME | FUNCTION |
|  | Terminal | The beginning or end of a process. |
|  | Flowlines | The flow of information, work or logic. |
|  | Process | Job tasks or activities. |
|  | Decision | A comparison, question or decision that determines alternative paths to be followed. |
|  | On-Page Connector | A break in the path of a flowchart that is used to continue the flow from one point on a page to another. This connector symbol marks where the flow ends at one point on a page and continues at another point on the same page. |
|  | Off-Page Connector | Similar to the on-page connector but represents a break in the path of a flowchart that is used when it is too large to fit onto a single page. This connector symbol marks where the flow ends on one page and where it continues on another page or another process altogether. |

# APPENDIX D
## EXAMPLE KEY PERFORMANCE INDICATORS
## FOR SMALL BUSINESSES

**Marketing**
- Number of networking events attended per month
- Lead to client conversion per month

**Operations**
- Number of customer complaints received per week
- Total service errors reported per week

**Accounting**
- Amount of Aging Receivables between 30 and 45 days
- Amount of avoidable late fees per month

**Human Resources**
- Staff turnover per 90 days
- Total overtime hours per week

**Legal**
- Number of contract disputes per quarter
- Number of failed inspections per quarter

**Technology**
- Amount of money spent in equipment and digital repairs per month
- Number of support tickets resolved vs. unresolved per week

# APPENDIX E
## 10 Factors to Consider When Outsourcing Process Design, Documentation and Optimization Work

1. **Educational Background.** Process Specialists are not created equal, starting with the roles assigned to them. Some of those roles include technical writer, process engineer, lean and/or six sigma consultant and process analyst. Technical college degrees are not always required for some of these roles, but certifications usually are. The exception is the process engineer role. This role has perhaps the most misused title and is the least understood in business today. Process engineers are actually chemical engineers and performance in that role definitely requires a degree. Types of certifications include Project Management Professional (PMP), Scrum/Agile, Lean and Six Sigma. In recruiting the best help, analyze the type of project you have (i.e., manufacturing, data programming, service transaction) and seek resources who possess the optimal combination of educational and work experience for your process project.

2. **Technical & Analytical Skills.** Technical and analytical acumen are required for successful process work. Process mapping, for example, is more than just drawing a flowchart showing how various tasks are connected. Technical skills are needed to observe and collect raw data methodically on the process, and analytical skills are needed to interpret that data to identify improvement opportunities.

3. **Troubleshooting Skills.** One major way to gauge a person's ability to troubleshoot is by assessing the candidate's work experience. Troubleshooting is a natural skill extension of those with experience in designing, programming and producing/manufacturing a tangible good. Another way to gauge is by asking the candidate to provide specific details of when s/he helped a company determine the sources of bottlenecks and constraints using process mapping and other analytical tools.

4. **References & Work Samples.** *Always* ask for and seek references and recommendations of potential candidates. Check online sources to confirm a reference's identity. When meeting in person, ask candidates to bring samples of their work so that you can visualize the quality, thoroughness and organization of their work. Be prepared to provide and/or sign a mutual non-disclosure agreement (NDA) that protects confidential information.

5. **Ability to Scope Your Project.** Listening is critical to carefully scoping a process-related project. It's important for you as the business owner to describe the project first, as you see it. Then, ask the candidate to describe or offer potential strategies for fine-tuning the scope. Do you understand the candidate's suggestion? Does it sound logical? Pay close attention to the types of questions the candidate asks. This will give insight into his/her ability to accurately define and articulate the problem to solve.

6. **Personality.** Process work is like police work; it requires keen investigative skills. Job shadowing and data collection are integral to process work and require a Process Specialist with excellent interpersonal communication skills. You can use a combination of logic, intuition and personality tests to determine if you are about to hire a person that others will feel comfortable about divulging details of their daily work.

7. **Knowledge of Intellectual Property Laws.** Business processes are your company's intellectual property. A qualified, experienced Process Specialist will be sensitive toward the proprietary and confidential nature of protecting your "secret sauce." As you review the candidate's work samples, look for clues like *For Internal Use Only, Controlled Copy, Copyright* and *Confidential.* Seeing something as simple as these phrases on the candidate's work samples gives assurance of a basic understanding of and respect for protecting proprietary company information.

8. **Freelancer/Contractor, Consultant or Employee?** The type of engagement for performing process work is just as important as the type of Process Specialist you hire. This factor depends on a combination of your budget, the time commitment and level of experience required, as well as the length and complexity of your process work. Hiring a full-time employee assumes you have a permanent, ongoing need; whereas, hiring a freelance or contractor indicates your need is temporary. Avoid legal infractions by doing your re-

search on the differences between the two in the country in which you operate. Hiring a consultant gives you the freedom to have a subject matter expert manage all work required from conception to completion.

9. **Ability to Work Remotely/Virtually.** Process work requires extreme concentration. For this reason, many Process Specialists often find themselves having to work in isolated areas to minimize distractions. The need for remote or virtual work can arise if you also work from home or you simply do not have the physical space to accommodate the Process Specialist. Make sure candidates have a secure home office with access to high speed internet. Keep in mind that some people have trouble working in isolation and you should figure this out sooner rather than later.

10. **Flexibility.** Many Process Specialists are accustomed to working on enterprise-level projects with larger budgets, compared to smaller companies. Employees like this are a high turnover risk as they may find it difficult to adjust to the culture of a small business where there is usually no immediate opportunity to climb a corporate ladder.

# NOTES

## INTRODUCTION

1. Perry, Ben Edwin. (2007). *Aesopica: A series of texts relating to Aesop or ascribed to him or closely connected with the literary tradition that bears his name.* Champaign, IL: University of Illinois Press.

## CHAPTER 1: EMERALD CITY

2. Baum, L. Frank. (1900). *The Wonderful Wizard of Oz.* Chicago, Illinois: George M. Hill Company, 101.
3. Liker, Jeffrey. (2004). *The Toyota Way: 14 Management Principles from the World's Greatest Manufacturer.* New York: McGraw-Hill, 23. "JIT [Just in Time] is a set of principles, tools and techniques that allows a company to produce and deliver products in small quantities, with short lead times, to meet specific customer needs. Simply put, JIT delivers the right items at the right time in the right amounts."
4. When combining chemicals, compute the total number of atoms on both sides of the equation by multiplying the number placed in front of an element (the coefficient) by the number of atoms shown with the molecule, usually represented by a subscript. Molecules without a coefficient or subscript assume a value of one. Therefore, a 2 in front of $H_2O$ ($2H_2O$) is equivalent to stating four (2 x 2) Hydrogen atoms and two (2 x 1) Oxygen atoms.
5. Gladwell, Malcolm. (2000). *The Tipping Point: How Little Things Can Make a Big Difference.* Boston, MA: Little, Brown and Company.

## PART TWO: APPLYING THE METHODOLOGY

6. Kimbro, Dennis, Ph.D. (2013). *The Wealth Choice: Success Secrets of Black Millionaires.* New York, NY: St. Martin's Griffin, 58.

## CHAPTER 2: IDENTITY CRISIS

7. Adu, Sade. (2000). *King of Sorrow.* [Recorded by Mike Pela]. On *Lovers Rock* [CD]. New York, NY: Epic Records.
8. Peter, Dr. Laurence J. & Hull, Raymond. (1969). *The Peter Principle: Why Things Always Go Wrong.* New York, NY: William Morrow and Company.
9. Kardes, Frank R. (2002). *Consumer Behavior and Managerial Decision Making* (2nd ed.). Upper Saddle River, NJ: Pearson Education, 405.
10. Miller, George A. (1994). "The Magical Number Seven, Plus or Minus Two: Some limits on our capacity for processing information." *Psychological Review, 101* (2), 343-352.

## CHAPTER 3: CHILD'S PLAY

11. SCRUMstudy™. (2017). *A Guide to the Scrum Body of Knowledge (SBOK™ Guide): A Comprehensive Guide to Deliver Projects Using Scrum* (3rd ed.). Avondale, AZ: SCRUMstudy™, 2. "Scrum is…an adaptive, iterative, fast, flexible, and effective framework designed to deliver significant value quickly and throughout a

project. Scrum ensures transparency in communication and creates an environment of collective accountability and continuous progress."

## CHAPTER 4: THE PRINCESS VS. THE POLITICIAN

12. Liker, Jeffrey K. (2004). *The Toyota Way: 14. Management Principles from the World's Greatest Manufacturer.* New York, NY: McGraw-Hill, 7. "The Toyota Production System [TPS] is Toyota's unique approach to manufacturing. It is the basis for much of the 'lean production' movement that has dominated manufacturing trends (along with Six Sigma) for the last 10 years or so. Taiichi Ohno, founder of TPS, said…'All we are doing is looking at the time line from the moment the customer gives us an order to the point when we collect the cash. And we are reducing that time line by removing the non-value added wastes.' (Ohno, 1988)."
13. Harry, Mikel, Ph.D. & Schroeder, Richard Schroeder. (2005). *Six Sigma: the Breakthrough Management Strategy Revolutionizing the World's Top Corporations.* New York, NY: DoubleDay, vii. "What is Six Sigma? It is a business process that allows companies to drastically improve their bottom line by designing and monitoring everyday business activities in ways that minimize waste and resources while increasing customer satisfaction. It provides specific methods to recreate the process so that defects and errors never arise in the first place."
14. Bagehot, Walter. (2009). *The English Constitution.* Oxford, England: Oxford University Press, 7, 41. "No one can approach to an understanding of the English institutions…unless he divides them into two classes…first, those which excite and preserve the reverence of the population,—the dignified parts [Royalty]…and next, the efficient parts [Government],—those by which it, in fact, works and rules. Royalty is a government in which the attention of the nation is concentrated on one person doing interesting actions. A Republic is a government in which that attention is divided between many, who are all doing uninteresting actions. Royalty will be strong because it appeals to diffused feeling, and Republics weak because they appeal to understanding."
15. Andrews, Ted. (2004). *Animal Speak: The Spiritual & Magical Powers of Creatures Great & Small.* St. Paul, MN: Llewellyn Publications.

## CHAPTER 5: THE LEVEE & THE LEVY

16. Ehrmann, Max. (1927). *Desiderata: A Poem for a Way of Life.* New York, NY: Crown Publishers.
17. Vogt, Lloyd. (2003). *New Orleans Houses: A House Watcher's Guide.* Gretna, LA: Pelican Publishing Company, 22-23. "The shotgun double is a two-family house composed of two shotgun singles joined under one roof and separated by a center wall. The shotgun single is a rectangular house with all the rooms arranged directly behind one another in a straight line, front to back. The camelback is a shotgun single or double with one story in the front and two in the rear."
18. Centers for Medicare & Medicaid Services. (2018). Retrieved July 8, 2018, from https://www.medicaid.gov/about-us/index.html. "Medicaid provides health coverage to low-income people and is one of the largest payers for health care in the United States."

19. In this context, Karen Benoit, a New Orleanian, uses the term *dirty bird* to be insulting; an indication of the intense rivalry between fans of the Atlanta Falcons football team (whose mascot is the falcon bird) and the New Orleans Saints football team.

## CHAPTER 6: RED PILL OR BLUE PILL?

20. Shakespeare, William. Edited by Furness, Horace Howard. (1890). *As You Like It* (Vol. VIII). Philadelphia, PA: J.B. Lippincott Company. Act II, Scene VII, 122-128.

21. Droar, David. (2015). *In the Matrix, which pill would you take, the red or the blue?* [Web log post]. Retrieved July 20, 2018 from http://www.thematrix101.com/contrib/darrod_wpwyttrotb.php. "The question of which pill to take illustrates the personal aspect of the decision to study philosophy. Do you live on in ignorance (and potentially bliss) or do you lead what Aristotle called 'the examined life'… The blue pill will leave us as we are, in a life consisting of habit, of things we believe we know. We are comfortable, we do need truth to live. The red pill symbolises risk, doubt and questioning. However, in order to investigate which course of action to take we need to investigate why the choice is faced."

22. Harry, Mikel, Ph.D. & Schroeder, Richard Schroeder. (2005). *Six Sigma: the Breakthrough Management Strategy Revolutionizing the World's Top Corporations.* New York, NY: DoubleDay, vii. "What is Six Sigma? It is a business process that allows companies to drastically improve their bottom line by designing and monitoring everyday business activities in ways that minimize waste and resources while increasing customer satisfaction. It provides specific methods to recreate the process so that defects and errors never arise in the first place."

23. Shakespeare, William. Edited by Crawford, Jack Randall. (1917). *The Tragedy of Hamlet: Prince of Denmark.* New Haven, CT: Yale University Press. Act III, Scene I, 66.

## CHAPTER 7: VENI, VIDI, VICI

24. Tzu, Sun and Sawyer, Ralph D. (1994). *The Art of War.* New York, NY: Barnes & Noble Books, 179.

25. United States Department of Labor – Occupational Safety and Health Administration. (2018). *About OSHA.* Retrieved July 19, 2018 from https://www.osha.gov/about.html. "…Congress created the Occupational Safety and Health Administration (OSHA) to assure safe and healthful working conditions for working men and women by setting and enforcing standards and by providing training, outreach, education and assistance."
United States Department of Justice – Civil Rights Division. (2018). *Introduction to the ADA.* Retrieved July 19, 2018 from https://www.ada.gov/ada_intro.htm. "The Americans with Disabilities Act (ADA)…is one of America's most comprehensive pieces of civil rights legislation that prohibits discrimination and guarantees that people with disabilities have the same opportunities as everyone else to participate in the mainstream of American life -- to enjoy employment opportunities, to purchase goods and

services, and to participate in State and local government programs and services."

26. Farlex Dictionary of Idioms. (2018). *Get out of jail free card.* Retrieved May 31, 2018 from https://idioms.thefreedictionary.com/get+out+of+jail+free+card. "Something that will immediately resolve or relieve an undesirable situation, especially that which results in no or minimal consequences. A reference to the board game Monopoly, in which this card allows players to leave the jail space without missing a turn."

27. Sang, Master Larry & Luk, Helen. (2004). *The Principles of Feng Shui* (6th ed.). Monterey Park, CA: The American Feng Shui Institute, xv. "Feng Shui, a Chinese mathematical system developed by scholars through observations accumulated over thousands of years, is a method of harmonizing a man-made environment and the calculation of time and space. It is a science incorporating astronomy, geography, the environment, the magnetic fields, and physics. Contrary to popular belief, it is not a religion or superstition. Modern science has proven it to be a complex mathematical system."

## CHAPTER 8: EMERALD TABLET

28. WebFinance, Inc. (2018). *Full Time Equivalent (FTE)* [definition post]. Retrieved on July 20, 2018. "The ratio of the total number of paid hours during a period (part time, full time, contracted) by the number of working hours in that period Mondays through Fridays. The ratio units are FTE units or equivalent employees working full-time. In other words, one FTE is equivalent to one employee working full-time."

29. Muspratt, Adam. (2018, July 11). *A Guide to Robotic Process Automation (RPA)* [Web log post]. Retrieved July 20, 2018 from https://www.processexcellencenetwork.com/rpa-artificial-intelligence/articles/a-guide-to-robotic-process-automation-rpa. "Robotic Process Automation (RPA) is a software-based technology utilising software robots to emulate human execution of a business process. This means that it performs the task on a computer, uses the same interface a human worker would, clicks, types, opens applications uses keyboard shortcuts and more. It is predominantly used to automate business processes and tasks, resulting in reductions in spending and giving businesses of all size a competitive edge."

## CHAPTER 9: SANKOFA

30. The Board of Trustees of the University of Illinois. (2018). *Meaning of the Sankofa Bird.* Retrieved April 16, 2018 from https://www.uis.edu/africanamericanstudies/students/sankofa/.

31. Stevenson, Robert Louis (2010). *The Strange Case of Dr. Jekyll and Mr. Hyde.* London, England: HarperCollins. "All human beings, as we meet them, are commingled out of good and evil. After taking an elixir created in his laboratory, mild mannered Dr. Jekyll is transformed into the cruel and despicable Mr. Hyde. Stevenson's quintessential novella…epitomizes the conflict between psychology, science and religious morality, but is fundamentally a triumphant study of the duality of human nature."

32. Freeth, Nick. (2009). *Made in America: From Levi's to Barbie to Google.* New York, NY: Fall River Press, 151.
33. Price, Steven D. (2011). *Keeping up with the Joneses.* Retrieved May 31, 2018 from https://idioms.thefreedictionary.com/keeping+up+with+the+joneses. "Making an effort to match your neighbors' social and financial status."
34. Perry, Ben Edwin. (2007). *Aesopica: A series of texts relating to Aesop or ascribed to him or closely connected with the literary tradition that bears his name.* Champaign, IL: University of Illinois Press.

**APPENDIX C: STANDARD PROCESS MAPPING SYMBOLS**

35. Chapra, Steve C. & Canale, Raymond P. (1988). *Numerical Methods for Engineers* (2nd ed.), 31. Note the functions cited in the table are slightly modified from the original content to suit this book's audience. ANSI stands for American National Standards Institute.

# INDEX

# ABOUT THE AUTHOR

Alicia Butler Pierre is the founder and CEO of Equilibria, Inc., where she first formulated the Kasennu methodology for her clients. She has since successfully applied this methodology in over 30 different industries and counting. Alicia has a B.S. in Chemical Engineering from Louisiana State University and an MBA from Tulane University. She is also a certified Lean Six Sigma Black Belt and has authored over 200 articles, case studies, videos and white papers in the areas of business infrastructure, process im-provement and operational excellence. Combined, her content has received over a quarter of a million views on SlideShare.net alone. Her ability to blend scientific, business and mathematical methodologies to solve complex operational problems enables her to bring a unique, tactical and realistic perspective to her clients, who have also included larger enterprises like The Coca-Cola Company, Lowe's and Shell Oil Company. She lives in Georgia with her husband. Committed to doing the right things the right way, Alicia's mantra is "to leave it better than you found it."

Visit **BusinessInfrastructure.TV** to listen to podcasts, watch videos and read articles to learn more about the benefits of business infrastructure and various applications of the Kasennu methodology.

# BONUS STORY

## How to Use Business Processes to Increase Cash Flow
## — The Olivia DuMonde Story —

In *Behind the Façade*, you met entrepreneurs who were each faced with the challenge of sustaining their successful businesses during periods of fast, unmanageable growth. Unlike these business owners, Olivia DuMonde is struggling from the lack of business infrastructure as well as poor cash flow. With this bonus story you will:

- Follow Olivia (a muralist in San Francisco) as she applies the Kasennu methodology to better manage her growing small business' cash flow;
- Understand how it's possible to have more business than you can handle, but no cash to show for it; and
- Learn how to look at a process flowchart to visualize operational bottlenecks and develop techniques for streamlining the process.

**FREE download available at BehindTheFacadeBook.com**

CPSIA information can be obtained
at www.ICGtesting.com
Printed in the USA
BVHW060143020720
582423BV00013B/226/J